STUDENTS WITH AUTISM

HOW TO IMPROVE LANGUAGE, LITERACY AND ACADEMIC SUCCESS

KATHARINE BEALS, PhD

First published 2022

by John Catt Educational Ltd,
15 Riduna Park, Station Road,
Melton, Woodbridge IP12 1QT
UK
Tel: +44 (0) 1394 389850

4500 140th Ave North,
Suite 101, Clearwater,
FL 33762-3848
US
Tel: +1 561 448 1987

Email: enquiries@johncatt.com
Website: www.johncatt.com

ISBN: 978 1 915261 37 3

Set and designed by John Catt Educational Limited

Finally, a book with a truly comprehensive focus on autism-friendly curriculum and instruction, rather than another re-hash of how to create an autism-friendly classroom! Beals provides the best description of teaching language and cognition to children and adults with autism I have seen to date. I heartily recommend her book to all autism ABA practitioners.

Kent Johnson, Founder & Executive Director, Morningside Academy

I gained great insight into how language and emotion are different in autism. As a person who thinks in pictures, it was interesting to learn more about how a trained linguist interprets autism. There are some parts of this book I disagree with but the first part about problems with joint attention and slow "sticky" shifting of attention were really helpful.

Temple Grandin, Author, *Thinking in Pictures*

Student with Autism is a revelation. Katharine Beals tells us what is and is not affected by autism; what unique strengths autism brings to the world; and which programs and treatments will bring those strengths to the fore. Parents of the newly diagnosed will be heartened by Beals' explanation of the difference between empathy, which isn't affected in autism, and "theory of mind," which is. And her sections on "sticky" attention and the relationship between verbal and nonverbal learning (a current topic in cognitive science) help us see the difference between autism itself and the downstream effects of having autism.

This is the book I wish I'd had when I was starting my life as a parent of young children with autism.

Catherine Johnson, Ph.D., is the co-author, with John Ratey, of *Shadow Syndromes* and, with Temple Grandin, of *Animals in Translation* and *Animals Make Us Human*

The modern classroom -- noisy, fluid, collaborative and unstructured -- can be overwhelming for students with autism. Katharine Beals explains how to teach to the strengths of children with autism at school and at home.

Joanne Jacobs, Author, *Our School: The Inspiring Story of Two Teachers, One Big Idea, and the School That Beat the Odds.*
joannejacobs.com.

ACKNOWLEDGMENTS

First and foremost I would like to thank Mark Combes of John Catt Educational for his advice and encouragement throughout this project, from the initial outline to the final manuscript. Mark sent insightful feedback on each chapter within days after I produced it, his energy and enthusiasm helping me maintain mine.

I also owe special thanks to an anonymous copy editor whose help went well beyond basic line editing to thoughtful suggestions about terminology, clarity of formatting, and references.

Several friends read parts of the book and offered valuable feedback and encouragement: Jane Avrich, Olga Beloded, and Amy Lutz. To one friend, Steve Fischer, I owe a much snappier title than the tongue-twister I had originally slapped onto the manuscript.

Finally, I thank my husband, David, who cooked suppers and quietly cheered me on outside my closed office door during many long evenings throughout the past year.

ABOUT THE AUTHOR

Katharine Beals is the author of *Raising a Left-Brain Child in a Right-Brain World: Strategies for Helping Bright, Quirky, Socially Awkward Children to Thrive at Home and at School.* She has a PhD in linguistics and is an adjunct professor in the Autism Program at the Drexel University School of Education, where she designed two of the program's five courses.

She also teaches courses on autism at the Graduate School of Education at the University of Pennsylvania. She specializes in language and literacy acquisition in autism, language technologies for autistic individuals, educational challenges for students with autism, and the problems with Facilitated Communication as an intervention in autism.

She is a contributor at FacilitatedCommunication.org and also an autism parent.

CONTENTS

PREFACE

A note on terminology

One question that arises throughout this book is how to refer to individuals on the autism spectrum. Should we say, for example, "on the autism spectrum," "with autism," or "autistic"? My answer is to use all three. In part, this is because I'd like to reflect the variety of preferences among different stakeholders in the autism world. Many parents and some disability rights advocates prefer person-first language: "person with autism," "child who has autism," "adults on the autism spectrum." Many autistic self-advocates and other disability rights advocates, however, prefer identity-first language: namely, "autistic person/child/ adults."

But most of the time I opt for the adjective "autistic." I do this for two reasons. First, "autistic people" is more compact than "people with autism," let alone "people who have autism" or "people on the autism spectrum." Indeed, by the end of the book, I shorten things even further, sometimes referring to "autistics" versus "non-autistics."

Second, as the initial chapters will show, autism involves deep social, cognitive, and communicative idiosyncrasies that go well beyond what characterizes, say, people with social anxiety or people with attention deficits. Given this, "autistic people"—as compared with "people with/ who have autism"— avoids the conceptual problem of trying to separate people from their autism.

A second question has to do with how to refer to people at different functioning levels. As I'll discuss, autism is a spectrum of symptom intensity. Traditionally, that spectrum has been divided into "Asperger's" and "autistic," or "high functioning" and "low functioning," or "mild," "moderate," and "severe," But Asperger's, which has proved difficult to distinguish from high-functioning autism, is no longer an official diagnostic category. Some people, furthermore, argue that terms like "low functioning" and "severe" are stigmatizing. Accordingly, in the most recent version of the official diagnostic criteria for autism, adjectives have been replaced with numbers: level 1, level 2, and level 3. But these euphemisms are sufficiently non-transparent that most people still use the adjectives. For these two reasons—transparency and common usage—I will as well.

Another more transparent set of new euphemisms describes people in terms of "support needs" (e.g., "high-support-needs people"). I avoid these in part because they're so linguistically cumbersome.

But there's a more general reason why I stick with "autistic," "high functioning," "low functioning," "mild," "moderate," and "severe." One of my goals throughout this book is to be honest about the fundamental socio-cognitive nature of autism and about the severity of the linguistic and cognitive challenges of individuals across the spectrum. Only in confronting these factors head-on can we begin to improve communication, literacy, and academic success in all students with autism.

CHAPTER 1

WHAT IS AUTISM? A REVIEW OF WHAT'S IMPAIRED AND WHAT'S INTACT

Introduction: Red flags and first steps

She sits apart, apparently daydreaming, oblivious to the chatter of the children nearby. He's so absorbed with the gears of a toy clock that he doesn't look up when we call his name repeatedly. Are these children merely unsocial, dreamy, and/or hyper-focused? Or is there more going on? When should we worry?

The worry at the back of many of our minds—whether we're parents, teachers, or clinicians—is autism. As with most mental disorders, autism is a diagnosis based entirely on behavioral symptoms. There is no way for us to peer directly inside someone's brain and see autism—nor is there even any certainty about what "autistic brains" look like. And so it is up to those of us who spend time with children to notice the external signs that may indicate autism. And, to ensure that our children get whatever support they might need, it is up to us to take the next steps: to follow up with specialists who do the formal evaluations that determine whether a diagnosis applies; or, if we're teachers or clinicians, to diplomatically nudge parents in that direction.

In America, autism diagnoses are based on the symptoms laid out in the most recent version of the *Diagnostic and Statistical Manual of Mental Disorders*, the DSM-V-TR, published by the American Psychiatric Association. The DSM-V-TR divides symptoms into two categories: 1) deficits in social communication and social interaction; and 2) excesses in restricted, repetitive patterns of behavior and interests. Each of these, in turn, is broken down into subcategories of symptoms.

In the case of social communication and interaction, difficulties and/or deficits occur in the following areas:

1. **Social-emotional reciprocity**: social initiation, back-and-forth interactions, and sharing emotions and objects of interest

2. **Nonverbal communicative behaviors**: eye contact, understanding people's body language, and using expressive gestures for communicative purposes

3. **Developing and maintaining relationships**: showing interest in one's peers, adjusting one's behavior for different social contexts, and engaging in imaginative, social play

In the case of restricted, repetitive patterns of behavior and interests, symptoms fall within at least two of four categories:

1. **Repetitiveness**: repetitive motor movements, repetitive use of objects, or repetitive speech patterns

2. **Inflexibility and rigidity**: "insistence on sameness, inflexible adherence to routines, or ritualized patterns of behavior"

3. **Interests**: "highly restricted, fixated interests abnormal in intensity or focus"

4. **Sensory issues**: hyper- or hypo-reactivity to sensory stimuli or "unusual interests in sensory aspects of the environment"

All these symptoms are matters of degree. One child might be only somewhat infrequent in her social overtures and in her sharing of objects of interest; another might never initiate or share. One child might be only mildly inflexible about routines and only sometimes unusually focused on narrow interests; another child might seem largely oblivious to the world outside his areas of fixation or have meltdowns whenever there's even the slightest change in routine. Autism is now considered a spectrum disorder—autism spectrum disorder or ASD—and different symptoms appear to different degrees in different ASD individuals.

If you've met one child with autism, the saying goes, you've met one child with autism.

Despite this heterogeneity, however, researchers have devised an effective preliminary screening tool that can be used in children between 16 and 30 months of age: a 20-question survey known as the Modified Checklist for Autism in Infants and Toddlers-R (M-CHAT-R) (Kleinman, Robins, Ventol, Pandey, Boorstein et al., 2008). Over its many years of use, it has turned out that, out of these 20 questions, a mere six do most of the work in identifying which children warrant evaluations. The six so-called "critical items" are:

- Does your child take an interest in other children?
- Does your child ever use his/her index finger to point, to indicate interest in something?
- Does your child ever bring objects over to you (parent) to show you something?
- Does your child imitate you (e.g., you make a face–will your child imitate it)?
- Does your child ever respond to his/her name when you call?
- If you point at a toy across the room, does your child look at it?

While the M-CHAT-R is a parent survey, these six questions are ones that others who work closely with young children can also consider. Indeed, if you're one of these people, your broad exposure to children's typical (and atypical) patterns of social behavior potentially puts you in a better position than parents are in to notice the warning signs of autism. There is some awkwardness, of course, in taking the next step: approaching the parents about screening and evaluations. Some teachers report being discouraged by higher-ups from doing this. Under the Child Find Mandate of the Individuals with Disabilities Education Act (IDEA), however, educational agencies are obligated to identify students who are suspected of needing special education services.

Identifying what kinds of special education services a child with autism needs, however, requires much more than a formal evaluation. To understand how to prepare him for K-12 schooling, and how to tweak the K-12 curricula and learning environments to maximize his academic success, we need an in-depth understanding of his learning challenges. While researchers are nowhere near mapping out the underlying neurology of autism, they have identified a number of perception- and attention-based idiosyncrasies that seem to lie near the root of the various language and learning challenges. Becoming familiar with these key idiosyncrasies is our first step towards doing what we can to maximize the educational achievement of our ASD students.

Orienting to voices: Spoken words versus beeps and buzzes

She seems deaf when we call out her name but turns around to the sound of a dog barking. He doesn't react when we yell, "Stop!" but startles at the sudden rumble of the refrigerator. One of the earliest idiosyncrasies in autism is a tendency to be much less aware of people's voices than of other sounds in the environment: something the autism literature calls a lack of "orienting to voices." Not orienting to voices, of course, means not attending to speech.

To most of us, however loud the other noises that surround us, the most salient sound is the sound of speech. In fact, so effectively do we tune out the ambient noises that it's only when everyone goes silent that we suddenly notice the hum of the HVAC system, the buzz of the overhead lights, the roar of outdoor trucks, and the chirps of birds and crickets. Even when these noises are objectively louder than the speech sounds they're competing with, we still pay them little to no attention. Stop for a moment to consider the sounds of crickets. Because we often notice them only when people stop talking, "crickets" has come to signal "silence." And "silence"—as in "the room was silent"—can simply mean that no one's talking.

Imagine how different the world would be if the opposite were true: if we mostly ignored speech and tuned in to everything else. Imagine what it's like, at home or in the classroom, to be constantly noticing the creaking of chairs and the fall of footsteps and the rustling of papers and the tones of car horns and the patter of raindrops against windows, but not the voices of the people around us. Imagine if, on top of it, we experience some of these sounds—as happens frequently to individuals with autism—as so grating or piercing that they completely distract us away from all other noises, including those that are truly meaningful.

Separating "signal" from "noise" is an essential and—for most of us—automatic step in making sense of our environments. Many of the most important, meaning-charged signals in our world, of course, involve the words that people pronounce. Attending to speech is essential for acquiring language, and acquiring language is essential for learning about people, learning things from them, and, later on (as we'll discuss in Chapter 2), learning how to read. Reduced attention to speech, therefore, means reduced language learning in particular and reduced learning in general. One of the first steps to helping children with autism reach their educational potential, as we'll discuss in Chapter 3, is successfully competing against the many things that distract them—and in some cases distress them—away from spoken and written language.

Joint attention: Who is looking at what?

She rarely looks up and makes eye contact, even when someone walks into the room. Try as we might to point something out to him, it's really hard to get him to look where we're pointing.

Related to the tendency in autism to preferentially attend to environmental sounds over speech is a tendency to preferentially attend to objects over faces—something that, similarly, emerges in early infancy and has consequences for language acquisition and learning.

By the time they're nine months old, typically developing children, increasingly tuned in to social stimuli, have begun engaging in what's called "joint attention" behaviors. Joint attention, in essence, is two or more people focused on the same thing, with both (or all) of them conscious of sharing a moment together. The object of joint attention can be anything: a raccoon in the backyard, a cheetah at the zoo, a bedtime story, a math lesson on the classroom whiteboard. But, regardless of what the object of joint attention is, reaching that moment of joint attention involves first attending to the other person—specifically, to his or her face.

Stripped down to the basics, joint attention is a two-step process: Person A gets Person B's attention; B responds by looking up at A's face, then A either points or simply shifts their eye gaze over to the object of their attention. B's eyes then follow A's pointing gesture or eye gaze over to that object. Voila—both people are attending to the same object. And, assuming that each is sufficiently tuned in to the other, both people are also conscious that this is a shared moment. The entire process of coordinating attention, from Person A's initial attraction of Person B's attention all the way up to their moment of shared focus, is largely automatic. Typically, neither party needs to think consciously through any stage of it. But while the shared moment is often achieved instantaneously, it can last long enough to encompass substantial amounts of shared material and shared experiences.

The human brain is said to be the most complex object in the known universe. But the essence of joint attention is in some ways more complex still: It is multiple brains working in sync. It's often effortless, but also magical: the closest we get to telepathy. More importantly, for our purposes here, joint attention moments are prime moments for teaching and learning. Teachers cannot teach effectively if they are unable to direct their students' attention to relevant aspects of the lesson—to the tens place of the numbers being added; to the quadrant of the water cycle diagram that shows evaporation. And students cannot learn efficiently if they're unable to coordinate their focus with that of their teacher.

A deficit in joint attention, unfortunately, is a core characteristic of autism. We see it reflected in many of the core social symptoms— particularly those pertaining to social reciprocity. Emerging research indicates that, while social stimuli like faces and eyes are rewarding to most infants and children, eye contact, in particular, is aversive in autism. This is one reason why ASD children typically prefer non-social stimuli and objects over people. And it is one reason why ASD children resist disengaging from their preferred, non-social activities in order to look up at the face or, worse, the eyes of the person who's trying to get their attention. Those crucial initial steps toward joint attention—looking up at someone's face and then following their eye gaze—are therefore much less likely to occur than with typically developing children. Indeed, the more profound the autism, the less frequent the joint attention.

One way we attract people's attention—and initiate joint attention—is by speaking. But the tendency of autistic children not to orient to voices makes even direct statements like "Look at where I'm pointing" much less effective than with other kids. The combination of not attending to speech and not attending to faces, indeed, is one of autism's most challenging aspects—for student and teacher alike. We will discuss strategies for dealing with this in Chapter 3.

Reading faces: How are they reacting?

When we chase after her, she'll sometimes turn around and smile, but she never looks up at our faces: She's smiling not at us but at our scissoring legs. Once when his mother was worried, he cried out, "Eleven! Eleven!," rushed over to her face, and delightedly traced his finger along the two vertical lines of her furrowed brow.

Related to the relatively infrequent attention that autistic children pay to eyes and faces is their greater difficulty in reading facial expressions: in perceiving, for example, a furrowed brow as a sign of worry—as opposed to a representation of the numeral 11. We often think of the mouth area of the face as the most obvious conveyer of emotions—through smiles, frowns, or grimaces. And, indeed individuals with autism tend to pay more attention to the mouth region of people's faces than to the eye region.

But the area around the eyes is packed with more subtle information about people's emotions, conveying more information, in fact, than the mouth area. The size of the pupil, the position of the eyelids, the position of the pupil relative to the whites of the eyes, the speed of the eyes' motion, where the eyes are focused, and the shape of the eyebrows—all of these comprise a sort of "language of the eyes." Different values and combinations of these variables of size, position, shape, and speed can express emotions as specific as fear, pride, jealousy, playfulness, and longing. Follow someone's eye gaze over to the objects or people they're looking at—perhaps a bunch of different items in quick succession—and one can sometimes come close to reading their mind. Yet, as with joint attention, this variety of near-telepathy is also less available to individuals with autism.

While individuals with autism can often glean some information—particularly about the more basic emotions like happiness, sadness, and anger—from people's mouths, their avoidance of eye contact gives them much less practice in making sense of the language of the eyes and in noticing the crucial clues about people's emotions. Additional brain differences in areas of the brain involved in facial processing may add to these difficulties. Whatever its source or sources, however, difficulty with facial expression reading is well-documented in autism and has subtle but extensive consequences for learning.

For starters, how often and how accurately we read faces affects how much we're able to learn about emotions, about the emotional make-up of specific individuals, and about how people react to different situations. Hand in hand with this worldly knowledge is all the associated language: the many words and phrases that go with different facial expressions—for example, "Wow!" (surprise), "Yuck!" (disgust), and "Whoops!" (regret). Learning such vocabulary, in turn, enables us to learn about the emotional characteristics and responses of people who aren't physically present, but appear, say, in the stories we're reading.

The emotional landscape of stories, indeed, is a big part of what makes them compelling and comprehensible: what drives the plot and gets us into the characters' heads. Think of how much less engaging and accessible, say, *Beauty and the Beast* or *Frog and Toad* or *Ramona the Pest* would be if we were only able to take in the bare plot, with no insight into the characters' states of mind. The more compelled we are by stories, the more stories we attend to, and the more we learn about human psychology and acquire the associated language. Such is the virtuous cycle set in motion by accurate facial expression reading.

When that cycle stalls, the consequences are widespread. To one degree or another, autistic children struggle to understand the psychological landscape of the world around them, to make sense of character-driven stories, and to access and internalize the large amount of language that is grounded in human psychology and human-centered narratives. We'll return to these issues in Chapter 2.

Attention switching: Looking up and tracking human interactions

The discussion is lively. It crisscrosses the circle from mouth to mouth. Heads and eyes shift back and forth as different students take the floor. But one girl stands out. Sometimes she looks straight ahead, gazing into the middle distance; sometimes her head moves slowly towards the speaker, but there's a delay. Her eyes often hit their target only when the speaker is almost done; they then linger there even after another classmate has taken over.

Sticky attention. Often associated with attention deficit-hyperactivity disorder (ADHD), it also occurs frequently in autism. When a new person walks into the room, or someone calls out your name, or a new voice starts speaking, how long does it take you to disengage from what you're doing and attend to the person in question? With sticky attention, it takes significantly longer than average: longer than average to look up from what you're doing; longer than average to switch back and forth between speakers. Even when you're highly motivated to do so, you struggle to keep track of the back-and-forth interactions between family members or schoolmates.

On average, each "turn" in a conversation lasts only about two seconds, and the gap between them is about one-fifth of a second. The slightest lag in switching your attention can therefore greatly impede your ability to follow what's going on—let alone join in with the right words at the right time.

Conversations, just like facial expressions, provide vast amounts of information—both social and non-social in nature. The more conversations we follow, the more we learn about conversations: their rhythm, when someone is done talking, when it's OK to interrupt, when it's OK to change topic. Conversations also give us more general information about human interactions: about what people are interested in, about humor, about the conventions of small talk. Conversations that go beyond small talk—say a classroom debate about school lunches or the upcoming election—can be rich sources of information about the world and about the multiple perspectives on that information.

But for someone with sticky attention, all of this is hard to access. If your sticky attention is part of an autism diagnosis, such that you're easily distracted by noise and not so readily attentive to voices and faces, you'll find it especially challenging to follow and participate in class discussions—even if you summon up the motivation to try your best. We'll return to these issues in the next chapter.

Breadth of focus: Taking in the whole scene

When asked to describe his classroom, he writes almost exclusively about the electric outlets next to the computers. Her summary of the Renaissance Fair field trip is a list of details, mostly about the different breeds of dogs that some of the spectators happened to have with them.

Compounding the sticky attention challenges in autism is a tendency towards depth over breadth: a tendency, that is, to laser-focus on small details at the expense of the big picture. Some autism researchers call it weak central coherence, likening it to missing the forest for the trees, or, further still, missing the forest and the trees for the twigs. Others liken it to looking at the world through a telescope. While you can point the telescope in any direction and view everything around you in a sequence of high-resolution, circular slices, it's hard to compile these piecemeal disks into a single big picture. Combining the similes of tree and telescope, picture how hard it would be to conceive of the forest if all we have is a whole bunch of high-resolution close-ups of twigs.

To some extent the narrow bandwidth is cognitive in nature: Studies show that individuals with autism are better at noticing and remembering small details than in processing images as wholes and better at noticing differences between similar items than at generalizing across them. But, as with so many other aspects of autism, there is probably also an element of preference: Recall the tendency, codified within the core symptoms of autism, towards narrow, all-consuming interests. If electric outlets are what fascinate you, why would you bother shifting your metaphorical telescope in any other direction?

Weak central coherence—this focus on details at the expense of the big-picture—has subtle effects on learning. Specifically, it makes it difficult to do the following:

- Organize, make sense of, and/or abstract away from details
- Extract general concepts from specific situations and generalize learning from one environment to the next
- Use context clues to deduce the meanings of unfamiliar words and phrases—an essential skill in language acquisition, language comprehension, and reading comprehension in particular

- Extract the gist, summarize information, and take useful notes

As we'll see in Chapter 6, a great many school assignments assume a much broader cognitive bandwidth than what comes naturally to students with autism.

School assignments also tend to assume a broader range of interests—and only occasionally overlap with the often-idiosyncratic obsessions of autistic students. How interested and motivated a student is, as we all well know, has a huge effect, regardless of diagnosis, on how much he engages and on how well he performs. The motivational aspects of the narrow focus in autism will, therefore, be another subject covered in Chapter 6.

Social connectedness: Showing and listening

He'll point to an old toy he wants that's up on a high shelf, but not to the brand-new toy on the floor that someone just gave him and that the person he's addressing has never seen before. She'll carry on at length about her rock collection but doesn't seem to really care whether people are listening and doesn't seem interested when they start telling her about their own hobbies.

Reflected in many of the core symptoms of autism is a diminished interest in showing things to people and in engaging with what they say. Starting in infancy, compared to their non-autistic peers, autistic children point to things more often out of a desire to have them in their hands (the old toy on the high shelf), and less often out of a desire to call attention to them as objects of interest (the brand-new toy on the floor). Just as ASD children are less likely to look up, follow someone's eye gaze, and attend to what they're attending to—joint attention—they're also less likely to initiate joint attention. They're less likely, that is, to try to get you to look up at them and follow their eye gaze and pointing gestures over to an object that they want you to look at with them. Similarly, they're less likely to bring an object of interest over to show you, and less likely to check your reaction to something that they're doing or saying. Finally, they're less likely to reciprocate: to show interest when you're the one showing, doing, or talking.

Spontaneously sharing, caring about people's reactions, and engaging with what they say and do—all of this presupposes a level of social connectedness that is often missing, or at least manifested less frequently and with less intensity, in autism. Once again, there probably are both cognitive and preferential aspects to this facet of autism. On the preferential side, there's the preference for non-social sounds and objects, the aversion to eye gaze, and the narrow interests. On the cognitive side, there's the difficulty reading facial expressions, difficulty detaching one's attention from objects of interest to attend to others, and difficulty tracking conversations.

Regardless of the ultimate causes, however, the diminished social connectedness in autism has major effects on learning and on quality of life in K-12 classrooms. For one thing, diminished social connectedness means diminished awareness and knowledge of the social and psychological spheres of human existence, difficulty making friends and getting along with classmates, difficulty doing group activities and collaborative projects, and difficulty making sense of character-centered stories (both fiction and nonfiction).

In addition, diminished social connectedness means not experiencing, or experiencing with much less intensity than most people do, a host of social emotions. These are emotions that depend on being aware of and interested in how people react to you or think about you: emotions like embarrassment, modesty, shame, and humiliation. Many of these are sentiments that people might happily live without. But if, say, you've never experienced humiliation, or have felt only mild inklings of it, it's harder to truly appreciate what it is and to empathize with someone who's feeling it. Also tough to relate to are a host of common social goals: fitting in, gaining status, getting noticed, being influential. In these ways, the diminished social connectedness of autistic students only compounds their difficulties in engaging with character-centered stories. Think of how much great fiction is driven by humiliations, social climbing, or the drive for power: *The Scarlet Letter, The Great Gatsby, Macbeth.*

Finally, diminished social connectedness means diminished appreciation of social institutions and concepts: concepts like community, organizations, political parties, ethnicity, and nationalism. These are the backbone of history, politics, and civics—making social studies, among all K-12 subjects, one of the least accessible to students with autism.

All of these are issues that we'll revisit in later discussions of K-12 classrooms, academic subjects, and reading comprehension.

Perspective-taking: Getting into other people's shoes

Anne watches as Sally puts her marble in the basket. Sally leaves the room. Anne takes the marble out of the basket and puts it in the box. Sally comes back. Where will Sally look for her marble?

In the basket, of course. This is the response that most non-autistic kids will give you by the time they reach three and a half years of age. By this point in development, most children are able to put themselves in Sally's shoes and realize that Sally didn't see where Anne moved the marble. Autistic kids, on the other hand, take much longer to grasp this; many never do. The capacity to put oneself in Sally's shoes, sometimes called Theory of Mind or "false-belief" reasoning (the ability to deduce other people's beliefs, even when those beliefs don't match reality), depends on reaching a certain threshold in language acquisition: Language appears to provide the mental scaffolding needed for working out other people's beliefs. We see this with language-delayed deaf children, who, even if otherwise socially connected, have trouble grasping Sally's perspective— they have trouble, that is, until they catch up linguistically, whether through speech or through sign language.

But autistic children appear to depend even more on language than their non-autistic counterparts do. To do as well on the Sally–Anne test as others do, autistic children typically first need to attain higher levels of linguistic mastery—which, given the many difficulties with language associated with autism, is both ironic and unfortunate. It is also one of the reasons why many autistic individuals never pass these false-belief tests: Many never reach the requisite language levels.

As for those autistic individuals who do pass false-belief tests, their above-normal dependence on language is one indication that they're using mental processes that differ from those used by their non-autistic counterparts. Another indication is that autistic individuals tend to be slower in working out Sally's perspective and more error-prone on false-belief tasks outside the laboratory setting, out in the messy real world. Researchers hypothesize that, while most people automatically acquire an intuitive ability to put themselves in other people's shoes—quickly and effortlessly simulating Sally's perspective—autistic people need to reason through these situations deliberately via language: "Sally was out of the room. That means she didn't see that Anne moved the marble. So she'll think it's still where it was when she left the room." This sort of reasoning takes longer than an automatic simulation does, is more susceptible to error, and is more likely to fall apart in the midst of real-world complications and distractions.

Some researchers have compared difficulties with intuitive, automatic perspective taking to difficulties with map reading. Most people are able to read maps intuitively, effortlessly rotating the layout and geometry of streets, as needed, in their heads. But a small subset of people are so deficient in automatic visual processing that, if they want to get from point A to point B on a map, they need to translate the cartography into verbal directions: "Go two blocks, then turn left; go another three blocks, then turn right…" When it comes to social reasoning in general, and perspective taking in particular, autistic students may similarly depend on verbal translations or verbal directions.

All this has important implications for classroom instruction. The impairment in automatic, intuitive perspective taking further complicates what we've already seen of the social challenges in autism. It also exacerbates the difficulty that autistic students have in making sense of the many character-centered narratives and the many narratives involving multiple points of view that they will encounter throughout their school years. The compensatory strategy of verbal translation—of spelling out the social dynamics explicitly in words—therefore is something we'll return to in subsequent chapters.

What's intact: Empathy, attachment, imagination, intellectual capacity

While it's important to understand the many idiosyncrasies in autism that pose challenges for autistic students, it's also important to be aware of a number of autistic traits that present potential advantages: traits that parents, teachers, and clinicians can harness when providing instruction. But before we discuss these, let's discuss a related caveat: the importance of not overgeneralizing the deficits we've just finished covering.

It's easy, for example, to look at the various aspects of social disconnection in autism and conclude that autistic individuals are uninterested in emotional attachment and incapable of empathy. But studies have shown both attachment behaviors and basic empathy to be fully intact in many autistic individuals. To understand how this is possible, we need to recall the basic elements that interfere with social connection in autism: preferentially orienting to environmental sounds rather than voices, aversion to eye contact, difficulty reading facial expressions, particularly from eyes, and difficulty with automatic perspective taking. None of these prevent a child from yearning for emotional connection, from enjoying and seeking out physical contact even as she avoids making eye contact, or from getting upset when a parent leaves the room and feeling relief when they return. Nor do they prevent her from feeling distress at someone else's pain: the canonical example of basic empathy.

As far as empathy goes, it's important to draw a distinction between the basic emotional capacity to feel someone's pain and the higher order cognitive capacity to quickly and automatically simulate their cognitive perspectives—for example, Sally's take on where the marble is in the Sally–Anne experiment. Mistakenly assuming that Sally already knows that the marble is in the box doesn't rule out feeling distress if Sally becomes upset and starts crying. Furthermore, as we've seen, autistic individuals who acquire sufficient language are able to work out other people's cognitive perspectives—albeit more laboriously and less reliably than non-autistic people do.

There are other sorts of empathy difficulties in autism that do not preclude the capacity for basic empathy. For example, an individual with autism may fail to empathize only because of his difficulty reading facial expressions—in particular, the expressions in and around people's eyes. If he doesn't witness Sally getting her feelings hurt and the only evidence is the look in her eyes, he may well remain clueless. On the other hand, if Sally is clearly frowning, he may be able to infer that she's upset or disappointed.

In addition, he may have difficulty empathizing with social emotions like shame and embarrassment and difficulty appreciating other people's goals or interests. But such difficulties may simply be consequences of not having personally experienced these social emotions himself, or of not having many social goals of his own, or of not having interests that are in any way similar to those of the other person (recall the "highly restricted, fixated interests abnormal in intensity or focus" of the diagnostic criteria). Autism aside, the more different your emotional reactions and goals are from someone else's, and the less your interests overlap, the more difficulty you'll have in putting yourself in their shoes. Some of the empathy challenges in autism, therefore, simply boil down to the fact that autistic people often have very different reactions, goals, and interests from those of their non-autistic counterparts.

Another empathy challenge in autism is in knowing how to respond to someone's pain or distress. The more what comforts you or cheers you up differs from what people typically find comforting or cheering, the less successful you may be at offering comfort or cheer, and the more you may come across as not caring—when in fact you may care a great deal. In her memoir *The Siege: A Family's Journey into the World of an Autistic Child*, Clara Park (1995. P. 290) recounts how her daughter Jessy, when distressed, could be comforted by hearing the call letters of her favorite radio station, WMNB-FM. Accordingly, Park reports, when Jessy noticed one of her caregivers in tears after learning that her father was in a coma after a collision, "She said, not 'I hope that you feel better,' but 'WMBN-FM.'"

In short, as far as empathy goes, far from being cold, indifferent psychopaths, autistic individuals are the exact opposite. Psychopaths lack basic empathy but have the social skills to act quite convincingly as if they care.

Imagination is another area in which autistic individuals often get short shrift. A deficit in imaginative play is one of the diagnostic symptoms of autism. But the sort of imaginative play that diagnosticians typically have in mind here is social in nature: Does the child play house or engage in other joint imaginative play activities with other children? In no way do deficits in this area preclude the possibility of the child producing, say, highly imaginative drawings or stories, or having an active fantasy life inside her head that may be completely invisible to others. In fact, many autistic kids turn out to have very active, if idiosyncratic, imaginations. Jessy Park, for example, became a renowned artist of unusually creative paintings. As Park reports in *Exiting Nirvana: A Daughter's Life with Autism*:

> Only a mind as free [as Jessy's] of conventional perceptions would make lightning out of a migraine illusion, or convert the dramatic disorder of nature into [an] orderly vision, or transfigure a deteriorating church with colors beyond the rainbow. (2001, p. 4)

Indeed, we find a number of areas of strength in autism. For starters, let's revisit weak central coherence. This, recall, is the lack of big-picture awareness: a tendency to miss the forest and the trees for the twigs. We focused earlier on the associated deficits—the many consequences of missing the big picture. But what we left out were the advantages to seeing the twigs: the advantages, that is, of that narrow, laser-sharp focus. Those who excel at zeroing in on details can be great proofreaders, debuggers of computer programs, and all-round trouble-shooters, for example. Readily ignoring the big picture also makes it easier to perceive the precise size or shape of its individual components, and harder to fall for optical illusions. In the auditory arena, a possibly related skill is perfect pitch, which is, in part, the ability to process musical notes out of context. A rare skill, perfect pitch has been found to be significantly more common in individuals with autism than in the population overall.

Another strength lies in what has been called "reflective," as opposed to "intuitive," reasoning. Reflective reasoning is deliberate, logical reasoning, while intuitive reasoning is less logical and more gut-driven. Many non-autistic people, including highly intelligent college students, can be led astray by an overreliance on intuition, frequently falling for patterns of false logic like this one:

"All flowers need water. Roses need water. Therefore roses are flowers."

Autistic individuals, on the other hand, rely less on intuition and more on deliberate reflection: The illogic here leaps out at them. As one young autistic man observed, "That's like saying 'All people need water. Birds need water. Therefore birds are people.'" While intuitive reasoning is faster than reflective reasoning and helpful in many messy, fast-moving, real-life situations, those who are more prone to reflective reasoning can offer us all what is often a much-needed logical reality check.

Still other strengths turn up in the IQ patterns seen in autism. Verbal IQ, typically, is significantly lower than performance IQ. Given the language challenges in autism and given that some of the questions on

Verbal IQ tests measure social awareness and social reasoning, this is no big surprise. The Performance IQ, on the other hand, not only is often average to well-above average in autism, but also tends to turn up marked strengths in visual reasoning and pattern recognition. In general, the more we factor out the linguistic and social components, the more likely we are to find intact skills. Mathematical reasoning, mechanical reasoning, logical reasoning: all these are potentially immune from the cognitive problems in autism. So is analytical reasoning more generally—so long as we're sure to eliminate the linguistic and social confounds.

It's important for people who work with autistic children to actively seek out these strengths—especially because of how the language weaknesses and attention behaviors can distort our impressions. One of the first things we notice about people, typically, is how well they express themselves orally, how well they understand what we say to them, and how alert and tuned in to the world they seem to be. A child who has trouble putting words together, doesn't appear to understand us, and looks unfocused and out of it can easily appear more cognitively impaired than he really is. Indeed, particularly in the more severe cases of autism, where the linguistic and attention issues are at their most salient, people easily and routinely overgeneralize the weaknesses and overlook the strengths.

Even the core weakness in autism, the deficits in social connection, can sometimes have silver linings. Diminished interest in what other people think can be liberating: it can empower people to form more objective opinions, un-warped by social pressures, and, for better or for worse, to state those opinions openly and directly.

Autism, of course, is a spectrum of severity across multiple dimensions, and it's important to keep in mind that in the more severe cases the strengths may be both more limited and more difficult to access. When working with an individual child, it's essential to avoid any up-front assumptions based on how she initially comes across to us, but to probe, subskill by subskill, her strengths and her weaknesses. The goal from the start is to meet her exactly where she is.

References

American Psychiatric Association. (2022). *Diagnostic and statistical manual of mental disorders-V-TR*. (5th ed., text rev.). Author.

Kleinman, J. M., Robins, D. L., Ventola, P. E., Pandey, J., Boorstein, H. C., Esser, E. L., et al. (2008). The modified checklist for autism in toddlers: A follow-up study investigating the early detection of autism spectrum disorders. *Journal of Autism and Developmental Disorders, 38*(5), 827–839. https://doi.org/10.1007/s10803-007-0450-9

Park, C. C. (1982). *The siege: A family's journey into the world of an autistic child* (p. 209). Back Bay Books.

Park, C. C., & Sachs, O. (2001). *Exiting nirvana: A daughter's life with autism* (p. 4). Little, Brown.

CHAPTER 2
NOT ATTENDING TO THE RIGHT THINGS: HOW THE CORE DEFICITS AFFECT LANGUAGE AND LEARNING

In Chapter 1 we discussed the various core challenges in autism. We began with those challenges that are also considered diagnostic features: what autism, by its very definition, entails. In particular, we discussed how autistic individuals show diminished social reciprocity and restricted, repetitive behaviors. We also looked at some of the factors that research has shown to underlie these traits. We reviewed the reduced tendency of autistic individuals to attend to speech sounds and to people's faces; their difficulty in reading facial expressions; and their frequently "sticky" attention—their difficulty, that is, in 1) disengaging from current activities and redirecting their attention elsewhere, and 2) switching their attention back and forth between different speakers. Finally, we looked at challenges in higher order cognition, in particular big-picture thinking, with individuals with autism tending toward a narrow, fragmented focus on details rather than a wide-angled focus on wholes. In this chapter, we'll connect these tendencies to the various language, literacy, and learning challenges in autism.

One reason why it's important to flesh out these connections is that, if we look through the diagnostic criteria for autism, we find no mention of specific language, literacy, and learning challenges. These challenges, rather, are consequences of the core deficits of autism. Autism, meanwhile, is a spectrum of severity across multiple dimensions—as we discussed in the previous chapter. One consequence of this heterogeneity is that different autistic individuals have different levels and types of challenges in language, literacy, and learning. We begin with language.

The language challenges in autism range from difficulties in producing clear speech, acquiring vocabulary, and putting words together into grammatical sentences, to difficulties understanding language in social contexts and using language in socially appropriate ways. In addition, the degree of language impairment varies from individuals at the more severe end of the spectrum who are nonverbal or minimally verbal, to those at the mildest end of the spectrum who communicate fluently in fully grammatical, linguistically sophisticated sentences.

Even among those autistic individuals who communicate fluently, however, there are linguistic challenges. While their overall levels of vocabulary and command of syntactic structures may be normal to above normal, they nonetheless, by the very definition of autism and by virtue of qualifying for an autism diagnosis, experience deficits in social communication and higher order comprehension: in conversation skills, in narrative skills, and in comprehending socially sophisticated language. Social communication deficits, indeed, are the one sort of language deficit that is universal across the autism spectrum—especially if you include a new diagnostic category that we didn't discuss in the first chapter: a condition called social pragmatic communication disorder (SPCD).

SPCD, introduced into the *Diagnostic and Statistical Manual of Mental Disorders* (DSM-V, American Psychiatric Association) in 2013, is intended for those who meet the social and social communication criteria for autism but who lack some of the other core traits—particularly restricted and repetitive behaviors and obsessive interests. For the purposes of this book, most of what we say here about language and learning challenges (and, later on, about interventions) will apply to the SPCD population as well.

At the same time, our discussion of language will mostly focus on aspects that aren't just about speech. That is, we'll mostly be considering vocabulary, grammar, sentence structure, language comprehension, and the social uses of language. All these factors arise not only in speech, but also in written language (whether handwritten, typed, or texted) or sign language, and so play a role in many aspects of language, literacy, and school performance. We will begin, however, with a brief discussion of three idiosyncrasies in autism that are specific to speech.

One is the difficulty that some autistic children have in clearly articulating speech sounds—particularly consonants and multisyllabic words. Some researchers have proposed that this difficulty stems from a tendency of these children to have a co-occurring condition that goes by the name of "speech apraxia." Speech apraxia is an oral-motor disorder that interferes with the ability to plan and execute speech sounds. The evidence for the co-occurrence of speech apraxia in autism, however, is limited, and dissenting researchers have argued instead that what explains the speech articulation difficulties in autism—when they occur at all—is the diminished tuning in to the other people's speech (including their moving lips). Typically developing children, constantly attending to speech and to faces, spend many hours imitating speech sounds, particularly during the early phase of language acquisition known as babbling. Over time, these children experiment with their mouths, tongues, throats, and vocal chords, gradually figuring out which vocal movements make which speech sounds. The less a child tunes in to speech sounds and lip movements, and the less socially motivated that child is to sound like other people, the less the child will engage in this "tuning in and tuning up" behavior. Even if he produces some speech-like sounds, these may remain limited and poorly articulated.

A second speech-production issue sometimes seen in autism relates to an underlying deficit in phonological processing, or in the processing of speech sounds, as measured, for example, by a person's ability to accurately repeat nonsense words. This difficulty may be another consequence of diminished attention to speech sounds and lip movements. At a higher level, it has implications for learning how to read, and so we'll cycle back to it later on in this chapter.

A third speech-production issue in autism is a tendency toward odd patterns of speech tone and prosody. Some individuals with autism use a nasal or high-pitched speaking tone—in what is possibly yet another consequence of a diminished interest in attending to and imitating other people's speech. Additionally, some autistic individuals appear to have poor control over their speech volume, or to speak in a continuous monotone with few expressive pauses—in what may be manifestations of the broader social-communication deficits that we'll discuss below.

We turn first to vocabulary.

Figuring out what "modi" means: Problems with learning new words

A child is given a toy to play with; an adult opposite her has a different toy in a bucket. While the child looks at the toy in front of her, the adult looks at the toy in the bucket. Suddenly, the adult says "It's a modi!" What does the child do next?

If he is a typically developing child over the age of 18 months, he will look up at the adult, follow her eye gaze, and deduce that "modi" must refer to the adult's toy in the bucket. Put another way, typically developing children typically use joint attention to learn the meanings of novel words.

Joint attention, recall from Chapter 1, combines attention to a person with attention to an item that is a potential object of shared interest. Person A attracts Person B's attention (say, by commenting on something that they're attending to). B responds by disengaging from what he's doing and looking up at A's face to see where A is looking. B's eyes then follow A's eyes to A's object of attention. In one final step of social awareness or social reasoning, B then infers that A's comment is probably about the thing that A is attending to.

As noted in Chapter 1, diminished joint attention pervades the diagnostic criteria for autism and correlates tightly with autism severity. As it turns out, it also correlates tightly with word learning. If the child with the toy doesn't look up and follow the speaker's eyes upon hearing "It's a modi," she will miss out on an opportunity to learn what "modi" means. Worse yet, she may mislearn the meaning of "modi": She may assume that it refers to the toy in front of her rather than to the toy in front of the speaker. In one oft-cited anecdote of such a mistaken word mapping, an autistic child began referring to his toy truck as a "sausage" because his mother happened to be talking about sausages while he was looking at the truck.

Vocabulary is one of those areas of huge variation in autism. At the more severe end of the spectrum we find those who both use and appear to comprehend few to no words. At the opposite end we find individuals with sophisticated vocabularies of well-above-average sizes. Numerous studies suggest that how frequently a child engages in joint attention behaviors not only correlates with, but also is a causal factor in how much language the child subsequently acquires—particularly where vocabulary is concerned.

Reduced joint attention may also mean reduced appreciation of intentional communication—of why people talk in the first place. If you rarely look up at speakers, you may have little sense of why they are speaking. If you have little sense of the various reasons why people speak, you will have little sense that language is generally used for purposeful communication. Not seeing language as a tool for communication may reduce your own interest in using language. Finally, not realizing that language is a public, intentional communication system available to everyone, you may also not realize that you can use words the same way that others do. At the more severe end of the autism spectrum, even those children who do learn some words often use these words more to privately label the objects that interest them rather than to communicate something about these objects to other people.

Failing to appreciate language as a public communication system and other people as participants in it, in turn, may also reduce your interest in and motivation to ask questions about the meanings of specific words or the labels for specific objects. Think of how often a typically developing toddler asks, "What is that?" or "What's a robot?" Cumulatively over the years of childhood, questions like these result in a great deal of vocabulary acquisition.

Also facilitating word learning are the sorts of perspective-taking (or Theory of Mind) skills discussed in the previous chapter. These skills are measured, for example, by the Sally–Anne "false-belief" experiment: Can the child put herself in Anne's shoes and infer that Anne thinks the marble is still in the basket? As it turns out, appreciating the speaker's perspective can be crucial in deducing the meaning of a new word.

Imagine that the speaker and listener are looking at an array of stuffed animals belonging to animal categories known to both the speaker and the listener: a bear, a bunny, a dog, a cat. Imagine also that somewhere among these animals is one whose identity is unfamiliar to the listener. If the speaker says, "Look, a kangaroo!" a listener who is able to put himself in the speaker's shoes will naturally deduce that the speaker must intend this new word to refer to the unfamiliar animal. The listener would reason, in other words, that if the speaker had instead intended to refer to the dog, she would have used the familiar label "dog." In this way, the listener narrows down the possible referents of "a kangaroo" to the one stuffed animal that doesn't already have a familiar label. The capacity to reason about the speaker's perspective and intentions, therefore, can help listeners zero in on potential word meanings. The weaknesses in such reasoning in autism can limit this additional opportunity for word learning.

Finally, learning a word entails not just associating a particular utterance of the word with a particular situation, but also generalizing across all the situations in which the word is used. Except in the case of proper names like Barack Obama, no word refers to only one specific object, event, or situation. Instead, its meaning is a function of all the situations in which it could be used. Consider all the different shapes and sizes of dog that the word "dog" refers to. As we noted in the previous chapter, however, individuals with autism have difficulty generalizing across stimuli. As a result, they may also have difficulty learning the precise extent and generality of a word's meaning. Indeed, as the renowned autistic animal behaviorist Temple Grandin reports, "My concept of dogs is inextricably linked to every dog I have ever known. It's as if I have a card catalogue of dogs I have seen, complete with pictures" (1995, p. 28).

Technically, even the most linguistically limited, socially disconnected autistic individuals may appear to have picked up some words—at least inasmuch as we may hear them pronouncing those words. But pronouncing words isn't the same as knowing what they mean. Many children with autism have some degree of echolalia: a tendency to echo back words they hear, often without understanding their meanings. Such children may have reached a point in development where they attend somewhat to speech sounds and are motivated to figure out how to match their own speech accordingly. But they may do these things without having attained the levels of joint attention and generalization skills necessary to deduce word meanings or to appreciate the communicative functions of language.

Figuring out what "embarrassment" means: Problems with socioemotional vocabulary

> The summer she turned seven she acquired "sad" and "happy"… and when I drew a sad face and a happy one, Elly herself volunteered "mouth down" and "mouth up."… The comprehension of these crude approximations of emotion was light-years beyond her old imperviousness. Yet they bore the same relation to the subtleties of actual emotions as a road map bears to the colors and forms of a living landscape.
>
> Clara Park, *The Siege: A Family's Journey into the World of an Autistic Child* (1992, p. 212).

Related to joint attention, and also diminished in autism, is a phenomenon called "social referencing." This involves attending to people's facial expressions, tones of voices, and body language in order to assess their reactions to particular circumstances. When the airplane makes a weird noise, does the flight attendant look worried? In addition to telling us how we should be reacting to things, social referencing can provide more nuanced information about word meaning—as, for example, when speakers use evaluative terms like "icky" (with a tone and look of disgust) or "fantastic" (with a tone and look of approval). As we discussed in Chapter 1, while most information about people's emotional reactions comes from eyes rather than from mouths, individuals with autism tend to focus more on mouths than on eyes. Their resulting difficulty in reading facial expressions—and body language more generally—makes words with emotional connotations particularly challenging to learn, from reaction words like "icky" and "fantastic" (and "Wow!", "Yuck!," and "Whoops!," to name a few more) to emotion words like "surprise," "disgust," and "regret."

Relatedly, the same perspective-taking challenges that make the false-belief (Sally–Anne) tests hard for autistic individuals may also make it hard for them to fully grasp belief-related words like "know," "think," "believe," and "pretend."

Also challenging are words with social connotations—words that describe feelings about people ("love," "infatuation," "hate"), words that describe feelings inspired or caused by people ("jealousy," "embarrassment"), and words that characterize relationships between people ("friend," "enemy," "lover"). Finally, the sorts of vocabulary that are used mostly in unstructured social interactions—e.g., slang, idioms, small-talk expressions, and pop culture terminology—may be hard for autistic individuals to pick up. Among those with large vocabularies, indeed, there is a bias towards the more "bookish" words that appear disproportionately in structured, nonsocial contexts like lectures and textbooks.

Thus, even autistic individuals with large overall vocabularies often have weaknesses in subareas of vocabulary that pertain to emotional states, mental states, social relations, and slang.

English as a foreign language: Problems putting words into grammatical sentences

> Anybody who hears Jessy speak more than a word or two realizes that something is wrong. She has learned English as a foreign tongue, though far more slowly, and she still speaks it as a stranger… Pronouns get scrambled: "you" for "I," "she" for "he," "they" for "we." Articles and tenses are confused or disappear, verbs lose their inflections or are omitted altogether.
>
> —Clara Park, *The Siege* (1982, p. 292)

The middle of the autism spectrum contains a large number of children who acquire many dozens, or even hundreds, of words—even while remaining delayed and linguistically limited relative to their non-autistic peers. Within this broad subpopulation, vocabulary, in fact, tends to be a relative strength compared to grammar.

When we discuss grammar difficulties in autism, it's important to distinguish what we'll call "school grammar," on one hand, and "basic grammar," on the other. School grammar is what is taught to non-language impaired, native English speakers in school: topics like parts of speech, common punctuation and spelling errors ("its" vs. "it's"; "their" vs. "they're" vs. "there"), and finer points of style like dangling modifier errors and faulty parallelism. In contrast, basic grammar is more fundamental. It encompasses the sorts of topics that non-language impaired, native English speakers acquire without any explicit instruction. These include topics like subject-verb-object order ("The dog chased the cat" vs. "The cat chased the dog"); verb tenses ("She walks," "She is walking," "She walked," "She will walk"); and the word order and use of auxiliary verbs in questions ("Who gave the boy a cookie?"; "Who did the girl give a cookie to?"). Basic grammar is an area in which a significant portion of individuals on the autism spectrum experience limitations.

Most impaired in basic grammar are those who have no grammar at all: those who, however large their vocabularies, speak in one- or two-word phrases ("Cookie," "Go away") and don't use language to express subject-verb-object relationships. A child at this level might use the phrase "Go away" depending on his specific wishes, for "I want to go away," "I want you to go away," or "I want him/her to go away." This sort of speech, sometimes called "telegraphic speech," occurs in typically developing two-year-olds as a precursor to acquiring full sentences and grammar. In autism, unfortunately, a number of children plateau at this stage.

Some children in this pre-grammar group may appear from time to time to have the capacity to produce longer, fully grammatical utterances. But occasional grammatical sentences amid mostly telegraphic speech usually turn out to be mere echoes of other people's speech. As we discussed in the previous section, some children with autism echo words without necessarily knowing their meanings. What is more generally called "echolalia" can also include entire sentences and paragraphs.

There are various reasons for echolalia in autism. Sometimes it is merely a manifestation of the tendency of autistic individuals to engage in restrictive/repetitive behaviors; sometimes it is a self-soothing behavior. When used for communicative purposes, however, echolalia is a tactic to which an autistic person may default when she lacks the syntax skills to break a phrase or sentence into its component parts—e.g., subject, verb, and object. If she can't parse sentences into smaller groups of words and doesn't know the rules for recombining these word groupings in new ways to reflect new situations, her recourse is what some autism researchers call "gestalt processing." She simply takes certain prefabricated sentences that she's heard other people say—particularly at times that are personally significant to her—and memorizes them as wholes, with no sense of their internal syntactic and semantic structure.

Then, perhaps in an attempt to recreate the situations that she associates them with, she might later repeat these sentences verbatim in what's known as "delayed echolalia." In a bid to get another cookie, for example, she might say what she heard last time she got a cookie: "Do you want a cookie?" Whole-sentence echolalia, in other words, is a symptom of an inability to combine words into novel sentences.

The majority of those children with autism who acquire reasonably large vocabularies (in the dozens to hundreds of words), however, do move beyond telegraphic speech and echolalia to full sentences. Yet in constructing those sentences, a significant proportion of these children exhibit limitations in grammar.

Recent research into these grammar limitations has turned up two types of limitation, represented by two subpopulations of roughly equal size. First, there are children who use only a limited number of grammatical constructions and speak in shorter sentences. Compared to the other group, they make fewer grammatical errors. They also produce much less speech overall and use a more limited vocabulary, more jargon (meaningless strings of words) and more echolalia. Lastly, they have below-average nonverbal IQ scores. Those in the second grammar-impaired group, which has average nonverbal IQ and vocabulary scores, use a much broader range of grammatical structures and speak in longer sentences. On the other hand, they make many more grammatical errors. In their different ways, both groups are grammatically limited: one by its more restricted grammatical range, the other by its large numbers of errors.

Much has been written about grammar errors in autism. Autistic children often omit certain function words, particularly articles ("a" and "the"), auxiliary verbs (e.g., the "is" of "he is walking"), copula verbs (e.g., the "is" of "the ball is red"), and third-person and past-tense endings (e.g., saying "He walk" rather than "He walks" or "He walked"). They may also reverse pronouns (saying "I" instead of "you" or vice versa). In addition, compared to their same-aged, non-autistic peers, they tend to speak in shorter, less-complex utterances, to ask fewer questions, and to have difficulties with verb tense, relative clauses, and wh-questions. Beals and Hurewitz, in an unpublished study of wh-questions in autism, found problems not only with articles, tenses, and wh-questions, but also with possessive pronouns and verb agreement. Here are some of their data:

- Who washed the hands?
- What the girl brushes the teeth?
- What he washing him hands?
- What does the boys ride on?
- Which beds is bigger?
- When the boys bikes?
- What was the girls swim?
- Where is the boys?
- The girl brush her teeth?

Where do these grammar difficulties in autism come from? Some researchers have proposed that an additional language impairment, known as specific language impairment (SLI), frequently co-occurs in autism. Children with SLI, indeed, exhibit some of the same grammar difficulties as grammar-impaired children with autism. Other researchers argue that the grammar errors in autism are more extensive than what is found in SLI. Indeed, the range and types of grammar errors in autism recall the errors made by non-native English speakers (English language learners, or ELLs).

In a number of ways, individuals with autism are like nonnative English speakers. Attaining fluent, native-speaker-like grammar generally requires full immersion. But to benefit from full immersion, it's not enough to be immersed in speech. You also need to be paying attention. If you only occasionally attend to speech sounds and to the people producing them, and if you struggle to switch your attention back and forth between speakers when people are conversing, you are probably not accessing the full immersion necessary for fluency—even in your first language. It would be like living for years in a place surrounded by speakers of an unfamiliar language, but spending most of your time in their midst listening to loud music through headphones. Depending on how often you take off your headphones, you may pick up some words and phrases, but you will never attain native-speaker-like fluency, no matter how long you are "immersed" in the language.

The tendency of autistic individuals to not attend to speakers and speech sounds varies across the spectrum. This variation, in turn, is causally associated with language acquisition. Where speech attentiveness and joint attention behaviors are frequent enough, full fluency is possible, but in the majority of cases, it remains elusive.

Beyond these barriers to full immersion are additional obstacles to linguistic mastery in autism. One is a lack of sensitivity to feedback. All language learners make errors, and young children learning their first language are no exception. But most children overcome these errors by absorbing corrective feedback from the environment. Typically, this feedback is not explicit: Most children do not need to be explicitly corrected. Rather, children pick up discrepancies between how they talk and how others talk and gradually adjust their speech to conform to the community. If they say "eated" and most people around them say "ate," they start saying "ate" also.

But children with autism appear to be less responsive to such implicit, environmental feedback. Their errors are more likely to persist even when they hear everyone else speaking differently. These persistent errors, incidentally, include not only grammar mistakes, but also odd word choices and made-up words: The fact that no one else uses these words in the ways they do doesn't seem to faze them. In *Thinking in Pictures and Other Reports from My Life with Autism*, Temple Grandin reports on how she used word "prosecution" after she learned how to pronounce it when she was six:

> I had absolutely no idea what it meant, but it sounded nice when I said it, so I used it as an exclamation every time my kite hit the ground. I must have baffled more than a few people who heard me explain "Prosecution!" to my downward-spiraling kite. (1995, p. 32)

This imperviousness to implicit feedback may be partly a result of not fully tuning into how other people talk, but social factors may also play a role: Autistic individuals may feel less social pressure and/or social motivation to sound like other people.

Beyond these general impediments to language acquisition, some of the specific grammatical skills with which individuals with autism struggle require some social reasoning skills. To use articles—"a" and "the"—correctly, you need to be aware of what your conversational partner already knows. Whether you say, "The cat just walked by" or "A cat just walked by" depends on whether you think that the cat in question is familiar to your partner and salient in her consciousness. If you lack this sensitivity, you might choose the wrong article. Or not appreciating why articles matter, you might default to using the same article all the time—or not bother with articles at all.

Pronouns also involve social reasoning skills. The meanings of "I" and "you" shift depending on who is speaking and who they are addressing. To deduce these shifting meanings, children have to attend to third-party conversations and switch their attention from speaker to speaker. The meanings of "he" and "she," of course, depend on gender. Gender, as we know, is partially a social variable—and for many individuals with autism it simply isn't salient enough to motivate correct and consistent distinctions between the various pronouns they encounter. Finally, determining when it's appropriate to use a pronoun instead of a noun phrase depends on some of the same considerations that go into choosing between "a" and "the." Whether you say "the cat came back" or "it came back" depends on whether you think that the cat in question is salient in your listener's consciousness and whether she has enough contextual information to figure out what "it" refers to.

Finally, there are more general social factors at play in whether a child develops full fluency. The more socially tuned in he is and the more interested he is in interacting with others, the more motivated he is to communicate—and to communicate a broad range of messages. One particularly rich context for communication is in play with peers—particularly imaginative play where language is used in more elaborate and abstract ways to discuss objects and situations that are merely imagined. But as we've discussed, such peer interactions are significantly diminished in autism.

If a child is instead primarily motivated to express basic wants and needs, she will tend to limit her expressive language to basic sentences—either in the form of delayed echolalia ("Do you want a cookie?") or in simple statements of the form "I want X." Active practice, of course, is an important part of language learning—and so not using a variety of sentences severely limits the child's opportunities for expressive language mastery. In particular, if she's only expressing basic wants, she will rarely practice past and future tense, or ask wh-questions, or use relative clauses—or a whole host of additional grammatical structures.

Further limiting a child's linguistic opportunities are the communicative responses of other people. However eager his parents may be for him to communicate, and however motivated they may be to provide him with a linguistically rich environment, it can be difficult to keep up a one-sided flow of language towards someone who seems under-responsive and communicates little in return. Many parents nonetheless persist in initiating and sustaining these linguistic overtures. Siblings and peers, on the other hand, are generally less emotionally invested and motivated, and many peers reflexively move on to more responsive playmates.

Figuring out what "It's cold in here" means: the challenge of linguistic pragmatics

"It's cold in here." Perhaps the speaker is answering someone's question about the temperature of the room. Or perhaps she is talking to someone who is standing next to an open window. Or perhaps she is commenting on the chilly vibe she has sensed upon entering a room populated by silent, glaring people. Whether "it's cold in here" is simply a literal description of temperature, a request to close a window, or a metaphorical commentary on an emotional tone depends on the specific social context and on the communicative intent of the speaker.

What linguists and speech-language pathologists call "pragmatics" takes us beyond literal words and phrases to the social contexts of specific utterances. Pragmatics is pervasive: much of what people communicate goes beyond the literal meanings of the words they utter, and a listener will grasp the full message only by inferring what the speaker's likely intent is in the given context. Much of pragmatics—indeed, much of communication--thus taps into the social communication deficits that are universal across the autism spectrum.

The more indirect the language and the more social its context, the more elusive it is to individuals with autism. Humor and small talk are especially challenging.

As for their own pragmatic uses of language, autistic individuals tend to be less social and more instrumental. That is, they speak less often to initiate interactions, acknowledge their listeners, share impressions, and show off, and more often to express wants and needs or to carry on about topics that interest them.

Particularly in unstructured social situations with peers, the rates of spontaneous communication, conversational initiations, and sustained interactions are quite low in autism. Even highly motivated individuals with average to above average vocabularies and linguistic fluency may struggle to identify topics of conversation initiated by others, contribute relevant remarks, engage in appropriate conversational turn-taking, and formulate responses that take into account what their listener does and doesn't already know. Autistic individuals also have difficulty in guiding conversations—e.g., in changing topics smoothly and in eliciting remarks from their conversational partner(s). In larger group settings, their tendency towards "sticky attention"—difficulty switching their attention rapidly from speaker to speaker—may impede their ability to follow conversations and jump in at appropriate moments. Their often narrow range of interests, and the often all-consuming nature of those interests, may limit their participation in many discussions. Or, alternatively, it may propel them to abruptly switch the conversation to one of their favorite topics and carry on about that topic at great length without pausing to let their listeners get a word in edgewise. (For Temple Grandin, it might be cattle handling equipment; for Jessy Park, security systems.) All of this, of course, hampers their performance in class discussions—something we'll return to in Chapter 6.

These challenges also affect narratives. Autistic narrators have difficulty considering what their audience does and doesn't already know. They may not provide sufficient background information or connect ideas clearly. Or they may overemphasize material that is already familiar to the reader while leaving out information that is of far greater interest. Illustrating this second tendency is the "bee experiment." In this experiment, an individual (Person A) invites a child to take the perspective of someone (Person B) who misses out on part of a demonstration. Person A shows the child and Person B a mechanical bee, demonstrating how it can flap its wings. Person B excuses herself and leaves the room, at which point Person A shows the child how the bee can also nod its head. Then Person B returns and asks, "Now what can the bee do?" The results of this experiment showed autistic children to be just as likely to respond with "flap its wings" as "nod its head." In other words, they appeared not to have considered how, from B's perspective, the more informative answer is something that B did not witness—namely, the head nodding.

Beyond these idiosyncrasies, the narratives of autistic students tend to contain less of what some call a "landscape of consciousness"—i.e., fewer references to the psychological states of the people involved in the narrative, with less frequent use of the kinds of mental state terms we saw to be challenging for individuals with autism (embarrassment, friendship, infatuation). In addition, narratives may be skewed toward the autistic person's specialized interests, centering repeatedly on certain specific topics—e.g., ceiling fans, superheroes, or power stations.

All these factors have implications for school performance—both in essays and, even more so, in open-ended, creative writing assignments—issues we'll return to in Chapter 6.

What is an advertisement? Limitations on incidental learning

Related to the challenges in speaking, word learning, grammar/syntax, and pragmatics is a general challenge in language comprehension. The smaller your vocabulary, obviously, the harder it is to make sense of what you hear and read. The same goes for limited syntax: Those who speak in a narrow range of simple sentences tend to have trouble understanding longer and more complex sentences—the more so if they struggle to sustain attention to speech. As for pragmatics, difficulty understanding the many messages that are only implied rather than stated explicitly impedes overall comprehension. So does difficulty switching attention from speaker to speaker during fast-moving conversations.

Comprehension difficulties, therefore, are as pervasive in autism as difficulties with pragmatics. Worse, they can severely hamper learning—both learning about the thoughts and motivations of other people and learning about the world more generally. Most of what young children learn is not taught to them explicitly. Instead, they sponge it up from the everyday conversations they participate in or overhear—mealtime and bedtime conversations with parents, conversations with peers, or overheard third-party conversations—in person or in videos. In particular, much of the information that teachers assume students know by the time they start school—from what mailboxes are for to what an advertisement is—is learned, not explicitly from lessons, but incidentally through their attention to spoken language. Deficits in such knowledge can significantly hamper academic performance, particularly reading comprehension.

Learning from books instead of people? Obstacles to reading comprehension

Given all the challenges that autistic individuals have attending to and making sense of spoken language, especially open-ended conversations, might written texts, especially highly structured, non-social texts like textbooks, be promising alternative venues for learning? Unfortunately, however, challenges in spoken language may also affect reading skills.

As far as basic reading mechanics go, various estimates find that 6%-21% of autistic children have what is called "hyperlexia": a precocious ability to recognize and decode printed words (including words they don't yet understand) (Ostrolenk et al., 2017). In other children, however, mapping letters to speech sounds can be impeded by the phonological processing difficulties, discussed earlier, that sometimes accompany autism.

A more pervasive challenge harks back to language. Most of the language weaknesses that limit the comprehension of spoken language—in vocabulary, syntax, and nonliteral language—also limit reading comprehension. Put another way, whether it is channeled through speech or through text, language is language and English is English. Most language comprehension difficulties, therefore, are also reading comprehension difficulties.

A third challenge comes from deficits in general knowledge about the world. Much of what children read in school assumes that they have acquired a certain repertoire of worldly knowledge. This assumed repertoire, moreover, increases as students progress through school. It also plays a significant role in reading comprehension, as we see in the famous "baseball study" (Recht & Leslie, 1998). Here, 7th and 8th graders read a narrative about a baseball game and, as it turns out, poor readers who knew a lot about baseball performed as well on various comprehension measures as did more skilled readers. Beyond baseball, there are other popular pastimes; there are traditions and holidays; there are jobs and laws and businesses—there is, in short, a world of cultural activities, institutions, and norms, any of which may coincide with an autism-related knowledge deficit. The cumulative effects of years of diminished opportunities for incidental learning, potentially widening the gaps in general background knowledge between autistic individuals and their peers, may also increase the difficulties that autistic students have, relative to those peers, in making sense of grade-level texts.

Especially wide are the gaps involving knowledge that is social in nature. As we discussed in Chapter 1, social knowledge includes concepts like community, organizations, political parties, ethnicity, and nationalism—concepts that underlie much of history, politics, and civics and that make social studies textbooks particularly elusive to autistic students.

Deficits in social background knowledge can also impede comprehension of character-centered narratives. In general, the more social the narrative—the more it centers on social interactions and social reactions, the more driven it is by the psychology of its characters, the more overlaid it is with that "landscape of consciousness"—the more elusive it is. We see this, for example, in experiments involving the "Strange Stories Test" (Happé, 1994). Here, participants are presented with vignettes in which characters say things they don't literally mean—e.g., "It's lovely, thank you. It's just what I wanted", as a polite reaction to an unwanted gift. Individuals with autism, even those high functioning enough to pass the Sally–Anne tests, struggle to make the correct psychological inferences. Compounding this, as noted in Chapter 1, they may fail to understand or appreciate social motivations like humiliation, social climbing, or the hunger for power. Social motivations like these are what drive many of the classic texts assigned in school—e.g., *The Scarlet Letter*, *The Great Gatsby*, and *Macbeth*.

Besides their difficulties with social content and with psychosocial inferencing, autistic individuals also have reading difficulties that hark back to some of the big-picture thinking challenges we discussed in Chapter 1. Making sense of extended discourse often means integrating information from the broader context of the text as well as from one's own personal background knowledge. Such integrative thinking can be challenging for autistic students—even when they don't need to do any social reasoning, and even when they do have the requisite background knowledge. We see this, for example, in the trouble that some individuals with autism have disambiguating homophones—like the word "bank" in the context of running errands versus river settings. Typically, the setting is clear from the text's broader context, and the reader's background knowledge about errands or rivers will fill in the rest. But those who have difficulty integrating such context cues and background knowledge may have significantly impaired comprehension—even of texts that otherwise might appear accessible.

Effects on emotional health and behavior

Not being able to express yourself clearly—especially your basic wants and needs—can be a huge source of frustration. Compounding this frustration is not being able to understand what other people say to you. When what they say involves explanations about unexpected events or warnings about pending change (e.g., a fire drill, a non-routine trip, the temporary departure of a parent or aide), your comprehension difficulties can cause tremendous anxiety. After all, without explanations and warnings, the world is a much scarier, more unreasonable, and more unpredictable place. Suddenly a shrill noise goes off and everyone is lining up to leave the building—what is going on?

Many children will calm down and learn to regulate their emotions by processing them with other people. But autistic children have difficulty partaking in such conversations, and this makes it much harder for them both to regulate their emotions in the short term, and to learn emotional self-regulation skills over the long term.

Collectively, all these factors contribute to the frequent meltdowns and aggressive behaviors exhibited by some individuals with autism.

Besides frustration and anxiety, there is boredom. Difficulty understanding the language used in classroom instruction, classroom discussions, and interactions in the schoolyard and in the cafeteria can cause kids to tune out and grow bored. This boredom, which may be aggravated by narrow interests, can lead some to act up, or at least to squirm around in their chairs and appear rudely disengaged. As noted earlier, language limitations and narrow interests can also make it hard to participate in conversations and discussions—even for those who summon up the motivation to try their best.

When autistic individuals "misbehave" or fail to attend and cooperate in these various ways, it's important for those who work with them to be aware of the potential underlying causes. Much of this has nothing to do with ill will or bad attitudes, and everything to do with the challenges of language, communication, and narrow interests.

Language, literacy and learning—a quick recap

As we've seen, the core symptoms of autism, though primarily social, can result in a variety of linguistic challenges. In combination with the social and the big-picture thinking challenges, these linguistic challenges have downstream effects on incidental learning, the acquisition of background knowledge, narrative skills, reading comprehension, and, as we just saw, emotional health and behavior.

We'll start discussing how to address these various challenges in the chapters to come. As this chapter has suggested, language is the most urgent, and the most promising, place to begin.

References

Grandin, T. (1995). *Thinking in pictures and other reports from my life with autism* (pp. 28, 32). Doubleday.

Happé F. G. (1994). An advanced test of theory of mind: understanding of story characters' thoughts and feelings by able autistic, mentally handicapped, and normal children and adults. *Journal of autism and developmental disorders*, 24(2), 129–154. https://doi.org/10.1007/BF02172093

Ostrolenk, A., Forgeot d'Arc, B., Jelenic, P., Samson, F., & Mottron, L. (2017). Hyperlexia: Systematic review, neurocognitive modelling, and outcome. *Neuroscience and biobehavioral reviews*, 79, 134–149. https://doi.org/10.1016/j.neubiorev.2017.04.029

Recht, D. R., & Leslie, L. (1988). Effect of prior knowledge on good and poor readers' memory of text. *Journal of Educational Psychology*, 80(1), 16–20. https://doi.org/10.1037/0022-0663.80.1.16

CHAPTER 3
HOW TO DIRECT ATTENTION AND BREAK THINGS DOWN: EARLY INTERVENTIONS FOR LANGUAGE AND BASIC SKILLS

We've now reached the point in our book where we start turning to strategies—specifically, strategies for addressing the various barriers to learning described in the first two chapters. This chapter will focus mostly on the skills that are prerequisites to academic success in K12 classrooms: skills that typically developing students acquire without explicit instruction. As we suggested in the previous chapter, the most urgent skill is language. Language, we've seen, is an area of significant and wide-ranging deficit in autism. It is also essential for accessing the K12 curriculum.

By the time most students enter kindergarten, they've mastered nearly all the fundamentals of their native grammar—including syntactic structures that elude even some of the more verbal students with autism. Whether an autistic student is placed in a general classroom, an autistic support classroom, a special education classroom, or some combination, language is essential. The details of a child's placement will depend in part on her overall level of functioning, and in part on the specific options at her school. In all environments, instruction primarily occurs through language, and it is largely through language—spoken, signed, written, and/or typed—that students are expected to respond to teachers and classmates and to complete their work. Language, of course, is also essential for life at home, life in the community, and life in general.

Besides language skills, there are other basic skills that teachers may assume that students have mastered by the time they enter kindergarten, or, at least, that may help new kindergartners adjust to the novel expectations of elementary school. These include attending to teachers, following directions, familiarity with numbers and letters, basic conceptual skills, and, of course, basic social skills. Therefore, while our primary focus in this chapter will be on language, we'll also discuss strategies for teaching some of these other pre-K skills as well. "Early intervention," the cover term for interventions for preschool-aged children with disabilities, is thus another way to characterize what we're focusing on here.

The primary audience for this chapter is parents who are making decisions about which sorts of early interventions are most appropriate for their children. A secondary audience is pre-K teachers who have one or more students with autism in their classrooms as well as some latitude to select particular programming or interventions on their behalf.

We'll begin by discussing the standard, established therapies—therapies that are often delivered, at least in part, by trained therapists, whether in the home, at the clinic, or at center-based early intervention programs. Some of these therapies are so intensive—running up to 40 hours per week—that parents and other nonprofessionals may also play major roles in delivering them. After discussing the standard therapies, we'll turn to some less formal, more ad hoc, therapies or strategies that parents and teachers might consider trying on their own.

"Look at me": Jumpstarting the process of language learning

In the very earliest stages of language instruction, "Look at me," delivered in an exaggerated sing-song or a slightly raised volume, is a common way to begin a teaching session. One might alternatively, or simultaneously, hold the child's preferred toy near one's eyes. One might withhold this toy, or a coveted cheerio, until the child looks up and responds. Tactics like these are typical openers to the initial therapy sessions for children with autism. After all, if the child isn't paying attention to the therapist, therapy can only go so far.

As we discussed in the first chapter, many of the basic language and learning challenges in autism trace back to idiosyncratic attention patterns: the narrow focus of attention, the tendency not to attend to speech and to speakers, the tendency to get distracted by incidental sensory stimuli, the tendency not to attend to the things that speakers attend to, and the difficulty switching attention back and forth between speakers. In extreme cases, these tendencies and difficulties not only limit the child's full immersion in her native language, but cut her off from most opportunities for learning language and acquiring basic knowledge about the world around her. Accordingly, embedded in the various therapies and strategies that we'll discuss below are techniques for directing or motivating attention to the appropriate targets in order to teach basic categories; basic concepts; and, first and foremost, basic language.

Most of these therapies and strategies are tailored specifically to children on the autism spectrum. However, a more general therapy is also routinely prescribed to children diagnosed with language impairment (with or without autism): namely, speech-language therapy. Typically limited to one to two hours per week, speech-language therapy is among the least intensive therapies provided to children with autism.

Speech-language therapists address a variety of linguistic challenges, from pronunciation to vocabulary; from syntax to conversational pragmatics to overall comprehension. They also use a variety of techniques, including visual supports like gestures, pictures, and sign language, as well as behaviorist and naturalistic techniques, many of which we'll discuss below in connection with autism-specific therapies.

Speech-language therapy typically runs in parallel with other, much more time-consuming, autism-specific therapies—therapies that typically range between 20–40 hours per week. These therapies are also more expensive and correspondingly more difficult to get insurance companies to pay for. Increasingly, however, insurance will cover more standard, evidence-based therapies—particularly if a doctor deems them medically necessary.

The two standard therapies most likely to be covered by insurance, besides speech-language therapy, stand in diametric opposition to one another. One is a behaviorist, instructor-centered approach; the other is a naturalistic, child-centered approach. (To anyone familiar with the debate between traditional and progressive education, the differences and issues involved should be familiar.) After discussing these two approaches, we'll look at some alternative interventions that parents may encounter and/or should be aware of, including high-tech computer and tablet-based interventions.

Prompting at the table: Behaviorist approaches

A child and a therapist sit on opposite sides of a small table. The therapist places a toy cookie in front of the child and says "Touch cookie." He waits a second as the child lifts her arm and touches the cookie. The therapist praises the child, removes the cookie from the table, pauses, and then puts the cookie back on the table along with a doll. The cookie is to the child's right; the doll to his left. "Touch cookie," the therapist says again (trial two). The child hesitates. A few seconds pass. The therapist directs the child's hand to the cookie.

In the third "trial," the therapist leaves out the doll. After "Touch cookie," the child immediately touches the cookie and the therapist praises her.

The fourth trial is like the second one: The cookie is to the child's right; the doll to his left. But this time the child correctly touches the cookie, and the therapist praises her with extra enthusiasm.

In the fifth trial the therapist switches the positions, putting the cookie on the child's left and the doll on his right. "Touch cookie." The child hesitates, moves his hand back and forth, and touches neither. The therapist directs the child's hand to the cookie. The therapist then removes both objects from the table.

The process continues until the child consistently touches the cookie regardless of which position it's in. The task then switches, and the child is asked to "Touch doll." When the child masters this, the therapist alternates between "Touch doll" and "Touch cookie." Once the child is reliably labeling both objects, the therapist adds a third object, then eventually a fourth. He also might start expanding and varying the verbal prompt, alternating between "Touch the cookie," "Show me the cookie," and "Where is the cookie?" The entire process may require several dozen sessions spread over several weeks.

The underlying teaching protocol goes by the name of "discrete trial training," "discrete trials," or DTT. The child is asked to do something in response to a verbal prompt. Additional prompts are added as needed, then gradually faded until the child consistently responds with accuracy. Correct responses are rewarded with praise—"Good job!", "Nice!"—initially accompanied by a preferred toy or food. Praise, too, is gradually faded. Besides teaching a child to recognize and respond to object labels like "cookie" and "doll," DTT may target concepts like color, shape, and same versus different, categories like animal and clothes, and actions like "Stand up" and "Sit down." To secure the child's attention, early trials begin with commands to "look at me," rewarding the child when he makes eye contact. Early trials also focus on imitation, which is considered a foundational learning skill: The therapist models a particular action or gesture (e.g., standing up or sitting down) and prompts the child to "do this." Imitation figures prominently in early speech training. To teach the child to ask for a cookie, for example, the therapist might start by saying: "What do you want? [pause] Cookie," thus prompting the child to imitate "cookie." Over time she fades this prompt to just the initial "k"sound: "What do you want? [pause] K."

DTT is a core component of Applied Behavioral Analysis (ABA), the most generally accepted and commonly used intensive therapy for autism. ABA, in turn, is a form of behaviorist training. While it often occurs in structured environments as in the tabletop scene described above, it can be deployed in a variety of settings. Regardless of setting, however, the principles remain the same. Complex tasks—like language use or categories or concepts—are broken into simpler subtasks; each subtask is taught to mastery before new tasks are systematically introduced. Correct responses are reinforced with praise; incorrect responses are ignored or corrected; extra prompts are added as needed and gradually faded.

Behaviorists view all skills, language included, as forms of behavior— behaviors that are controlled, or motivated, by specific elements in the environment. The two most basic types of linguistic behavior are what behaviorists call "mands" and "tacts." A mand—think of the word "demand"—is a request. Mands include not just commands, but also questions—which are requests for information—though, as we'll discuss later, ABA training doesn't focus on question asking. A tact is the action of labeling or describing. A given word, say "cookie," can be used as either a mand (as a request for a cookie) or a tact (to label an object as a cookie). Because mands and tacts correspond to different behaviors, the two ways of using "cookie" are considered to have different meanings. Teaching the full meaning of a word, therefore, means teaching both its mand and tact "meanings." Given the discrete way in which behaviorism trains subskills, teaching these distinct meanings requires separate, dedicated training sessions: for example, a series of trials that teach a child how to use the word "cookie" to request a cookie, and a separate series of trials that teach a child how to use the word "cookie" to label a cookie.

The advantages of ABA's DTT include the large number of trials that the therapist can conduct during these across-the-table sessions. Evidence suggests that—in part because of the difficulties with generalization we discussed in earlier chapters—a great many trials are often required before a child with autism gains mastery of a given skill. Then there's the precision with which the therapist can plan out each session ahead of time and control how it plays out. This includes minimizing the extraneous environmental factors that, as we've seen, can often distract students with autism. In addition, the general DTT protocol potentially prepares students for the concentration and deskwork required in school.

Perhaps the biggest advantage of DTT is the degree of control the therapist has over the stimuli that motivate and shape the student's responses. With a gradual fading or reintroduction of prompts and reinforcements, the therapist eventually (ideally) teaches the student to produce the targeted responses spontaneously and precisely when appropriate. One of the common criticisms of DTT, however, is that the skills learned in such structured, tabletop environments may not generalize to real-life situations. A related criticism is the artificiality of the training environments as compared with the real-world environments in which the student ultimately needs to function. Finally, many young kids with autism are unable or unwilling to sit still for long periods of time.

For all these reasons, much of ABA therapy is conducted in the child's preferred environment using preferred activities and toys—in what is sometimes known as "milieu training." The therapist, however, still exerts control. She arranges the environment ahead of time with carefully chosen stimuli, motivators, and reinforcements. Then, during play, she might prompt the child to produce the appropriate mand by moving a favorite toy out of reach. If the child responds incorrectly, just as in DTT, she models the correct response—a strategy called "recasting" —and prompts him to try again. The upside of naturalistic ABA is that children may be more motivated and may more readily generalize and apply what they learn to other real-life settings. The downsides are that the pre-planning can be more complicated and the extraneous, potentially distracting environmental factors more difficult to limit. In some cases, those extraneous factors (e.g., the pattern of a particular rug) may be so distracting that they actively impede generalization to novel environments with different extraneous factors (e.g., a rug with no pattern).

What about what ABA has to offer, specifically, in terms of language training? Consistent with its focus on language as an environmentally induced behavior rather than as an abstract construct, ABA's guidelines for language instruction focus more on the environment than on general linguistic concepts. The most extensive set of guidelines for ABA-based language instruction, *Teaching Language to Children with Autism and Other Developmental Disabilities* (2010), focuses on ways to modify the environment and elicit certain types of responses, but not on how to teach the linguistic details or address linguistic errors. If the child says, "Me wants cookie," the therapist simply models (recasts) the correct response and prompts the child to imitate it. If the child consistently says, "me" instead of "I," or "wants" instead of "want," there is no systematic drilling of pronoun rules and verb rules. Trials instead focus on specific linguistic behaviors (e.g., mands for cookies) in specific situations (e.g., hungering for a cookie).

What about the more complex linguistic structures that we discussed in Chapter 2 as challenging for individuals with autism? *Teaching Language to Children with Autism and Other Developmental Disabilities* (2010) discusses the complex manipulations of the natural environment, such as how to arrange a bunch of toy cars of different sizes and colors, that may be necessary to elicit certain types of complex responses (e.g., "The red car is bigger than the white car"). But, once again, the book doesn't discuss the general linguistic rules—for example, how to use comparative adjectives like "bigger"—or how to teach them. Nor does it explain how to elicit, let alone teach, abstract word meanings—such as general nouns like "animal," abstract words like "idea," "pretty," "carefully," "think," and "until," and social words like "friend" and "jealousy."

Teaching Language to Children with Autism and Other Developmental Disabilities (2010) does dedicate a section to pronouns—which is only appropriate, given the challenges that individuals with autism have here. The book suggests alternating prompts like "Touch your shirt" and "Touch my shirt" and eventually expanding to a group setting so that multiple individuals can model multiple pronoun references to multiple people. But it doesn't flesh this out in detail. Nor does it broach the other pronoun challenge in autism: when to use a pronoun in the first place.

Beyond pronouns, the most advanced linguistic topics addressed by the various ABA language materials are past tense and wh-questions. Again, however, the focus is on elicitation rather than on linguistic instruction. Therapists may elicit past tense by asking, "What did you just do?" right after an event just happened and then by gradually increasing the time interval. Therapists may elicit wh-questions by opening up a robot's battery compartment and then prompting a child to ask, "Why did you open it?" But there's no discussion about teaching the general rules for past tense—for example, the regular past tense "ed" ending ("walked," "jumped"), or the irregular past tense ("ran," "went")—which are independent of specific environments. Nor does the book address how to teach the placement and form of "do" in questions ("why do/ does/did…"), except via the general procedure of recasting (modeling the correct response) when the child's response contains an error. No protocol exists for systematically drilling specific linguistic skills—even though there is nothing in principle about behaviorism that should rule out such an approach.

Beyond this, there are many linguistic concepts that the ABA language materials simply do not cover. *Teaching Language to Children with Autism and Other Developmental Disabilities* (2010) acknowledges, for example, that there are multiple ways to frame questions and answers beyond the scripted language of their suggested prompts and targeted responses. For example, one might mand a cookie by saying, "Is it OK if I have one of those cookies?", and one might tact a cookie by saying, "A homemade chocolate chip cookie!" The book, however, leaves these multiple possibilities, along with the more advanced syntax—articles and other function words, complex verb tenses, relative clauses—mostly unaddressed. It suggests, rather, that once a child reaches a certain level of functioning and is able to ask others for linguistic information, he will be able to learn from his natural environment as non-autistic children do.

Playing on the floor: Naturalistic approaches

The child sits in the middle of a toy-strewn floor, moving a red toy truck around in circles. His dad sits down next to him and says, "Look at that truck go! It's going around in circles!"

The child continues to move the truck around, not looking up.

"Hey, I want to play too," says the dad, and picks up a blue truck. He rolls it over to the red one and says, "Hi, I'm Mr. Blue Truck. Can I play with you, Mr. Red Truck? Can I follow you around in circles?" The dad rolls the blue truck behind the red truck. The child stops playing with the red truck and moves his hand over to the blue truck. Before the child can grab it, the dad picks it up and says, "Wee! Now I'm a flying truck! Look where I can go!" The adult moves the truck up to his temple, right next to his eyes. The child looks up and finally makes eye contact. "Do you want the blue truck to fly back down? Truck back down?" asks the dad. The child reaches for the truck. "Wait, wait, wait!" says the dad, backing away a bit. "If you want Mr. Blue Truck to come down, you need to tell him. Do you want down truck?" The child keeps reaching and the dad keeps inching away. "Do you want down truck? Down truck?" the dad repeats. Finally the child says, "Down."

"Oh, you want me to go down. OK, daddy down." The dad lies down on the floor, continuing to hold the truck up in the air and away from the child. The child keeps reaching for the truck. "OK, time for daddy to get back up!" says the dad, sitting back up. "Now is it Mr. Blue Truck's turn? Do you want down truck?"

"Down" says the child.

"Down.... what? Daddy down?" The child shakes his head. "Daddy down or truck down?"

"Truck!" says the child.

"Ok, truck down," says the dad. "Let's let Mr. Blue Truck fly back to his friend, Mr. Red Truck." The child grabs the grounded blue truck and starts pushing it around in circles.

Many people criticize ABA for what they see as an overly scripted, artificial approach to fostering communication and other skills—even when ABA is conducted in naturalistic settings. As an alternative to ABA, some autism practitioners endorse naturalistic approaches. Known originally and informally as "Floortime," and more recently as "DIR" (the "Developmental, Individual differences, Relationship-based" model), or "DSP" (the "developmental social-pragmatic" model), these approaches reject the therapist-controlled, across-the-table setting of DTT. Instead, therapists, teachers, and—first and foremost—parents are supposed to get down on the floor and follow the child, join her in her world, and engage her in play and social interactions. Floortime antics include imitating the child and following her attentional lead (attending to what she is attending to rather than directing her elsewhere). The assumption is that all this fosters a more positive emotional adult–child relationship than do the more coercive ABA-based methods, and that this relationship, in turn, will motivate the child to engage and learn more.

While the ultimate goal of Floortime is direct interaction with other people, some of the general strategies of Floortime practitioners—play involving dolls and puppets, and play that treats toys like Mr. Blue Truck and Mr. Red Truck like characters—taps into recent findings about autism. Autistic children are more comfortable interacting with dolls and puppets than with people. Ideally, Floortime's play with non-human characters can serve as a gateway to more direct human interaction.

In terms of human interaction, one of Floortime's biggest contrasts with ABA is in its approach to joint attention. In ABA, as we saw, the child is directed to "look at me"; in Floortime the therapist instead attends to what the child is attending to. In both cases, the goal is for the child and therapist to be attending to the same thing such that, when the therapist refers to the thing in question, the child makes the appropriate linguistic associations. The difference is that in ABA joint attention is therapist-controlled, while in Floortime it is child-centered.

Proponents of naturalistic approaches like Floortime argue that ABA conflicts with what's known about language acquisition. Linguists, they point out, have convincingly argued that humans have a natural capacity to learn language. This means that children will discover the rules of their native languages without explicit instruction. Floortime proponents, assuming that this natural linguistic capacity is fully intact in autism, argue that there is no need to teach language explicitly to autistic children via scripted prompts and discrete trials. The challenges in autism, they propose, are not with language, but, rather, with attention (i.e., the diminished attention to speech and to speakers) and with motivation (i.e., a diminished motivation for social interaction). The role of the teacher (or parent, or therapist), according to Floortime, is to influence the child's attention or motivation by manipulating his social, physical, and linguistic environments—which, to some extent, takes us back to the environmental approach to language learning seen in naturalistic ABA.

Indeed, Floortime proponents implicitly endorse and practice some of the same behaviorist tools they criticize: prompting, imitating, and soliciting desired verbal behavior. Often, however, these solicitations are indirect. In order to motivate the child to communicate more or with greater clarity, for example, Floortime practitioners may perform what they call "playful obstruction." That is, they may playfully get in the child's way, or withhold a desired object, or pretend not to understand. Depending on how much prompting and playful obstruction there is, Floortime sometimes resembles naturalistic, milieu-based ABA. Or, at least, Floortime may often look like a hybrid of the more naturalistic variants of ABA and the more open-ended, child-centered approach that Floortime theoretically aspires to be.

On the other hand, the closest thing that the self-styled naturalistic approaches have to a language curriculum—*The Affect-Based Language Curriculum (ABLC)* (Greenspan & Lewis, 2005)—is strikingly different from that of ABA. The *ABLC* focuses on learning in the natural environment and on socially functional uses of language. To foster vocabulary development, for example, everyone working with the child should constantly label and describe the objects in the natural environment. As for pragmatics and grammar, these are to be learned mostly through incidental exposure and productive practice in the context of activities and games. For example, one of the *ABLC's* learning goals is "Combines three or more ideas in an interconnected plot." To work on this, the adult and child might enact an imaginary zoo outing, and then the adult might ask the child to recount what happened. If the child only combines one or two ideas, the adult might have one of the characters say, "Wait—we forgot to see the giraffe!" The *ABLC*, though, doesn't elaborate what to do next if the child fails to respond with more ideas. Unlike the ABA guidelines, the ABLC includes no protocols for systematic prompting to ensure that desired responses are eventually produced.

Other *ABLC* learning goals include sustaining back-and-forth exchanges for at least 15 minutes, reporting, requesting confirmation, elaborating, talking about other people, adjusting one's speech when it isn't understood by others, and talking about the immediate past and the imminent future. The ABLC suggests various general environmental manipulations to facilitate these goals—for example, activities with a variety of events, calling the child's attention to an unusual event, or talking about an event just before it happens and then right after it occurs. As with its discussion of teaching a child to combine three or more ideas, however, it doesn't spell out what to do if the child doesn't produce the desired response.

One of the weak points of the *ABLC*, thus, is in eliciting linguistic practice on the topics it seeks to teach. This is particularly problematic when the lesson goals are specific grammar skills. Here, the best the *ABLC* has to offer is a "wait-and-see" approach, suggesting things the child might say, but—as before—proposing no follow-up tactics if the child doesn't actually say them. Here, for example, are outlines of two of the ABLC's suggestions for teaching me versus you pronouns:

Via "Barnyard Bingo":

- Wait for the child to say, "My turn" in response to "Whose turn is it?"
- When it's the adult's turn, the child can say, "Your turn."
- When the child gets all the matching chips for her board, she can say, "Bingo!"
- The adult can ask, "Who won?" and the child can respond, "Me!"

Via Duplos:

- The adult could set up the bus with the driver and large Duplo blocks.
- The child could begin to build with the blocks on the roof of the bus saying, "Mine" when he goes to take a block.
- The adult could ask, "Who's going to put the driver in the bus?"
- The child could respond, "You do it!"

In addition to assuming that the child will naturally produce a response that uses the targeted grammatical feature, the *ABLC* also assumes that the child will use this feature more or less correctly (as in "me!" or "I won!") and doesn't address what to do if she doesn't (as in "me won!" or "you won!"). All this is consistent, of course, with the notion that autistic children, like all children, can discover the rules of their native language without any explicit instruction. The Floortime framework assumes that autistic children in fact already know these rules and just need the right sort of social and environmental motivation to use them. Similarly, the ABLC assumes that the autistic children it targets have acquired enough receptive language to make sense of prompts like "Whose turn is it?" or "Who's going to put the driver in the bus?"

Teacher-directed vs. child-directed: What does the evidence show?

Ultimately, the choice of therapy should depend not on abstract preferences between teacher-directed and child-directed approaches, but on efficacy. Comprehensive reviews of all the empirical studies of both approaches show significantly more support for the behaviorist approaches to language and basic skills instruction than for the naturalistic approaches, though there is some evidence for hybrid approaches that combine the two (Smith & Iadarola, 2015). These findings are consistent with what we have discussed in Chapter 2: Autistic children show patterns of attention that inhibit their ability to learn from the natural environment. Approaches that focus primarily on boosting the child's motivation through playful interactions, as Floortime does, may be limited in their ability to reduce the autistic tendencies not to attend to speech, speakers, or the things that speakers attend to. It's important to note, however, that behaviorist approaches have not succeeded in fully addressing these issues or in bringing many autistic kids to mastery in language and other skills. ABA has produced a wide range of outcomes across children that depend largely on autism severity. But ABA's more active, behavior-shaping interventions appear better suited to altering children's habits of attention than Floortime's more child-centered tactics do.

Both approaches have additional weaknesses, however, that further limit their efficacy. Neither ABA nor Floortime teaches linguistic concepts explicitly and systematically. Neither approach provides explicit linguistic feedback about linguistic errors: At most, there is some corrective feedback when a therapist recasts (models the correct response) and (in the case of ABA) prompts the child to repeat it. Crucially, both frameworks assume that language will eventually be picked up by those autistic children who are capable of it: that at some point, the natural environment will take over. ABA assumes that this will happen following mastery of what its proponents consider to be the linguistic basics; Floortime assumes that correct grammar will follow automatically from a growing motivation to communicate and from an increasingly purposeful use of language. However, as we saw in the previous chapter, there is a significant cohort of children on the autism spectrum who have learned the basics of language and communicate purposefully but still are limited in their correct use of grammar and syntax. However naturalistically typically developing children pick up language, it is evident that the same assumptions cannot be made of most children with autism.

Singing, signing, drawing, and writing: Alternative media for language

Given these limitations, it's worth asking about alternative approaches to teaching language and basic skills that can either substitute for some of the standard strategies or help make them more effective. We should note that, as with speech-language therapy, neither ABA nor Floortime is committed to any particular mode of communication: Both approaches acknowledge that many autistic children struggle with spoken language and may potentially learn and communicate more efficiently through alternative media like sign language and/or pictures and/or text. Thus, some of what we discuss below will include techniques that are already deployed in the standard therapies. Nonetheless, it's still worth considering each of these modes of communication its own right.

Before looking at these alternative modes, however, let's look at two interventions that aim to boost children's facility with the mode that most surrounds them: the oral mode.

Given the tendency of autistic children to preferentially orient to environmental sounds over speech sounds, might there be a way to make speech sounds less like speech and more like other sounds in the environment? It turns out that singing, which converts regular speech into speech that is closer to musical tones, has shown some promise as a language intervention in autism. These results are consistent with Clara Park's anecdotal reports about her daughter Jessy, who has already made several appearances in this book. Jessy Park was initially much more responsive to words and phrases when they were sung rather than spoken. Clara Park also reports that Jessy responded more readily to loud, exaggerated pitch (and gestures) than to regular speech (Park, 1992).

Another approach to the speech issues in autism assumes that the underlying problem has to do with the processing of speech sounds. This is the rationale behind "auditory integration (AIT)" training. Here, children listen through headphones to a customized regimen of filtered and modulated music at different frequencies. The goal is to reduce supposed hypersensitivities to certain sounds. However, comprehensive research reviews find no support for AIT as an effective treatment for auditory sensitivities in autism.

Two properties of speech make it potentially challenging for autistic children with speech delays. One is that speech happens inside the mouth and throat, where it is largely invisible and difficult to model or demonstrate to those who have difficulty producing it. The other is that speech—like auditory information more generally—is fleeting. It comes and goes, and thus runs afoul of attention problems in autism. If a child doesn't shift her attention quickly enough or sustain her attention long enough, she inevitably misses part of the message. Visual information, in contrast, can be static and enduring: if a child takes a while to attend or looks away and then back again, the printed words or pictures are still there.

For the teacher or therapist, visual information has one additional advantage: A child's eyes are more revealing than his ears. It's easier to tell what he is looking at than what he is listening to. It is, therefore, easier to know when his attention needs to be redirected, and, in an ABA framework, easier to shape and reward proper attention behaviors.

Beyond all this (though perhaps partly as a consequence of it), some studies suggest that in autism, visual processing, as opposed to auditory processing, is an area of relative strength (though others have rebutted this finding).

With this in mind, let's look, first, at sign language. Especially in children with minimal speech, sign language has proven an effective autism intervention—perhaps because it is easier to imitate external hand movements than internal mouth movements. Sign language also lends itself well to ABA's behavior shaping and reinforcement strategies. When a child struggles to produce a sign, the therapist can mold the child's hand into the correct shape. Readily observing the child's increasingly close approximations of the targeted shape, she can reinforce them accordingly. Sign language, of course, can be used in combination with speech, raising the possibility of gradually fading the signs and transitioning into oral language. A disadvantage to sign language, however, is that, like speech, it comes and goes: signed sentences don't linger in the air any longer than spoken sentences do. Sign language, therefore, runs into the same attention challenges that speech does.

Other visual systems are less fleeting. The most widely used of these is PECS (Picture Exchange Communication System) (Bondy & Frost, 1985). In place of spoken or signed words, PECS represents words through small, laminated, Velcro-backed pictures (including photographs) or icons, often customized to the child's particular interests and sometimes captioned with printed words. Strict PECS training follows ABA protocols. The difference is that instead of prompting a child to produce a targeted spoken or signed response, the PECS therapist prompts him to select one or more picture/icons, assemble them onto a Velcro strip to form a message (e.g., "want" plus "cookie"), and then hand the strip to her. As with sign language, PECS can be used in combination with speech, and there is some evidence that it can facilitate oral language acquisition in children with minimal speech.

One criticism of PECS is that children may not be able to make sense of the sequences of pictures and icons and understand the semantic relationships (subject vs. verb vs. object) between the different symbols in a given sequence. While they may memorize specific formulaic sequences for requests (e.g., "I want cookie," "I want juice"), they may be unable to combine pictures and icons in the variety of ways necessary for more open-ended communication. Without more explicit instruction, they may not understand the difference between "Girl sees boy," "Boy sees girl," or "Does girl see boy?"

A newer picture/icon-based approach, however, does provide systematic instruction in picture/icon sequencing. The Visual Immersion System (VIS) (Shane et al., 2015) begins with tabletop activities in which students are prompted via recorded animations to use 3-D objects to copy or reenact animations of specific scenes (e.g., a video of a particular doll climbing a toy ladder). After a student can accurately reenact animations of various permutations of, say, who is doing the climbing (e.g., Kermit climbs the ladder; Woody climbs the ladder), he is then prompted to reenact static representations of these same scenes (e.g., a photograph of a particular doll climbing the ladder). As it progresses, VIS training introduces linear sequences of pictures and icons (e.g., a picture of the doll, followed by an icon for climbing, followed by a picture of the ladder). The child is prompted both to reenact scenes based on these sequences, and, conversely, to sequence pictures and icons based on enacted or animated scenes.

The pictures/icons are often customized to reflect the child's daily activities, allowing the VIS to be deployed both in instructional, table-top settings (in a behaviorist approach where prompts are faded or re-introduced and correct answers are modeled as needed), and in naturalistic settings, with all the child's caregivers using the same sets of pictures and icons, for milieu-based learning. The goal is to move children beyond the limitations of PECS to a deeper understanding of the semantic relations within sentences and more open-ended, generative language production. VIS practitioners have found, however, that the transition from static pictures of scenes to sequences of picture/icons can be challenging. As they continue to develop strategies for facilitating this transition, they're also field-testing different icons for more abstract words like prepositions.

This takes us to a major limitation of all the picture/icon-based interventions. Many linguistic concepts are extremely difficult to depict through pictures and icons. This is a problem even with nouns. Nouns that denote concrete objects, of course, are readily depicted by pictures of those objects. But nouns denoting complex and variable scenes ("supper") and abstract meanings ("friendship") are more elusive. Any particular depiction of these concepts—say, a specific meal at a specific table with specific people, or a picture of two people holding hands and smiling at each other—may be interpreted by an autistic child in an overly specific way. Given the tendency in autism toward detail focus and difficulty with generalization, the child may either fail to abstract the general meaning (concluding that friendship means holding hands) or link the meaning to a specific detail in the picture (e.g., "supper" to the chandelier depicted above the table), ignoring the scene as a whole—particularly its social aspects. Potentially, a large number of pictures of different supper events (different foods at different tables with different people) could help with proper generalization, but this quickly becomes impractical, and, indeed, existing picture-based systems typically limit themselves to one picture or icon per word.

Verbs—even concrete action verbs—are generally harder to depict than nouns. Depicting "jump" with a picture of someone jumping, for example, may be misinterpreted as a picture of a person rather than a picture of the person's action. Depictions of adjectives (e.g., "red," "blue") and prepositions (e.g., "over," "under") raise the same concerns: The child may focus on the objects in the pictures rather than, say, their color or position. Furthermore, as with nouns, many verbs, adjectives, and prepositions simply aren't visual enough for clear or unambiguous depiction ("yell," "rough," "of"). The same is true of function words ("and," "or," "if," "then"), verb tenses ("walked," "will walk"), and pronouns ("I" vs. "you," "he" vs. "him").

Of course, those children for whom picture/icon-based systems are most appropriate are those who are not yet ready for the more complex elements of grammar. However, even if the main priority is concrete nouns, obstacles remain. An apple need not be red; an egg need not be white. For proper generalization of these words, particularly given the generalization challenges in autism, multiple pictures may be necessary. Furthermore, a child who is especially interested in color or shape may focus on the redness or greenness or roundness of the depicted apple, as opposed to its apple-ness. Of course, some of the same challenges arise when we teach language using actual objects, situations, and actions: The child may need to see multiple examples of actual eggs or actual apples (or suppers, or jumping) to make the appropriate generalizations.

Potentially bypassing the limitations of pictures and icons—for those autistic children who are able to make sense of it—is written language. It is estimated, in fact, that somewhere between 6%-21% of autistic children have hyperlexia, or a precocious interest in letters and a precocious ability to recognize printed words (Ostrolenk et al., 2017). For them, written language may be a more engaging medium than spoken language. Indeed, both PECS and VIS sometimes deploy cards that contain text in addition to or instead of pictures.

There are additional advantages to written language. While speech and sign language are dynamic and fleeting, and while PECS's laminated pictures are static, written language has both static and dynamic features. It is dynamic when the person communicating is in the process of typing or writing; it is static on the page once completed. Handwriting is particularly dynamic, as the letters, line by line, take their shape—a process that teachers can deploy to attract and hold a student's attention. For example, as Park, working with Jessy, reports, "I printed slowly and clearly; her eye followed the word as it took shape. I wrote the label before I drew the picture, hoping anticipation would tempt her into recognition" (Park, 1982, p. 221)

Written language can also be used to highlight challenging aspects of word pronunciation. Park, for example, found that particular letters could direct her daughter's attention to the consonant sounds that she tended to mispronounce or omit.

The challenge in using written language, particularly with those who are highly interested in letters, is to ensure that the child doesn't just learn printed words as sequences of abstract symbols. By default, many autistic, hyperlexic children focus more on letter sequences than on meanings—even if they can read written words out loud. Thus, written language interventions must ensure that the child not only recognizes printed words, but understands what they mean.

Teaching English as a Second Language

As we've seen, both ABA and Floortime fall short in addressing the grammar difficulties of many individuals with autism. As we discussed in the previous chapter, these individuals resemble nonnative English speakers. Why not, then, supplement the standard autism therapies with materials designed for ELL (ESL) students—particularly those that focus on the grammar rules that the autism therapies neglect? ELL texts that teach the fundamentals of grammar include *Practice Makes Perfect: English Grammar for ESL Students* (Swick, 2018), which covers basic tenses, articles, auxiliary verbs, and comparative adjectives, and *Understanding and Using English Grammar* (Avar, 1989), which covers more complex verb tenses, pronouns, passives, and a variety of complex sentences. Both books include grammar exercises and online activities.

Since ELL materials, however, aren't tailored to the autistic population, teachers of autistic students may need to substantially adapt and supplement them.

Beyond language to other pre-K concepts

As we discussed earlier, there are other early intervention targets besides language that can prepare children with autism for elementary school. ABA training, accordingly, also includes basic numeracy, literacy, penmanship, and cognitive skills. So does an offshoot of ABA known as Direct Instruction (DI). DI, however, mostly focuses on grade school skills, and so we'll return to it in Chapter 6.

To teach basic cognitive skills, visual representations, as we saw with visual modes of language, are a promising venue. One might draw Venn diagrams around pictures or names of different animals to teach general categories like "animal" or "pet," or multiple concentric circles within circles to show "country," "state," "city," "neighborhood," and "home." Or one might draw tree diagrams with names or pictures to show family relationships like "parent," "sister," and "cousin," or power hierarchies like "king, "duke," "knight," and "peasant." Or one might draw maps to illustrate concepts like right or left and provide practice following directions. Or one might draw flow charts with arrows to teach concepts like event sequences (washing hands before eating food), or cause and effect and if-then (if you turn off the light, then it gets dark).

Visual representations can be dynamic as well as static and using them dynamically may help hold a child's attention. A teacher might ask a child for input (e.g., "Where should I move my pencil?") as she slowly draws a circle in a Venn diagram, or a branch in a tree diagram, or a road in a map, or an arrow in a flowchart. She can also prompt the child to contribute his own circles, branches, roads, or arrows—or to draw his own complete diagrams.

Turning, finally, to noncognitive pre-K skills, ABA protocols can shape behaviors like sitting, listening, and making eye contact. To develop more open-ended social skills, Floortime's naturalistic approach may be more promising. In addition, some clinics offer pre-K social skills classes: classes where, under the guidance of trained psychologists, young children with social difficulties practice various aspects of interpersonal interaction during play and conversation-based activities.

Learning on the screen: Computer and app-based interventions

These days, myriad computer programs and apps promise children (and their parents) instruction in all sorts of academic and cognitive skills. While it's debatable how useful these programs are for most children, studies have shown that computerized environments can be a boon for those with autism. This is because autistic children often find screen-based environments more comfortable than in-person environments. Screens bypass the face-to-face interactions that many autistic children find aversive. The regularity and predictability of software programs give many autistic individuals respite from the comparative chaos of real-world environments. While we want to help autistic children function and interact in the real world, we also want—for that very reason—to boost their cognitive and linguistic skills as effectively and efficiently as possible.

Certain cognitive and linguistic skills are conducive to computerized instruction. These skills involve the kinds of systematic rules and procedures that can be abstracted away from real-world environments, fully and efficiently captured by software programs, and taught separately from other skills. Two good candidates are arithmetic and grammar. Less suited to computerized instruction are other aspects of language like vocabulary and conversation skills. Computerized depictions of word meanings ("supper," "friendship") run into the same limitations as the low-tech depictions we discussed earlier. And even today's most sophisticated software programs aren't great conversational partners, let alone great conversation coaches.

Provided they stick with the things they're best at, software programs offer several potential advantages over in-person instruction. They can deliver unlimited hours of practice at relatively low cost; they can automatically adjust to the learning curves of specific users; and they can provide consistent, systematic feedback, never tiring, ever patient.

Potential aside, what do we find in the programs actually on the market? Turning first to grammar-teaching programs—programs like SentenceBuilder, Rainbow Sentences and Laureate's Autism Packages—we do, indeed, find relatively low cost (at least as compared with in-person therapies), many hours of practice, and consistent feedback. Unfortunately, however, these programs have some of the same limitations as the standard in-person autism therapies. None of them provide feedback about linguistic errors that goes beyond recasting (modeling correct responses). None of them elicit full linguistic responses that come entirely from students. Some instead have students passively click on the pictures that match specific linguistic structures. Others do much of the work for the students—either by having them fill in the blanks of partially constructed sentences, or by having them assemble sentences from a small set of pre-chosen words.

Finally, while these programs cover some combination of basic sentence structure, basic prepositions, basic verb tenses, and basic pronoun distinctions, none delve into the more complex areas of grammar that stymie many of the more verbal students with autism. Thus, while these programs may serve as cost-effective reinforcements for skills that in-person therapies, to some extent, already cover, they tend not to supplement these therapies with additional material that children wouldn't otherwise encounter. Nor are these programs backed by rigorous studies demonstrating their efficacy.

Turning to other potentially useful pre-K cognitive skills, we find three programs:

- HearBuilder: a program that gives children practice following increasingly complex, multistep, oral directions
- TeachTown: a program that uses an ABA framework to teach listening skills, basic math, and basic categories
- Time4Learning: a program specially recommended by those who work with autistic students (including homeschooling parents) that teaches math and literacy skills

But these programs, too, lack rigorous data supporting their efficacy. A recent study in the Philadelphia public schools found TeachTown to be no more effective than instruction as usual.

One of the problems with some of these programs is that their screens tend to be busy—cluttered with color, objects, details, and sound effects that may be especially distracting to students with autism. Unsupervised, autistic users may click around randomly or focus on irrelevant details, particularly with programs that prompt them to click on pictures rather than to input words and numbers. Anecdotally, in fact, teachers report this happening frequently.

One program that keeps its screen clean and simple is Montessorium's Intro to Math, a Montessori-based math app that teaches pre-K number concepts (quantity, relative size, counting, and penmanship practice for writing numbers) through simulated hands-on activities and games. Also stripped down and straightforward is the Khan Academy preschool math program, which covers counting, shapes, and telling time. A potential downside of Khan Academy for autistic students, though, is that its explanations assume a typical level of oral language comprehension.

Answering versus asking questions: Broader limitations

This brings us back to language—the top priority in preparing autistic students for school. As we've seen, the standard therapies potentially take them a certain distance but fall far short of raising most children with autism to age-level linguistic mastery. What the standard therapies lack is comprehensive coverage of English grammar, sufficient focus on general linguistic rules, and feedback that targets specific linguistic errors. In the next chapter, we'll attempt to fill these voids.

We conclude this chapter with an observation. In the course of their many hours of therapy, autistic children are expected to spend a great deal of time answering questions. "What do you want?" "What is that?" "What did you just do?" "Do you want Mr. Blue Truck to come down?" "Who's going to put the driver in the bus?" But when do autistic children ever ask questions? Question asking, as much of the linguistic research has noted, is remarkably rare in language-impaired children with autism. And, while some practitioners consider question asking a "pivotal" skill that supports further learning and have had success in teaching it (Koegel et al., 2018), most interventions don't prioritize it. Part of the problem is that it's much easier to elicit an answer than to elicit a question. But eliciting a question isn't the only difficulty.

Indeed, there are several ways in which asking questions is more challenging than answering them. Pragmatically speaking, you need to understand what a question is and what kind of question gets you what kind of answer. Grammatically speaking, as we'll see in the next chapter, you need to know about auxiliary verbs, where to put the auxiliary verb, what to do if there's no auxiliary verb, what to do with the tense of the main verb and the tense of the auxiliary verb, and whether and which wh-word to use. If you say "What it happened?" instead of "When did it happen?" people won't understand you.

Knowing how to ask questions, arguably, opens up far more possibilities than knowing how to answer them. A child who knows how to ask questions can play a more active role in her interactions with others, including her therapists and teachers. She can ask people to clarify what's confusing, validate her conjectures, and fill in knowledge gaps that they might otherwise not be aware of. She can exert some control over her learning—feeding what is, hopefully, a growing curiosity about the world around her.

One of the focuses of the next chapter, therefore, will be on how to teach autistic students, who spend so much of their days being asked to answer questions, the pragmatics and grammar of formulating questions of their own.

References

Avar, B. D. (1989). *Understanding and using English grammar (Azar English Grammar), 2nd Edition*. Pearson.

Bondy, A., & Frost, L. (1985). *Picture Exchange Communication System* (PECS). Pyramid Educational Consultants.

Koegel, L. K., Camarata, S., Valdez-Menchaca, M., & Koegel, R. L. (1998). Setting generalization of question-asking by children with autism. *American Journal on Mental Retardation*, 102, 346-357.

Ostrolenk, A., Forgeot d'Arc, B., Jelenic, P., Samson, F., & Mottron, L. (2017). Hyperlexia: Systematic review, neurocognitive modelling, and outcome. *Neuroscience and biobehavioral reviews*, 79, 134–149. https://doi.org/10.1016/j.neubiorev.2017.04.029

Park, C. C. (1982). *The siege: A family's journey into the world of an autistic child* (pp. 83–84, 94, 209). Back Bay Books.

Shane H. C., Laubscher, E., Schlosser, R. W., Fadie, H. L., Sorce, J. F., Abramson, J. S. (2015). *Enhancing communication for individuals with autism: A Guide to the Visual Immersion System*. Brookes Publishing.

Smith, T., & Iadarola, S. (2015). Evidence base update for autism spectrum disorder. Journal of Clinical Child and Adolescent Psychology, 44(6), 897–922. https://doi.org/10.1080/15374416.2015.1077448

Sundberg, M. L., & Partington, J. W. (2010). *Teaching language to children with autism or other developmental disabilities*. AVB Press.

Swick, E., (2018). *Practice Makes Perfect: English grammar for ESL Learners, 3rd Edition*. McGraw Hill.

CHAPTER 4

TAKING LANGUAGE A STEP FURTHER: WHY SENTENCE GRAMMAR IS KEY AND HOW TO TEACH IT COMPREHENSIVELY

As we saw in the previous chapter, the existing autism interventions take kids a certain distance but then run into practical limitations, particularly when it comes to language instruction.

Some of these limitations reflect inherent teaching challenges. Teaching vocabulary, as we saw, runs into problems of depiction: How do we illustrate "helping" or "friendship"? Whether we use 2D pictures or actual real-world objects and events, many word meanings are difficult to demonstrate clearly and unambiguously. Furthermore, even if we succeed in teaching a child with autism that a particular (illustrated or actual) entity is, say, a "neighbor" or a "doctor," how do we help the child generalize "neighbor" or "doctor" to all neighbors or doctors? As we've discussed, the narrow, detail focus in autism can make proper generalizations difficult: Not all neighbors have curly hair; not all doctors wear thick-lensed glasses. A child with autism may need to see many more examples of neighbors or doctors than a typical child does before he truly knows the meanings of these words.

Also eluding formal instruction is conversational pragmatics, embedded as it always is in messy, real-world contexts. No one has been able to formulate simple, general, teachable rules for such things as when and how to jump into a conversation, how to make small talk, how much to say at a time, how to stay on topic, and when and how to change the topic or end a conversation. The most promising approach may be an indirect, naturalistic one: encouraging a child to tune in to and practice engaging in conversations. But some of the same things that cause conversational difficulties in the first place may limit this approach—namely, difficulty attending to speech and switching attention back and forth between speakers. Then there are the problems with generalization: Will the child be able to apply whatever he learns from one specific conversation to conversations in general? Going over recordings or transcripts of particular conversations may bypass an autistic child's attention challenges, but not his problems with generalization.

Compared with vocabulary and pragmatics, grammar is much more amenable to formal instruction. Grammar, after all, is all about word endings, word order, and hierarchical sentence structure—subjects and predicates, main clauses and subordinate clauses. It therefore is less about the real world, and more of an abstract, rule-based system. It also operates independently of specific nouns, verbs, and adjectives, and thus can be taught using those nouns, verbs, and adjectives that are easiest to represent in pictures (shapes, colors, and concrete action verbs). Grammar, therefore, is highly suited to focused settings that optimize rule learning and eliminate real-world distractions.

Grammar, however, has its own challenges, as we saw with the existing intervention tools. One of them is elicitation. As we saw, neither the ABA nor the Floortime protocols can guarantee that a child will produce a certain type of sentence structure—even one that is filled with errors. Instead, a child might not respond at all, or might respond with a simpler structure than the one that the therapist is hoping to teach.

As for the various software programs and apps, many of these elicit clicks and drags as opposed to productive linguistic output. Those that do elicit linguistic structures give so much guidance that what they elicit is only a small part of what it takes to produce the target structures. As we saw in the last chapter, some programs and apps provide partially constructed sentences for students to complete by filling in blanks; others provide small sets of words for students to order into sentences. Beyond the most basic phrase and sentence structures (e.g., "a blue truck"; "The cup is in the box"), no approach we've seen so far has a mechanism for eliciting a particular type of grammatical structure without partly giving away the targeted response.

In addition, few of these interventions provide systematic exposure to the underlying grammar rules—e.g., subject-verb agreement and past tense -*ed* endings. Instead, standard autism therapies like Applied Behavior Analysis (ABA) and Floortime assume that autistic individuals will eventually pick up these rules implicitly. But this, as mentioned, flies in the face of the widespread and persistent grammar difficulties seen in autism. Relatedly, the existing interventions fall short of full coverage and systematic sequencing of grammar topics.

Unlike the seemingly insurmountable challenges for vocabulary and pragmatics instruction, however, the shortcomings of grammar instruction are practical consequences of the particular approaches taken by different therapies. In this chapter we will attempt to overcome these shortcomings. We'll discuss ways to elicit particular grammatical structures, teach rules systematically, and cover English grammar comprehensively.

Why focus on grammar?

Beyond its teachability, there are other reasons to prioritize grammar. Grammar is a key part of what linguists call "communicative competence." In all but the most obvious, high-context situations, a person who doesn't know grammar won't be able to communicate clearly. When she says, "Mommy give," does she mean "Mommy, give me something," "Mommy is giving something," "Mommy gave something," or "Mommy will give something"? Imperfect grammar mastery may cause frustrations and misunderstandings that compound the various social challenges in autism.

Second, grammar is key to getting beyond the here and now. Many autistic children are only able to express immediate wants and needs and label things in the immediate environment. While this may reflect limited cognitive skills and/or limited motivation, it may also reflect incomplete language acquisition. Only after a child has mastered verb tenses can she express clear thoughts about things that have already happened or that will happen. Only after she has mastered conditional sentences—

like "If it snows, then school will be closed" and "If it had snowed, then school would be closed"—can she express hypotheticals. Only after she has mastered sentences with embedded clauses—like "Sally thinks that the marble is in the basket" and "Anne knows that the marble is in the box"—can she readily express the perspectives of different individuals, as in the Sally–Anne tests we talked about in Chapter 2.

Third, solid knowledge of grammar enhances a child's comprehension of what other people say—particularly when they are speaking of past and future events, hypothetical events, or other people's perspectives. These are common conversational topics, and so the greater a child's comprehension of the underlying grammar, the better poised she is to follow conversations. This, in turn, broadens her opportunities to develop her own conversational skills.

Before we dive into grammar instruction, however, we should note that this chapter is not relevant to all children with autism. Many do not reach, or have not yet reached, the linguistic threshold necessary for grammar. Reaching this threshold means progressing beyond nouns, proper names, and pronouns (e.g., "Mommy," "ball," "this") to verbs, prepositions, and adjectives. These, collectively, are the building blocks of phrases and sentences—as in "Throw the green ball under the table." Thus, this chapter is specifically focused on those children who have acquired—whether through ABA or Floortime and/or speech-language therapy—at least some vocabulary beyond nouns and pronouns.

This chapter is not relevant, however, to those at the mild end of the autism spectrum who become grammatically fluent on their own. Our target population, rather, are those in the middle: somewhere between minimally to fully verbal. Specifically, this chapter is directed at children who belong to the grammar-impaired cohorts we first discussed in Chapter 2.

Why the sentence is the locus of grammar instruction

In teaching grammar, there are various reasons to focus, in particular, on sentences. To begin with, sentences are the basic units of communication. They underlie ABA's various verbal behaviors—e.g., its mands (requests) and tacts (labels). Even though mands and tacts may consist of single words or short phrases, the underlying message is still a sentence. When "a truck" is a tact, it stands for "That is a truck"; when it's a mand, it stands for "I want the truck"; when it's a response to "What is the man driving?", it stands for "The man is driving a truck." Furthermore, even though in high-context situations only a fragment of a sentence needs to be said out loud, many low-context situations require full sentences for full clarity (as with "Mommy give"). Sentences—and knowledge of sentence structure—are thus central to pragmatics: to interacting conversationally, and to understanding what people are saying.

Sentences are also central to thinking. When we think in words, we're generally thinking in sentences—whether in statements (including hypotheticals like "If I leave now, I'd get there by 10:00"), in commands ("Stay calm"), or in questions ("Where did I leave my backpack?"). Even if you only hear your inner voice saying a short phrase like "backpack," such fragments are typically abbreviations of either statements, commands, or questions. Indeed, philosophers of language have argued that our capacity for verbal thought depends in part on our knowledge of sentence structure: that grammar and syntax provide the mental scaffolding for certain types of thinking. Language-deprived individuals, in fact, show evidence of limitations in thinking that reflect their limitations in sentence knowledge. The flip side is that expanding people's knowledge of sentence structure potentially boosts the range of ideas they can think about.

In terms of broader language pedagogy, there are practical reasons for sentence-focused instruction. Many linguistic phenomena only make sense in the context of sentences. This includes basic vocabulary: Most words besides nouns cannot be taught in isolation. Verbs (e.g., "jump," "pat") are best taught in the context of the subject who performs the action ("The girl is jumping") and, if there is one, the object that experiences it ("The boy pats the cat"). Prepositions are best taught not only with their associated objects ("behind the table"), but also with the entity that the prepositional phrase applies to ("The book is behind the table"). Function words like "and" and "if" cry out not only for a following clause ("and came running back"; "If you don't get up soon"), but also, for full clarity, for a larger sentence ("The girl went into the woods and came running back"; "If you don't get up soon, then you'll be late for school"). There is, thus, a feedback loop between learning new words and learning how sentences work.

With these considerations in mind, we turn now to strategies for teaching grammar in general and sentence grammar in particular in an intensive, systematic, comprehensive way. We'll begin by considering how to overcome the challenges of productive practice that we saw with the in-person and high-tech therapies we discussed in the last chapter.

General strategies for eliciting productive practice

In general, an essential ingredient of linguistics training—and of the various therapies we reviewed earlier—is eliciting the specific linguistic structures to be practiced. How do we get a child to utter a subject–verb–object sentence, or use future tense, or ask a "who" or "what" question? As we saw, children need to practice producing specific linguistic structures before they can master them, but how do we prompt such practice without telling them what to say?

The most direct way to get people to produce a particular linguistic response is to ask a question to which they are most likely to have some sort of specific answer—i.e., a question about a specific, familiar, here-and-now situation. The most obvious way to get people to produce a bunch of different responses is to ask a variety of questions about a variety of here-and-now situations involving familiar characters, objects, and events. Finally, the most convenient way to cycle through situations quickly is through pictures. Thus, the basic ingredients for intensive linguistic instruction are large sets of pictures of familiar characters, objects, and events and large sets of questions about them.

But how do we elicit the specific structure we want to teach without giving away the answer? One elicitation strategy is to start the lesson with a model of the correct response. This is the approach taken in the beginning ABA drills and in some of the early lessons of the ABA-inspired software programs. But are there ways to make this sort of guidance less of a giveaway?

One way is to show the child several different models that exhibit the target structure, only one of which is correct, and have the child choose from among them. For example, suppose we're trying to elicit a basic subject–predicate sentence of the form "The square is blue." We prompt the child with a picture of a blue square and the question "What color is the square"? So that the child doesn't simply answer "Blue," we might also prompt her with a set of choices that include, besides the correct one,

"The square is red," "The square is yellow," and "The square is green." Given the attentional difficulties seen in autism, and the fact that, for some, written language is often an area of strength, both the prompt and the choices might be presented both orally and in writing. But instead of prompting the child to circle what she thinks is the correct choice, the teacher can prompt her to reproduce it word for word—whether out loud or by typing/writing. This phase—selecting among several choices that correctly model the grammatical structure being taught and then reproducing it—both gives the child practice using the particular structure and primes her to continue using it as the lesson progresses.

After multiple rounds of such priming, the teacher can remove the choices and go through the same pictures and questions without them (phase two). But she must ensure that the child hasn't just memorized the answers to these picture–question combinations. Autistic kids often rely on intact rote memory—and develop great rote memory skills—when other skills are lacking. Thus, in a third phase of the lesson the teacher can introduce pictures the child hasn't seen before (e.g., a red diamond) and that aren't accompanied by multiple choices. By this time, the child should be sufficiently primed to produce the target structure—e.g., to say "The diamond is red" rather than just "red."

But if at any point the child reverts to a sentence fragment or some other paraphrase that doesn't involve the targeted structure, the teacher can interject a follow-up prompt. At the multiple-choice phase, she might go over the choices again. At a later phase, she might ask the child to include a particular word: one that doesn't give away the grammatical structure but that does help to elicit it. For example, if the child says "Red," the teacher might say, "Please use the word 'diamond' in your answer."

As the targeted grammar structures get more complex, eliciting them may become correspondingly more complicated. A third elicitation strategy—besides multiple-choice modeling and follow-up prompting—is to include a list of written words, or "word bank," representing the kinds of words the child should include in his response. Word banks, of course, risk giving a lot away. We saw this in the last chapter with apps like Rainbow Sentences, where all the words the child selects and assembles make up the answer. The word bank, therefore, should include all the different words and word forms a child might conceivably use in his response, including all the ones he might use by mistake. In the case of "The square is blue," the teacher could include not just "the," but also "a" and "an"; not just "is," but also "are"; not just "square," but also "squares." Nor should the word bank tell the child what order the selected words go in—indeed, for convenience, the words in the bank should be given in the same fixed alphabetical order each time. Collectively, all these measures preserve the goal of the lesson, which is to get the child, independently, to put the correct words in the correct order.

Finally, given how autistic students may rely on rote memorization of picture and answer sequences, it's important for teachers to randomize the elements wherever possible—for example, by shuffling both the exercises and the multiple choices.

Strategies for optimizing feedback

If the child gets the wrong answer, what's the next step? As we saw, most interventions focus on recasting (modeling correct responses) and imitation (having the child imitate the correct response). The software programs may also re-prompt the child with fewer choices or with the correct answer highlighted, and/or indicate via words or sound effects that the answer is wrong. But how much does the child learn from such feedback? The most explicit of it, flagging incorrect answers, is only minimally explicit. There's a huge difference between saying that something is wrong and saying *why* it is wrong. Was a particular word missing an ending? Were a couple of words in the wrong order? In cases where the child has filled in multiple blanks or arranged multiple words to construct a sentence, there are multiple possibilities for errors, and simply telling the child that she's wrong doesn't tell her very much.

Indeed, multiple studies indicate that language-delayed children with autism need more explicit feedback than what the existing therapies provide, and that limiting instruction and feedback to modeling, recasting, and imitation is both inefficient and ineffective. As we discussed in Chapter 2, one idiosyncrasy of autistic children is that they tend to be relatively impervious to incidental linguistic feedback from the environment, such that they often persist in making errors despite such feedback. All this suggests that, with language learning in autism, the more explicit the feedback, the more effective the instruction.

So, what would explicit instruction and feedback look like, say, in the case of the subject-predicate lesson described in the previous section? The teacher might begin by stating the general rule—for example, "To say what color a shape has, you say 'the', and then the shape name, and then 'is', and then whatever color it is." But those who are most in need of grammar instruction may also lack the linguistic comprehension necessary to make sense of this rule when it is formulated in so many words. A better approach might be to call the child's attention to the choices—"The square is red," "The square is yellow," "The square is green," "The square is blue"—and to the pattern they exhibit, and then have the child read or recite these choices. Listing the choices that model the structure being taught, therefore, serves not just as an elicitation mechanism, but also as a teaching strategy.

But such teaching will be only so effective in the absence of active practice by the child. Indeed, at first the child may answer the exercise prompts incorrectly—particularly after the multiple-choice phase is over. Perhaps she omits the "is," and/or says "a" instead of "the" ("A square blue"). How do we give explicit feedback that goes beyond simply flagging the answer as wrong? The most obvious approach is to tell her directly which words she left out and which words need fixing. Having her type or write out her response before providing this feedback, or writing it out for her, makes it easier to point out mistakes. The teacher can circle incorrect words or word endings, list the words that are missing, or insert blanks for missing endings. Then, to ensure that the child understands the feedback and internalizes it, he can prompt her to produce a corrected response. If this response still contains errors, he can provide additional feedback, as before, and solicit another corrected response. Once the child produces a response that is fully correct, the teacher can transcribe it and repeat it back to her for further reinforcement, praise her, and (ABA-style) provide additional rewards as needed or as appropriate. To ensure that she is able to do the given exercise on her own, the teacher should put it back into circulation until the child gets it right once or twice on her own.

When the child's response contains multiple errors, addressing them all at once risks overwhelming her. Instead, the teacher might start with feedback about missing or incorrect words. Once the response has all the right words, she can then focus on problems involving word endings or word order. Some mistakes may boil down to a single error, as when the child says, "The square is red" in response to "What color are the squares?," using singular forms instead of plurals. In this case, the teacher might highlight both mistakes at once: the absence of the plural ending for "square" and the fact that the verb also needs to be in the plural form ("are" instead of "is"). For errors involving word order—e.g., "The boy is carrying the girl" versus "The girl is carrying the boy"—the teacher might circle the words that are out of order ("boy" and "girl") and ask the child to look at the picture and identify which person is performing the action.

In cases where the child gets the correct answer the first time around, the teacher should reinforce it with extra praise and by repeating it back to the child. As for rewards, these can be deployed (and faded) ABA-style—and customized to the child's particular interests.

In the following sections, we'll give additional examples of the above strategies—strategies for both elicitation and feedback. We'll do this while showing how to teach some specific grammar topics, most of which are not covered by the existing therapies. Collectively, these sample lessons will help address the challenge we alluded to at the conclusion of the previous chapter: How do we get individuals with autism, who spend so much of their days answering other people's questions, to ask questions of their own? The first step is to deepen their comprehension of different types of questions.

Sample lesson 1: How to teach children to distinguish between questions

One of the most common prompts in the various language interventions are questions: "What do you want?"; "Where is the cookie?" But one skill that these interventions largely overlook is practice discriminating among different questions about the same object or picture. Such practice, however, is easy to provide—even in the case of simple objects like colored shapes. A teacher might, for example, intermix exercises from the subject–predicate lesson ("What color is the rectangle?") with "What is that?" questions. In order to produce the correct answer—is it "The rectangle is green" or "That is a green rectangle"?—the child needs to pay closer attention to the question than he may have earlier.

More advanced exercises might depict two side-by-side items with different shapes, sizes, and colors. One picture, for example, of a small blue triangle next to a large green oval, might appear with well over a dozen different prompts:

- What color is the oval?
- What color is the triangle?
- Which shape is green?
- Which shape is blue?
- Which shape is bigger?
- Which shape is smaller?
- Which shape is on the left?
- Which shape is on the right?
- Which shape is not blue?
- Which shape is not green?
- Where is the triangle?
- Where is the rectangle?

Given the challenge potentially posed by this much variety, the teacher may want to start with a smaller set and gradually introduce more questions. She might start with "what" questions, then move on to "where" questions, then "which" questions—which tend to be more complex—and then, finally, mix all three together.

Such lessons, of course, involve discriminating between questions only at the level of comprehension, not at the more demanding level of production.

Sample lesson 2: How to teach basic question asking

One reason why the existing therapies have neglected question asking is that it's much harder to elicit questions than answers. To get someone to produce an answer, one simply asks him a question. But how do we get him to do the asking?

One possible first step is to start with the most basic type of question—yes–no questions—and to drill students on the relationship between yes-no questions and yes-no answers. With the same shape and color pictures used in earlier lessons, the teacher might begin with a series of exercises in which there is a blank for a question and beneath it a blank for an answer, labeled accordingly:

QUESTION: _____

ANSWER: _____

While the student watches, the teacher fills in the QUESTION field with a yes–no question about the picture: e.g., "Is that a square?" or "Is the square red?" She then prompts the child to answer in full sentences as in earlier lessons, but also to include "yes" or "no," as appropriate, at the beginning of his answer. He either writes his answer into the ANSWER field, or the teacher transcribes it there for him.

After a series of exercises like this, the teacher switches things up. She starts filling in the ANSWER field instead of the QUESTION field, filling it with answers like those that the child was prompted to give earlier: "Yes, that is a square" or "No, it is red." She then, Jeopardy-style, prompts the student to produce the question that, given the picture, goes with her answer. After the child masters this set of exercises, the teacher mixes together the question-to-answer and the answer-to-question exercises.

In this way, a child who, over years of ABA training, may only have learned questions as prompts that he is supposed to respond to, can now gain a deeper sense of the essence of questions. They aren't just things that therapists say when they want him to respond but things that anyone can say to elicit specific answers. If he himself wants an answer then he, too, can ask the corresponding question.

In addition, in constructing yes–no questions, the child starts learning question syntax. The multiple choices should model the correct form and position of the verb "to be": e.g., "Is the square blue?"; "Are those squares?" If the child produces something in the form of a statement rather than a question—e.g., "The square is blue"—the teacher can circle the incorrectly placed "is" and prompt him to reposition it.

Once the child has mastered the basic answer-to-question process and the positioning of "is"/"are" at the beginning of the question, she can then move on to wh-questions. Here an additional challenge is to begin with the "wh" word ("What is that?") along with any accompanying noun ("What color is that?"; "Which circle is green?"). The other challenge, as with yes–no questions, is to discriminate between different sorts of questions—but now there is an even greater variety to choose from.

Given this, as with the earlier question-discrimination lessons, one might start with just one type of wh-question ("what"-questions are fairly straightforward) and gradually introduce others ("where," "which," "how many"). Ultimately, the child should be able, with a given picture (e.g., a blue circle next to a red triangle) and an ANSWER field filled out with a wide range of answers ("The circle," " Blue," "On the right side," "One") to produce appropriate answers ranging from "Which shape is blue?" to "What color is the circle?" to "Where is the circle?" to "How many circles are there?" Note that teachers, at this point, should give the answers as sentence fragments (e.g., "The circle"; "One"). Full-sentence versions of these answers ("The circle is blue"; "There is one circle") risk giving too much away about the corresponding questions ("Which shape is blue?"; "How many circles are there?").

For all their variety, these questions share one basic property: The main verb is either "is" or "are." More advanced questions require various forms of auxiliary verbs like "will" and "do" ("What did/will the boy give to the girl?"). Before teaching these, therefore, we should first introduce auxiliary verbs. The best time to do that is while teaching the basic verb tenses.

Sample lesson 3: How to teach basic verb tenses

Creators of some of the existing language interventions have found ways to elicit present versus past tense. They might, for example, have the child comment on an ongoing action and then talk about it after it has occurred, perhaps via a photograph or animation. Eliciting future tense is harder, as it is difficult to depict things that haven't yet happened.

An alternative for all tenses is to annotate pictures with time captions. Many children with autism who are ready and able to learn verb tenses are also high functioning enough to have already learned about clock and calendar time. Indeed, calendars are sometimes an area of intense interest in autism.

So, we select pictures of easily depicted actions—e.g., a person walking, running, swimming, carrying someone, pointing to someone, or giving someone something—and add time captions that correspond to different tenses. We might use "now," perhaps accompanied by the current clock time, for present progressive ("is sleeping," "is helping"); "yesterday" or "in 2020" for past tense; "tomorrow" or "in 2040" for future tense; and "on weekends" or "Saturday and Sunday" for the simple present or "habitual" tense ("she sleeps," "he helps her"). Relative terms like "tomorrow," "yesterday," "an hour ago," or "in ten minutes" might be accompanied by precise times, depending on what the current time is ("at 2:00," "on September 25th, 2021"). As for the word bank, it should include all the possible forms and tenses of the given verb. Calling attention, as needed, to the time caption or to the words in the word bank, we then simply say, "Describe the picture."

We first address each tense separately with multiple choices modeling the various tense patterns and verb forms—including not just the regular "-ed" past tense, but also irregular forms like "ran" and "swam." After the child has worked past the multiple-choice phases and mastered each tense by itself, we mix together all the time caption plus picture combinations. Now the child must choose among all the basic tenses, depending on the time caption, as the exercises shift randomly between present progressive, past, future, and habitual.

Mastering basic verb tenses means learning how use two types of auxiliaries: the "is"/"are" of present progressive and the "will" of future tense. Before the child is ready for more advanced questions, however, there is one more auxiliary verb to learn. This one is best introduced through negated forms of the basic verb tenses.

Sample lesson 4: How to teach negation

While it can be difficult to elicit negated verbs from real-life situations, picture prompts readily lend themselves to negation, as we see in the crossed-out pictures and icons, say, of "No smoking," No littering," or No pets allowed" signs. A series of exercises parallel to the basic verb tense exercises but with pictures crossed out can thus introduce the negated counterparts of these verbs. "Is swimming" becomes "isn't swimming"; "will walk" becomes "will not walk."

But in the case of the past and habitual tenses, where there is no auxiliary verb, negation can be expressed only after adding one. So, we add the auxiliary verb "do," give it the same tense and form as the main verb and negate it. At the same time, we revert the main verb back to its basic form. Thus, "walked" becomes "didn't walk"; "ran" becomes "didn't run"; "swims" becomes "doesn't swim," and "run" becomes "don't run." Guided by multiple choices that model complete sentences that use these negated phrases ("The boy didn't walk"), the child practices using the different forms of "do" and converting the main verb to its basic form. Once he has gotten beyond the multiple-choice phase and mastered these various steps, via different combinations of crossed-out pictures and time captions, he is ready to learn advanced questions.

Sample lesson 5: How to teach advanced questions

To introduce the use of auxiliary verbs in questions, the teacher can return to the QUESTION- and ANSWER-field formats used to teach basic questions. As before, he can start with simple yes–no questions with the questions filled into the QUESTION field. But this time he should select from the action pictures used to teach tense, along with their various time captions. The questions, accordingly, will express various tenses: e.g., "Is the girl swimming?", "Will the girl swim?" In the case of the past and habitual tenses, the questions require the same use of "do" that the child practiced with negated verb forms—e.g., "Did the girl swim?"; "Does the girl swim?"; "Do the girls swim?"

Via the filled-out QUESTION field, the teacher prompts the child to produce an answer for the ANSWER field that starts with "yes" or "no" and forms a complete sentence: "Yes she is swimming/did swim/will swim/does swim." After completing a certain number of such exercises, the child should be able—via the questions, the corresponding answers, and, initially, the multiple choices—to see the various patterns. At that point, the teacher should once again switch things up, start filling in the ANSWER field instead of the QUESTION field, and prompt the child, Jeopardy-style, to produce corresponding questions for the QUESTION field.

The child can continue practicing the auxiliary verb patterns of the yes–no questions when he moves on to wh-questions. The only complication is that when "who" or "what" stand for the subject instead of the object, no addition of "do" is necessary ("Who/what chased the girl?" vs. "Who/what did the girl chase?").

Once the child is ready for all the different wh-questions to be combined, the number of possible questions increases substantially, along with the challenge of constructing the correct one. As with the basic question lessons, a single picture, depending on what is in the ANSWER field and—here—what its time caption is, can target a wide variety of questions.

For example, a picture of a girl giving a boy a cookie, with time captions ranging from "10 minutes ago" to "in 2040," and with answers like:

- "The girl."
- "The boy."
- "A cookie."
- "Last year."

can target:

- "Who is giving/gave/will give/gives the cookie to the boy?"
- "Who is/did/will/does the girl giving/give a cookie to?"
- "What is/did/will/does the girl giving/give to the boy?"
- "When is/did/will/does the girl giving/give a cookie to the boy?"

As with basic questions, it's best at this point for teachers to give the answers as sentence fragments. Here, though, the problem isn't that full-sentence answers give away too much; rather, they don't sufficiently narrow down the target question. For example, "The girl is giving the boy a cookie" could be the answer to a "Who is giving the boy a cookie?", "Who is the girl giving a cookie to?", or "What is the boy giving to the girl?" "A cookie", in contrast, can only be the answer to the last of these. The side benefit to these sentence-fragment answers is that the child must do more linguistic work to figure out which auxiliary verb to use—relying solely on the time caption, and not (as he could with the yes-no questions) on any auxiliary verbs that appear in the ANSWER field.

Question asking, as we discussed earlier, is a major challenge for children with autism. It involves numerous grammatical complications that stump even the more verbal kids. In addition, it has posed elicitation challenges that the existing autism interventions have been unable to surmount. The multi-lesson approach laid out here is one way to address these linguistic and elicitation challenges. The entire process should be broken down, ABA-style, into incremental steps, with each subskill drilled to mastery. It may, therefore, depending on both the child and the intensity of the training, take many weeks or months to complete. Generally, the rule of thumb for what constitutes mastery in these sorts of drill-based interventions, ABA included, is something like an 80–90% rate of correct responding.

Toward a linguistically principled scope and sequence

Having discussed a sampling of grammar topics and how to address them, we now turn to questions of scope and sequence. To cover all the basic grammar structures of English, the curriculum must go far beyond what the current therapies cover. It must include:

- Not just spatial prepositions like "in the box", but time prepositions like "in an hour"
- Not just basic verb tenses, but complex tenses like "had eaten" and "will have eaten"
- Not just basic sentences, but negated, passive, and hypothetical sentences
- Quantifiers like "all," "each," "some," and "none"
- Comparative structures like "The square is bigger than the triangle" and "The more it rains, the wetter it gets"
- The gamut of yes–no and wh-questions
- The gamut of relative clauses ("the boy who is wearing a hat"; "the hat that the boy is wearing")
- Embedded clauses like "The girl wants the boy to talk to her" and "Sally says that the marble is in the basket"
- Embedded questions like "The boy asked the girl who she gave the present to"

As for how to sequence these topics, there are several factors to consider. One is the order in which the various linguistic structures are acquired by typically developing children. Another is the cumulative nature of some of the topics: e.g., tensed verbs, negated tensed verbs, auxiliary verbs, and tensed questions. A third is the relative abstractness and complexity (and therefore the potential difficulty) of the different topics.

The problem with ordering topics according to typical development is that typical developmental stages include errors. For example, one of the earliest types of utterances is "that dog," as in "that is a dog", which omits the verb and the article. Strictly following typical development would mean introducing errors that would later need to be un-taught.

A more promising course is error-free instruction, one topic at a time, with topics ordered according to how one topic builds to the next and, all else being equal, by how complex they are. A logical starting point is basic noun phrases: articles and plurals, as in "a square" and "squares." Indeed, noun phrase grammar is the one grammar topic that can be taught outside of the broader context of sentences. After basic noun phrases, the logical next topic is noun phrases that include adjectives ("a green circle"; "red squares").

Moving on to full sentences, the first lessons might build on these nouns and adjectives, as in the subject–predicate exercises discussed earlier ("The rectangle is yellow"). Then we might introduce the question discrimination lessons, starting with "What color is the rectangle?" and "What is that?" Later lessons might introduce basic prepositional phrases ("The triangles are under the rectangle"), comparative expressions ("The red star is bigger than the blue one"; "The squares in the middle are smaller than the squares on the top"), simple negation ("The oval is not green"), and quantified expressions ("All the squares are brown except the ones in the corners"). These lessons, too, provide opportunities for discriminating among different questions about a given picture.

Once the child has mastered these lessons, he is ready for the basic question-asking lessons as described above. For more advanced questions, as we saw, we first need to introduce auxiliary verbs via basic verb tenses and then via the negated forms of these verbs. How early we should teach basic verb tenses—relative, say, to the comparative expressions discussed above—may depend on the individual child and whether he has an understanding of the clock and calendar times that we use to prompt verb tenses.

To move from simple to complex, verb-focused lessons should begin with intransitive verbs ("The girl is sledding"; "The boy jumped"), then transitive verbs, i.e., verbs with direct objects ("The cat chased the dog"), then verbs with indirect objects or directional prepositions ("The girl waved at the boy"; "The snake went along the fence"), and, finally, verbs with direct and indirect objects ("The boy give the girl a book"; "The boy put the cup behind the box."). In lessons involving direct and indirect objects, teachers can also elicit the different forms of the third person pronouns: "he"/"him"; "she"/"her"; "they"/"them" ("He gave her a present"; "She gave him a present"). Lessons on complex verb tenses ("has broken," "had broken," "will have broken"; "has slept," "had slept," "will have slept") naturally occur later in the curriculum than lessons on basic verb tenses. But all verb tense lessons can also teach the abstract time expressions that go along with the time captions, like "an hour ago," "in an hour," "for an hour," and "until 3:00." Passive sentences should be taught after complex verb tenses: They use the past participles that appear in these tenses ("broken"; "slept") but also involve greater syntactic complexity ("The cup was broken by the boy"; "The bed was slept in by the girl").

One key challenge in autism that we haven't yet discussed is accurately distinguishing between first, second, and third-person pronouns. One way to teach these is through different permutations of one character addressing either another character or the child himself (breaking the "fourth wall") with a simple message like "I like you/him/her." Pictures of a character looking at another character or turned toward the student might be accompanied by a caption that reports what the speaking character said ("The girl said that she likes you/the boy"), or a speech bubble that contains the speaker's words. In the first case, the child could be asked to produce the words that go in the speech bubble; in the second case, to report on what the character said based on the words in the speech bubble. Eight different variations on these possibilities are depicted below.

95

For the first four exercises (top row), the child must determine who the girl is addressing and, therefore, which pronoun she is using for the person she's referring to. In the second four exercises (bottom row), the child also must determine who the girl is addressing and referring to and, based on the pronouns she is using, calculate which pronouns to use to report on her message. Parallel exercises with the boy talking, and with alternative subject–object patterns (e.g., "You/He/She like(s) me") should also be included. The multiple perspective-taking tasks here are challenging enough that teachers should first break the exercises down into smaller subsets of contrasting permutations before mixing them all together.

These exercises also introduce sentences with embedded clauses. In the first set of exercises, they appear in the prompt ("The girl said that she likes you"). In the second set, they appear in the child's completed response ("The girl said that _____"). To give the child more active practice with this type of complex sentence, subsequent versions of such exercises might replace the "Fill-in-the-blank" prompt with "What did the girl say?" and have the child produce the entire sentence himself— e.g., "The girl said that you like her."

Subsequent lessons should introduce more complex embedded clauses, including relative clauses ("The stool that the girl is standing on"), clausal subjects ("Climbing the hill is easy for the girl"), clausal objects ("The hill is easy for the girl to climb"; "The boy wants the girl to come to his house"), and conditional/hypothetical clauses ("Since/If it snows/ had snowed...."). One of the most complex advanced grammar topics is embedded questions ("He asked the girl where she went"; "She asked the boy who cleaned up the room"). These should be introduced only after the child has mastered both advanced questions and the various other types of embedded clauses, including sentences with multiple-embedded clauses like "The boy said that the girl needs to help him to do his work." Final exercises in the curriculum might include embedded questions containing embedded clauses: "She asked the boy who he thought helped him clean up the room."

Putting all this together, a comprehensive sequence of productive grammar topics might look something like this:

1. Simple noun phrases
2. Simple subject predicate sentences
3. Basic prepositional phrases
4. Simple negation of the above types of sentences
5. Comparative expressions
6. Quantified expressions
7. Question counterparts to all the above
8. Basic tense and negation of intransitive verbs
9. Basic tense and negation of transitive verbs
10. Basic tense and negation of verbs with indirect objects
11. Basic tense and negation of verbs with double objects
12. Complex verb tenses (all verb lessons including practice with abstract time expressions)
13. Advanced questions
14. Passive sentences
15. Pronoun distinctions and basic embedded clauses
16. Relative clauses
17. Clausal subjects and objects
18. Conditional/hypothetical clauses
19. Multiple-embedded clauses
20. Embedded questions

Automating the curriculum—the SentenceWeaver

The comprehensive curriculum and component lessons described above represent hundreds if not thousands of hours of instruction that may take years to deliver. The demands of an in-person implementation of this curriculum—both in terms of person-hours and in terms of linguistic expertise—are prohibitive. Can the instruction be automated?

As we noted earlier, the limitations of automated grammar instruction are less about the inherent, real-world simulation issues that dog the vocabulary and pragmatics programs, and more about the practical limitations that the existing programs have in eliciting independent responses and providing explicit feedback. These are problems, however, that sufficiently sophisticated software can overcome. In principle, software can be powerful enough to automate both the specific elicitation and the specific feedback mechanisms we've discussed throughout this chapter.

In terms of elicitation, the program can be designed to deliver, both through text and through computerized text-to-speech, all the different prompts we've surveyed—including the prompts for the student's responses, any multiple-choice models, and any follow-up requests that the child include certain words in his answer. It can also display the above-described word banks. In addition, for eliciting verb tense, it can automatically display and read out dates and clock times, calibrating them to the internal clocks of particular devices.

In terms of feedback, the program can deploy an algorithm that first checks for missing or incorrect words; then, once the user fixes these, for incorrect word forms; and, finally, for incorrect word sequences. If articles, in particular, are missing (a common problem in autism), the program can highlight the specific noun that needs an article. In addition to explicitly stating what the mistake is (via text and computerized text-to-speech), the program can also automatically highlight the incorrect words, incorrect word endings, and words out of sequence. To make this highlighting more explicit, the program can put the incorrect words or endings in different colors depending on the type of error: red for wrong words, wrong endings, missing endings, and words out of order; and then green, say, for words that are in the wrong form ("swim" instead of "swam") or that are missing an article.

A sufficiently powerful program, thus, can simulate both the therapist-delivered elicitation procedures and the therapist-delivered feedback protocols described earlier. In addition, it can improve upon several aspects of the in-person lessons. First, it can more easily and quickly randomize things than humans can—for example, the order of the multiple choices and the sequencing of exercises.

Second, a screen-based interface allows a child an easy way to input his responses. Many students with autism, including those with grammar impairments, are rapid typists. To broaden accessibility to non-typists, the program might present the words in the word bank as clickable word buttons, allowing users to click in their responses word by word. To broaden accessibility to non-readers, the program can also be designed to read the word buttons out loud when the child hovers his mouse over them.

Third, to further broaden accessibility, the program can deploy speech-recognition software that allows users to speak their responses rather than type them. Such software will automatically transcribe spoken responses into printed responses that the program can then annotate, as above, with any needed corrections.

Fourth, a computer program can provide all of its feedback—annotations included—much faster than a human can, allowing students to see, nearly instantaneously, if their answers are correct and what kinds of mistakes they made. In addition, the program can place the cursor exactly where it needs to be to make corrections—e.g., right next to the red word marked as wrong, or right before the green noun that is missing an article—so that the student not only doesn't have to reproduce a revised response from scratch but also can fix mistakes quickly.

Fifth, as we saw with many of the programs we reviewed earlier, for all their other shortcomings, computerized programs are better than human beings at keeping track of which exercises have been completed, optimizing when and how quickly to advance the student through the program, and determining when she has mastered a particular topic. Computerized programs are also better and faster at collecting and displaying a student's progress data.

In short, computerizing the curriculum with sufficiently powerful software can vastly accelerate lesson delivery, response submission, feedback, advancement, and data collection. In addition, computerization readily lends itself to student-specific customization. For example, some students may not need word buttons; others may find it easier to navigate through the buttons if they are organized according to part of speech (e.g., nouns, verbs, articles) rather than being displayed all at once. Some students, moreover, may not need or like the spoken voice-over.

All the above-described details of lesson delivery, response elicitation, feedback, customization, advancement, data collection, and comprehensive coverage of English grammar can be found in a new program created by the author. The program, the SentenceWeaver, is a 20-module computerized curriculum for English grammar, consisting of 135 lessons and 5,480 exercises (Beals, n.d.). Below are some screenshots of some lessons from its Advanced Questions module. First is an example of its multiple-choice phase; this is followed by three screenshots of its feedback algorithm in action.

Every day (Monday-Sunday)

CHOICES:
Who gives the girls presents? ◀)
Who do the girls give presents to? ◀)
Who gives the boys presents? ◀)
Who do the boys give presents to? ◀)

Type or click on the buttons to match the correct CHOICE. Then click 'Enter'.

QUESTION: ⸮

Enter | Delete Word/Ending | Clear All | I don't know

◀)
ANSWER: The girls.

Nouns | Pronouns | Main Verbs | Auxiliary Verbs | Prepositions | Articles | WH Words

Yesterday (Saturday, September 11th)   Today's points: 3

You need the word do (**does, did**). Please click it in.

QUESTION: who the girl carried?

Enter | Delete Word/Ending | Clear All | I don't know

◀)
ANSWER: The boy.

Nouns | Pronouns | Main Verbs | Auxiliary Verbs | Prepositions | Articles | WH Words

carried | carries | carry | carrying

Yesterday (Saturday, September 11th)   Today's points: 3

Fix the green word and the red ending.

QUESTION: who do the girl carried?   Enter Delete Word/Ending Clear All I don't know

◄))
ANSWER: The boy.

Nouns Pronouns Main Verbs Auxiliary Verbs Prepositions Articles WH Words

are be been can can't did do does has have is was were will

Yesterday (Saturday, September 11th)   Today's points: 3

Getting next exercise...

Right!

QUESTION: Who did the girl carry?   Enter Delete Word/Ending Clear All I don't know

◄))
ANSWER: The boy.

Nouns Pronouns Main Verbs Auxiliary Verbs Prepositions Articles WH Words

At the time of this book's publication, the SentenceWeaver was new enough not to have undergone formal efficacy testing. Unpublished pilot data of dozens of users, however, indicates that individuals with autism-related language delays are able to progress through the program and to improve within modules from pretests to post-tests.

From computerized grammar instruction to broader goals

As we've discussed, some studies indicate that autistic individuals find computerized environments and computerized voices more comfortable and conducive to learning than in-person teaching environments and human voices. While we ultimately want language-delayed children to use their developing language skills in the real world, we also want them to acquire those skills as quickly as possible.

Language in the real world is primarily spoken. Several components of the interventions discussed in this chapter, on the other hand, are grounded in written language—particularly the multiple choices, the word buttons, and the text-based feedback and color-coded annotations in written versions of the child's responses. But regardless of whether it is written or spoken, language is language, and learning about word use, word endings, and word order in one medium generally transfers to the other. The hope, therefore, is that autistic children will eventually be able to generalize what they learn not just to their real-world written output, but also to their spoken utterances and conversational interactions.

Another hope is that a growing mastery of sentence grammar will boost the frequently impaired reading comprehension skills of autistic students, as written texts typically involve more complex sentences than spoken language does. Additional ways to boost reading comprehension in autism will be one of the main focuses of the next chapter.

Reference

Beals, K. (n.d.). *SentenceWeaver.* Autism Language Therapies. https://autism-language-therapies.com

CHAPTER 5
FROM SENTENCES TO EXTENDED DISCOURSE: STRATEGIES FOR TEACHING BROADER COMPREHENSION AND LITERACY

In this chapter we will go beyond the mostly word-, phrase-, and sentence-level comprehension challenges and interventions that we have covered and turn to issues of language use, also known as pragmatics. In addition, we'll be focusing on the larger tracts of language of the sort that await autistic children—particularly those who will be included in general education classrooms—when they enter the K12 system. We should note here that before they are ready to tackle language at this level, children need to have attained a certain degree of phrase- and sentence-level mastery. This chapter, therefore, has in mind children who have amassed reasonably large vocabularies—that is, of at least a few hundred words—and who comprehend simple sentences, basic verb tenses, and pronouns.

The larger units of language we'll review in this chapter include narratives and dialogue (spoken and written), lectures, and expository texts like passages in textbooks. The umbrella term we will use for these is "extended discourse." As we'll see, extended discourse imposes additional demands beyond those of individual words, phrases, and sentences. Some of these demands are particularly daunting for individuals with autism, including those who function well at the sentence level.

We'll begin by discussing the challenges involved in making sense of extended discourse, and then we'll turn to the various strategies that have been proposed to address them.

Discourse-level challenges

Before we get into discourse-specific challenges, however, we must first acknowledge the role of basic language skills—i.e., vocabulary and syntax. Basic language skills are a major contributor to discourse comprehension, even when we're talking about tracts of text. This is because language is language, regardless of whether it's spoken or written, and because discourse, no matter how extended, is still made up of words, phrases, and sentences. Thus, for all the differences between language at the level of phrases and sentences and language at the level of extended discourse, it turns out, not unsurprisingly, that the same core language skills that figure into the former also figure into the latter.

Turning now to discourse-specific challenges, we find several that can particularly stump individuals with autism. For one thing, the longer stretches of language in both narrative and expository discourse mean there's more to keep track of. To make sense of the whole, readers or listeners must integrate all the relevant information from within the discourse. In addition, they must factor in any relevant background information from the outside world that the speaker or writer is assuming is at their disposal. This potentially wide-ranging integration requires big picture thinking skills that run afoul of the detail-focused, weak central coherence tendencies in autism. The child may focus narrowly on details about individual word choices ("fall" vs. "autumn") or word orderings ("all the leaves are brown" vs. "the leaves all are brown"). Indeed, he may be so quickly overwhelmed by the details that he misses the broader meaning—or gist—even of smaller discourse components like paragraphs or turns in a conversation.

Besides weak central coherence, two additional cognitive challenges in autism affect reading comprehension—challenges that we will discuss in greater detail in the next chapter because they also affect broader academic skills.

First, many individuals with autism have deficits in executive functioning. Executive functioning includes the ability to control your attention—to sustain attention on a given focus, or to switch attention from one focus to another, as appropriate. It also includes working memory capacity (how many items you can remember and mentally manipulate at once) and meta-cognitive skills like self-monitoring (keeping track of what you are doing). We've already encountered one specific executive function difficulty in autism—namely, the difficulty with switching attention back and forth between different participants in conversations. This may also apply to conversations, or dialogues, that are embedded in narratives. Similarly, difficulty sustaining attention, combined with working memory limitations, can make it hard to keep track of extended passages and long sentences.

But the component of executive functioning most implicated in comprehension, particularly in reading comprehension, is self-monitoring. Self-monitoring includes attending to one's developing understanding of the text, noticing incongruities, and taking steps to repair, as needed, one's preliminary understanding—e.g., by going back and rereading. Precisely these skills have also been implicated as deficient in autism. Researchers have found that autistic readers seldom stop to verify their comprehension or go back and reread even when it's obvious to observers that things aren't making sense to them.

Related to executive functioning is the processing of complex information—information that contains large amounts of wide-ranging detail and/or that flows from multiple sources. Making sense of extended discourse often means contending with such complexity, particularly when readers must factor in relevant content from the outside world. Effectively processing this complex information, in turn, often requires organizational strategies and structures. As we'll discuss in the next chapter, students with autism have difficulty coming up on their own with the organizational strategies and structures needed to process complex information.

Another challenge for listeners and readers with autism is that extended discourse is often removed from the immediate here and now. This is true even of extemporaneous speech: A speaker may be recounting something that happened earlier or elsewhere, or he may be sharing new information or arguing a point. Making sense of extended discourse thus often requires readers and listeners to ignore and abstract away from sights and sounds in the immediate environment. As we discussed in Chapter

1, environmental stimuli can be particularly distracting to individuals with autism. This potentially impedes both their comprehension of extended discourse, and their ability, even when they do comprehend it, to sustain their attention for its duration.

Relatedly, part of comprehension involves figuring out what various pronouns—"it," "they," "this"—stand for in different situations. When they are embedded within extended discourse, these words derive their meanings not from people and objects in the immediate environment, but from proper names and noun phrases within the narrative or text. Making these discourse-internal connections, as we will discuss, can pose challenges to readers with autism.

Meanwhile, dialogues in particular and social narratives in general— whether they are spoken or written—run up against the social difficulties of autistic readers and listeners. Indeed, social knowledge—including the Theory of Mind skills we talked about in Chapter 1—is a major predictor of reading comprehension in autism, especially with texts that are more social and character-driven. Deficits in Theory of Mind can impede the reader's ability to understand the characters, particularly their perspectives, emotions, and interrelationships.

Part of making sense of discourse involves inferences, and teachers and standardized tests alike often assess students on their ability to draw correct inferences from reading passages. Individuals with autism struggle with two types of inferences that are key to making sense of discourse: bridging inferences and gap-filling inferences. An example of a bridging inference is one that connects "Susan opened up the trunk" and "The dog leapt out": namely, the inference that the dog of the second sentence leapt out of the trunk of the first sentence. An example of a gap-filling inference is one that combines "The eighteenth hole was the hardest at all" with background knowledge about golf courses to infer that "the hole" is the last hole of a golf course. Studies have found that autistic individuals are able to make inferences that might be appropriate outside the story (e.g., based on their own personal experiences, say with holes in the ground) but not within the context of the story. This may reflect a failure to consider the story as a whole (weak central coherence), or, alternatively, a difficulty suppressing irrelevant facts from their own lives and obsessions—an issue we will return to later in the chapter.

Sometimes individuals with autism are able to make automatic inferences while they're reading but have trouble answering inferential questions later on after they finish—perhaps a result of the above-discussed difficulties in integrating all the relevant information into a coherent understanding. Especially difficult are inferences that require taking into account the text as a whole (consistent with weak central coherence), and inferences that involve Theory of Mind and an understanding of emotions. Here is one example that involves the latter, from a study of reading comprehension difficulties in autism:

> Billy has made a drawing of the family home. When his mother sees the drawing, she says "This looks like something we should hang on the living room wall."
>
> Question: How does Billy feel? (Loukusa, Mäkinen, Kuusikko-Gauffin, Ebeling, & Leinonen, 2018).

Answering this question involves two Theory of Mind-based inferences: imagining what Billy's mother intends to convey to him about her feelings about his picture, and putting oneself in Billy's shoes to imagine his likely reaction.

Written discourse in particular

Written discourse—novels, textbooks, articles—bring additional challenges to all readers, beginning at the most basic level: the decoding of individual written words.

As we discussed, decoding (along with encoding, or spelling) tends to be a relative strength for many on the autism spectrum, with an estimated 6%-21% exhibiting hyperlexia, or a precocious interest in letters and a precocious ability to recognize printed words (Ostrolenk et al., 2017). This decoding ability, moreover, often co-occurs with low comprehension—further corroborating that the reading comprehension problems in autism go above and beyond the recognition of written words.

It's important to keep in mind, however, that the majority of children with autism do not have precocious decoding skills. Indeed, one study of autistic first graders found that 56% performed below expectations in reading accuracy on a standardized assessment of decoding. Most of those who are ready to learn to read, therefore, will need some sort of deliberate intervention.

In some cases, correctly identifying a written word requires broader comprehension skills. This arises with words that have different sounds when spoken but look the same in writing. Consider, for example, "tear" in "a tear on her cheek" versus "a tear in her dress." Some researchers have found that individuals with autism tend not to use the context of the sentence to determine the intended word—something that non-autistic readers do automatically.

Beyond these basic word-recognition challenges, written discourse often uses more sophisticated vocabulary than we have addressed in earlier chapters, as well as sophisticated figurative language—e.g., idioms and metaphors. Figurative language, written and spoken, poses particular challenges to individuals with autism. As we've discussed, autistic readers and listeners tend not to automatically put themselves in other people's shoes and take into consideration a speaker or writer's likely intent. When someone says, "It's raining cats and dogs," most listeners, even if they've never heard this expression before, will automatically rule out the idea that the speaker actually thinks that dogs and cats are literally falling from the sky. However, a listener or reader who doesn't consider the communicator's viewpoint, but only the words that come out of her mouth or appear on the page, may default to the literal meaning. And, if he doesn't monitor his comprehension and re-think things that don't make sense, he may fail to override those meanings—however much they defy reality.

Some types of figurative language are especially challenging in autism. So-called "conventional" figures of speech—"rain cats and dogs," "skate on thin ice," and "kick the bucket"—have fixed forms and frozen meanings that individuals with autism may simply not have picked up incidentally as other kids do. Far greater barriers to understanding come from non-conventional figures of speech. These include metaphors like "He was a volcano" or "She is the sun"—metaphors that haven't entered common usage and become attached to specific, invariant meanings. Their meanings instead vary depending on the specific context and the intents of specific speakers, and research suggests that deducing these meanings requires Theory of Mind skills. The same is true of verbal irony—a phenomenon that pervades the gamut of discourse from informal conversation to satire to the pinnacles of literature, from "He's a real genius" to "Brutus is an honorable man" to "A young healthy child well nursed, is, at a year old, a most delicious nourishing and wholesome food." However much these various figures of speech, taken literally, would contradict the broader context of the discourse in which they occur and/or the communicator's likely intent, individuals with autism, once again, may default to the literal.

Metaphor and irony aside, there are countless examples of mundane discourse where meaning varies by context. "It's cold in here," for example, might be a literal observation about the temperature, but it might instead be an indirect request to close a window. Indirect language, like figurative language, pervades both informal and informal discourse, and here, too, autistic listeners and readers tend to miss what's implied and once again default to the literal.

Comprehending extended discourse, particularly texts, also involves making sense of what are called "anaphora" or "anaphoric devices." Anaphora/anaphoric devices are umbrella terms for any linguistic device that takes the place of more explicit content words. The most familiar examples of these are personal and impersonal pronouns ("she," "they," "this," "that"), which we highlighted earlier as potentially challenging. But anaphoric devices also include various types of ellipses and substitutions, as seen in the following examples:

> Becky sang a song. Dan **did** too. ["Did" substitutes for "sang a song."]
>
> Are you leaving now? Yes I **am**. ["Leaving now" is elided.]
>
> Amy opened her wallet and took out **a quarter**. ["A quarter" is understood to be a coin that was inside Amy's wallet.]

These sorts of anaphora arise all the time, but especially in the more compact phrases of extended written discourse. Consider, for example, this excerpt from *From the Mixed-Up Files of Mrs. Basil E. Frankweiler*. The various anaphoric devices are highlighted, and the content that they stand for is in brackets:

In the meantime **she** [Claudia] almost forgot why **she** [Claudia] was running away. But [elided: "Claudia did"] not entirely [elided: "forget why she was running away"]. Claudia knew that **it** [running away] had to do with injustice. **She** [Claudia] was the oldest child and the only girl [elided: "in her family"] and [elided: Claudia] was subject to a lot of injustice. Perhaps **it** [running away] was because **she** [Claudia] had to both empty the dishwasher and set the table on the same night while **her** [Claudia's] brothers got out of **everything** [elided: "having to do with household chores"]. And, perhaps, there was another **reason** [elided: for running away] [elided: "that is"] more clear to **me** [the narrator] **than** [elided: "the reason is"] to Claudia. (Konigsburg, 1967, p. 5)

To make sense of this paragraph, the reader needs to deal with anaphoric substitutions and elisions in every single sentence. And, yet, this paragraph does not contain an unusually high number of anaphoric devices.

It's not surprising, therefore, that difficulty with anaphora is a major impediment to reading comprehension. Indeed, students who score low on comprehension tests tend to make frequent errors in interpreting these devices. In more extended discourse, as more words intervene between the anaphora and their antecedents (the words they stand in for), these errors increase. Some autistic individuals may have no difficulty interpreting pronouns and other anaphoric devices in simple texts, but struggle as texts become more complex and ambiguous.

Also important in reading comprehension, as research has shown, is background knowledge. Assumptions that readers already have encountered certain facts pervade both expository and narrative discourse. Among other things, background knowledge helps us make sense of figures of speech, ambiguous phrases, and anaphoric devices. Consider, for example, the metaphor "lawyers are sharks." To deduce the intended meaning, we need to know specific things about both lawyers and sharks. Or consider the headline "Florida man gets seven years in cello case." Here, familiarity with the legal system helps us rule out the interpretation in which the man spends seven years inside the case of a musical instrument. Legal system knowledge also helps us deduce the different people that "he" refers to in these two sentences:

- The prosecutor asked the witness about his relationship status, but he refused to testify about that.

- The prosecutor asked the witness about his relationship status, but he was stopped when the judge sustained the defense attorney's objection.

Depending on the text, relevant background knowledge can range from academic knowledge (e.g., history and math), to procedural knowledge (e.g., how to fix a car), to knowledge of common event schemas (e.g., what typically happens at birthday parties), to knowledge of psychological and social phenomena (including emotions and relationships).

Multiple studies show that individuals with autism have difficulty using background knowledge to make sense of what they read. In some cases, they have the relevant knowledge but don't deliberately integrate it into the reading process. But often there's a more fundamental problem: They have never acquired the requisite knowledge in the first place. Their diminished joint attention, imitation, pretend play, and attention to social phenomena reduce their opportunities to learn about cultural events like birthday parties and restaurant outings and their associated schemas. Diminished joint attention, as we discussed in Chapter 2, also diminishes opportunities for learning language, for informal incidental learning, and for formal academic learning. Meanwhile, all-consuming interests and a narrow focus on details may limit much of an autistic individual's background knowledge to restrictive stores of specialized facts. The end result is that individuals with autism may lack much of the basic knowledge writers assume readers have at their disposal and that is essential for making sense of the discourse.

One reason why background knowledge figures especially prominently in written discourse is that writing is more divorced from the immediate here-and-now than speaking. It therefore relies less on details in the surrounding environment and more on the reader's generalized knowledge. This is particularly the case with texts written for students in the upper grades, who are assumed to have accumulated considerable stores of knowledge—both informal cultural and commonsense knowledge, and formal academic knowledge.

Besides this, written discourse has several specific syntactic characteristics that require readers to draw on their background knowledge and/

or inferencing skills to fill in missing linguistic information. First, compared to spoken discourse, written discourse involves more frequent use of passive sentences, and these often omit the agent responsible for the action (as in "mistakes were made"). Second, written discourse tends to be more compact—connecting more ideas with fewer words. Much of this compactness comes from the use of nominalizations (or complex noun phrases) in place of clauses. Both passive voice and nominalizations make the relationships between concepts less explicit. Compare:

1. They regret that the damn flooded the valley.
2. They regret that valley was flooded.
3. They regret the flooding of the dam.

In example 1, an active clause specifies which entity caused the flooding (the dam); in 2, the passive structure omits this entity. In 3, where a noun phrase ("the flooding of the dam") replaces a clause, three pieces of information are lost. First, while the dam is mentioned explicitly, the valley goes unmentioned. Second, there is no longer a tensed verb ("flooded") to indicate that the flooding occurred in the past. Third, the relationship between the dam and the flooding is no longer explicit: Is the dam responsible for the flooding or a victim of it? Out of context, "the flooding of the dam" could denote a current or future event in which the dam is the thing being flooded. In general, the more the discourse relies on noun phrases like "the flooding of the dam," as opposed to clauses like "the dam flooded the valley," the more work the reader must do to figure out what's going on. Sometimes the broader context of the discourse will suffice. But sometimes background knowledge—for example, about the effects of new dams on water flow—is also helpful, or even essential.

Another grammatical phenomenon that makes written language more compact is the use of appositives. These are parenthetical remarks and remarks set off by commas, hyphens, and colons, as seen, for example in:

- Some piano teachers prefer to teach novices: people who haven't yet developed bad keyboard habits.
- Some piano teachers prefer to teach novices: people who are insecure about their pedagogical skills.

Here there is no literal clue as to how the two parts of the sentence fit together—i.e., who "people" refers to. The colon simply signals that there is some sort of a relationship between the phrases on either side of it. Figuring out what that relationship is requires some combination of background knowledge and inferencing.

More generally, beyond all this, extended discourse often places the listener (or reader) at greater remove from the narrator than shorter stretches of discourse do. Extended discourse, for one thing, often involves multiple audience members. In one-to-one interactions, speakers naturally adjust to the particular needs of particular listeners—for example, by slowing down and clarifying things when their interlocutor seems confused. One-to-many narration is less amenable to such adjustments. Nor is it appropriate, in many cases, for a single confused listener to interrupt the narrative with questions. Pre-recorded narratives, recited narratives, and written text, of course, are even less amenable to spontaneous adjustments to the needs of individual audience members.

What all this means is that individual listeners or readers of extended discourse are typically on their own when it comes to making sense of the language. At the same time, as we've seen, this sense-making entails additional challenges that do not arise in shorter and more interactive communications.

Why accommodations aren't enough

The widespread discourse comprehension problems in autism, as we have seen, stem from a combination of basic language deficits, social deficits, and deficits in background knowledge, big-picture thinking, and executive function skills. These sorts of challenges do not readily lead themselves to the kinds of accommodations typically given to children with reading difficulties: for example, text-to-speech devices, audiobooks, or enlarged print. The discourse comprehension challenges in autism largely transcend the particular medium of communication that is involved—e.g., oral versus written language. Even less relevant are superficial factors like print size and font style.

The more promising and productive approach, rather, is through effective interventions and teaching strategies. For most of the remainder of this chapter, therefore, we'll survey the strategies that have been proposed as remediations for the numerous comprehension challenges in autism.

Interventions

Many of the challenges we've surveyed here pertain to extended discourse in general, whether it is spoken or written. Most of the proposed interventions, however, specifically address written discourse. That's because, as we'll see, most of the interventions depend on the ability to review the discourse passages and/or to annotate them—something that oral discourse, which comes and goes, does not permit. To adapt such interventions for oral discourse comprehension, therefore, teachers would need to record the discourse and transcribe it into writing.

The most basic reading-specific challenge, as we discussed, is decoding. Here, all the evidence indicates that autistic children need precisely the same kinds of explicit instruction as their non-autistic counterparts. Indeed, reading programs that work for children in general tend to work, as well, for specific sub-populations. As far as decoding skills go, the overwhelming evidence favors direct, systematic phonics instruction. For the majority of individuals with autism who don't pick up phonics on their own, therefore, systematic phonics is the intervention of choice.

As we turn now to discourse comprehension, we will cover several general approaches ranging from question answering, to explicit instruction, to inference training, and, finally, to computerized approaches. We'll discuss each of these, in turn, before examining more targeted interventions. Finally, we'll look at what the overall efficacy data show about which approaches are most promising.

Question answering, question generating, and making predictions

One way to improve reading comprehension skills is to employ the same strategy used to assess comprehension skills—namely, prompting students with reading comprehension questions. Such questions potentially motivate students with autism to read, and to re-read, with greater focus and attention to meaning. Especially important, given the big-picture challenges in autism, are questions about main events and main ideas, as well as questions that solicit retellings or summaries. A second key ingredient of question-based interventions, of course, is providing readers with feedback on their answers and opportunities to revise them.

One specific question-asking strategy that has been used with some success with autistic readers is the "Question-Answer Relationships" (QAR) strategy. QAR focuses on teaching students to figure out, based on the specific type of question, where to find the answer. First teachers have students categorize questions according to whether the answer is "In the Book" or "In My Head." Then they have them subcategorize "In the Book" questions into literal "Right There" questions, for which the answer comes from a particular point in the text, and "Think and Search" questions, for which the answer comes from several points in the text that must be linked together. Finally, they have them subcategorize "In My Head" questions into "On My Own" questions, which they can answer based on their personal experiences, and "Author and Me" questions, which they can answer by connecting their background knowledge with the author's intentions. Some researchers report success with this approach, particularly when it is implemented along with the Applied Behavioral Analysis (ABA) strategies discussed in Chapter 3— specifically, systematic prompting and reinforcement—as well as with graphic organizers, which we'll discuss later in this chapter.

The converse is also promising: having readers generate the questions themselves—a strategy that's sometimes called "question generating." Question generating, indeed, has been deemed by the National Reading Panel to be the most effective reading comprehension strategy. Questions that originate with readers potentially have the same motivational effects—i.e., getting them to focus on meaning and to re-read as necessary—as questions that originate with teachers. In addition, by ultimately taking the teacher out of the equation, question generating potentially fosters improvements in independent reading skills. To help readers with autism achieve this independence, teachers can once again combine the intervention with ABA strategies like systematic prompting and fading. The teacher can first provide the child with an explicit script that helps her generate questions or suggests starting points like "What is the most important sentence in the paragraph?" Then he can fade the script to a few key words (e.g., "who," "what," or "how") until she is able to generate questions on her own. To guide her on when during reading to stop and ask questions, he can also have her use a self-monitoring checklist. (We'll say more about these later in the chapter.)

A related approach is having readers make predictions before they start reading—based, for example, on a passage's title and headers—and/or while reading. This potentially primes them to look for specific information as they read. It also potentially activates any information in long-term memory that may be relevant and boost comprehension. However, some evidence suggests that, for some students with autism, pre-reading questions can be counterproductive. The prior knowledge that is activated may be irrelevant or inaccurate and, as they read, students may perseverate on this knowledge at the expense of comprehension—particularly if it taps into their narrow interests. Furthermore, some autistic children may lack the relevant prior knowledge, or, even if they have such knowledge, may fail to recognize its relevance to a particular text.

A variation on question-asking strategies is reciprocal questioning. Here students are prompted to ask comprehension questions of one another— sometimes with partners, sometimes in group settings. Students with autism might be grouped together or, alternatively, grouped with non-autistic peers. Teachers might then prompt them to ask specific sorts of questions—i.e., prediction questions, questions about unfamiliar words, questions about plot and characters, and questions soliciting summaries of story excerpts. Initially, once again, teachers can provide students with scripts, key words, or other prompts.

Studies of reciprocal questioning in autism have found increases in unprompted question generating and responding, as well in overall comprehension. In addition, students report shifting their reading habits away from a mechanical process in which they skip over unfamiliar words toward a more comprehension-based process. Indeed, one of the main goals of the various question-asking and question-generating strategies is precisely this shift in reading habits.

Explicit instruction, Direct Instruction, and Precision Teaching

A more direct intervention for reading comprehension challenges is explicit instruction. Explicit instruction can target any number of skills, and shortly we'll examine its applicability to inferences and to figurative language. Here we mention an intervention used with autistic readers that included explicit instruction in identifying the main ideas of paragraphs and interpreting anaphoric devices. Researchers report that, following such instruction, students improved in both areas, and several months later they sustained their improvements in one area: identifying main ideas.

A specific variant of explicit instruction is Direct Instruction (DI). DI is a behaviorist approach to teaching, akin to ABA, that provides direct, systematic, subtask-by-subtask instruction, with prompting, modeling, and checks for retention over time. Unlike ABA, however, DI is typically done in classroom settings where teachers use scripted prompts and explanations and elicit choral responses from students. Teachers deliver scripted responses to incorrect or nonunison responses, model correct responses, guide students by responding along with them, and prompt students to respond independently.

Results from a nationwide comparison of reading programs (Project Follow Through) have shown that DI's reading programs produce the biggest gains in reading achievement, including with special needs populations. More recent studies have examined the effects of DI's curriculum on the comprehension skills, specifically, of students with autism; these, too, show efficacy. For example, DI's *Corrective Reading Comprehension B1* led to improvements on the Woodcock Reading Mastery Test (Ganz & Flores, 2009; Nelson Head et al., 2018).

DI's workbooks contain a number of comprehension exercises, including exercises that have students:

- Provide definitions or synonyms
- Differentiate what is explicit in a text versus what can merely be inferred
- Follow complex directions
- Fill out personal information forms based on passages that describe specific characters
- Put short action sentences in order based on a story's event sequence

- Choose between exercises that present pairs of sentences, one of which gives a reason for what's stated in the other (e.g., "Fred's house was robbed"; "Fred wants protection"), and "circle the sentence that says why."

DI's instructional strands, reflecting its behaviorist approach, break comprehension down into subskills. Besides linguistic skills like vocabulary, sentence manipulation, and basic comprehension, DI's reading comprehension subskills include cognitive skills: skills like analogies, inferences, induction, deduction, using facts, identifying contradictions, and identifying relevant and irrelevant information.

Some studies of DI's efficacy for reading comprehension, accordingly, have examined the specific contribution of some of its cognitive skills strands. One such study (Flores & Ganz, 2007) involved students with autism and used the picture analogies, induction, deduction, and opposites strands of *Corrective Reading Thinking Basics: Comprehension Level A*.

The picture analogies strand asks students to complete analogies expressed via pictures. In the deductions strand, they are presented with sentences, e.g., "Here is the only thing that Joe did; Joe sat in small boats," accompanied by four pictures, e.g., of a large tanker ship, a small life raft, a small kayak, and a large cruise ship. Students then must respond "yes," "no," or "maybe" to three statements, e.g., "Joe sat in a large cruise ship"; "Joe did not sit in a large tanker ship"; and "Joe sat in a small kayak."

In the inductions strand, students are given four facts, e.g., "On Sunday, the clouds came out and the horse ate an apple"; "On Wednesday, the clouds did not come out and the horse ate a carrot"; "On Tuesday, the clouds came out and the horse ate an apple"; and "On Thursday, the clouds did not come out and the horse ate a carrot." Students are then asked, "Tell me the rule about when the clouds came out," and "Tell me the rule about when the clouds did not come out." Finally, in the opposites strand, students are given a statement—e.g., "Muscles pull to move bones"—and are prompted to construct a statement that says the opposite—e.g., a sentence that replaces "pull" with "push." In the course of the intervention, all of the students mastered the targeted cognitive skills and, based on a DI-specific placement test that includes reading comprehension questions, placed into the next level of the corrective reading program.

A variant of DI, Precision Teaching (PT) also addresses reading comprehension skills. PT combines DI's behaviorism with an additional instructional goal—namely, fluency. Fluency, which is based on the speed of accurate responding, is viewed by PT practitioners as a key additional condition for mastery—besides the accuracy, generalization, and retention skills emphasized by ABA and DI.

Much of PT's approach was developed at the Morningside Academy, a school in Washington State serving students who are disadvantaged and/ or have special needs. Morningside has had so much success boosting students' skills that it offers a money-back guarantee to the parents of any child who starts out more than two grade levels behind and doesn't advance at least two grade levels in one year (Johnson & Street, 2012).

For reading comprehension skills in particular, Morningside has developed a program, based on methods designed originally for college students, called "Fluent Thinking Skills" (Robbins & Layng, 2010). Fluent Thinking Skills uses variants of the question-asking strategies we described previously. First, students practice these strategies in a non–text-based environment: The teacher presents a mystery and prompts them to ask her yes–no questions about it. Once they master this, students apply a similar strategy to texts. In pairs, they generate preliminary questions and predictions about a text based on its headings, subheadings, paragraph-initial sentences, and captions. Then, while reading, they look for discrepancies between these provisional answers and answers supplied by the text.

Fluent Thinking Skills, however, has not been evaluated for its efficacy with autistic students in particular.

Inference training

As we discussed earlier, numerous studies have noted that inferences— particularly those that require social knowledge—are challenging for children with autism and are a major source of difficulties with discourse-level comprehension. However, few studies have looked at interventions that directly target inferencing skills in autism. One of the most extensive inference interventions is a four-week training protocol that was tested back in the 1980s (Yuill & Oakhill, 1988). But its target population was individuals who were identified, simply, as being "poor comprehenders."

The inference training was called "lexical inference training." Students were asked what information specific words contribute in the context of the sentences that contain them. For example, in "Sleepy Tom was late for school again," "Tom" implies that the subject is male. Because it is a first name, "Tom" also implies, in combination with "school," that the subject is probably a student. Later in the training, the students made similar inferences in the context of whole narratives. They were also encouraged to link individual lexical inferences together, e.g., by using what they inferred about the story's setting from the word "wave" to infer that the word "tower" referred to a sandcastle.

In addition, the students underwent one session of what was called "prediction." They read stories that had some sentences covered up and made guesses about these based on the surrounding sentences. They then uncovered the sentences and checked their predictions.

Overall, this intervention was highly successful, resulting in an average reading comprehension gain of over 17 months in a period of 2 months. Nine of the thirteen children were classified as good comprehenders by the posttest.

Another variety of inference training is found in the Direct Instruction programs we discussed previously. In some exercises, as we saw, students are asked to identify statements that can be deduced from texts. Another strand of exercises prompts students to make inferences from descriptions. For example, "It has a tail. Name the three animals I could be talking about"; then, "It has a tail and stripes"; then "It has a tail and stripes and likes to eat zebras."

A third variety of inference training is offered by the Headsprout software program, which, as we'll discuss in the next section, has shown some promise with autistic students. The program presents students with a description—e.g., of a stoplight at an intersection where two big streets cross. It then asks them a question—e.g., "Why is a stoplight needed there?" Next, it prompts them to select, from a set of phrases, the one that makes them think about possible answers—e.g., a set that includes "to keep everyone safe." The program then highlights three phrases from within the original description—e.g., "where two big streets cross," "on one street from moving" and "when the light changes to green"—and students are asked to click on the phrase with the so-called "clue words":

the words that make them think of the answer to the initial question (e.g., "Why is a stoplight needed there?"). Finally, it presents them with three possible answers and prompts them to pick the one that makes them think about the clue words. All this, ideally, guides them to the correct answer (e.g., "because there are lots of cars coming and going").

We should note, however, that none of these inference interventions is tailored to students with autism. Nor do they specifically focus on the kinds of inferencing difficulties specific to autism: those that involve the appropriate use of background knowledge (including the suppression of irrelevant details from personal experience), and those that tap social awareness and perspective-taking skills.

We end this section with a cautionary point. One popular strategy for enhancing comprehension in K12 Language Arts classes, and for improving inferencing skills in particular, is to encourage students to make text-to-self connections. Text-to-self connections are connections between the world of the text and the reader's personal experiences. Given the difficulty that autistic readers have in suppressing irrelevant personal experiences, it may be not only counterproductive to encourage them to make text-to-self connections, but also necessary to *actively discourage* them from doing so.

Computerized approaches

Some of the above-described strategies have been incorporated into computerized reading instruction—as we've just seen with Headsprout and inference training. Computerized reading instruction often takes the form of "supported electronic text": texts that are digitally enhanced in various ways. For instance, the programs might sometimes highlight specific lines of text; or students might click on words to see their definitions, or, alternatively, on selected parts of the text to have them read out loud. Some programs go further, prompting students with multiple choice comprehension questions and giving them feedback on their answers. BookBuilder includes an "embedded coach" that guides students with questions and explanations; Headsprout highlights the relevant part of the reading passage and asks the student to re-read it.

Two recent studies suggest that Headsprout may boost reading comprehension in autism (Grindel et al., 2020; Nally et al., 2021). Earlier studies, however, have not found computerized reading instruction to be more effective than low-tech reading interventions—particularly when the low-tech comparison involves the same sort of intervention as the computerized version. A study of BookBuilder, furthermore, found definitive improvements in reading comprehension only when explicit, in-person instruction was added (Knight et al., 2014).

It's possible, therefore, that low-tech, in-person versions of Headsprout's computerized strategies—e.g., pointing to the relevant part of the passage and asking students to re-read it, or the inference training we discussed in the previous section—are just as effective in improving reading comprehension. However, as we noted in Chapter 3, individuals with autism often prefer computer-based interventions to in-person interventions. Furthermore, one study found that students tend to spend more time on task in the computerized reading environment (Williams, Wright, Callaghan, & Coughlan, 2002). To the extent that motivation and perseverance may boost learning over the long haul, there may be reason, in cases where both options exist, to choose a computer-based intervention over its in-person counterpart.

More targeted approaches: Figurative language, pronouns, and key words

Some of the interventions for discourse comprehension, and for reading comprehension in particular, target specific areas of reading weakness, such as difficulties with interpreting figurative language or anaphoric devices. We begin by looking at approaches that target figurative language.

As we discussed, some types of figurative language have fixed meanings—e.g., idioms like "rain cats and dogs," "skate on thin ice," and "kick the bucket"—while others—e.g., novel metaphors like "He was a volcano" and "She is the sun"—have meanings that haven't been conventionalized and, thus, vary according to context. Efforts to improve figurative language in autism have generally had more success with the former. This is because idioms and other expressions with fixed meanings are essentially like multiword vocabulary items. Just as with individual vocabulary words, therefore, the meanings of word complexes like "skate on thin ice" can simply be taught and memorized.

One possible strategy for teaching nonconventionalized figures of speech is seen in the similes exercises of some of DI's reading comprehension workbooks. These exercises present sentences like "The man had a fist like a brick" and "Her hands were like sandpaper," and ask students to "tell how these things are the same." We might expand the training from similes to metaphors via metaphorical counterparts to these sentences— e.g., "The man's fist was a brick" and "Her hand was sandpaper."

What about anaphoric devices? As we discussed earlier, these include personal and impersonal pronouns ("she," "they," "this," "that") and various types of ellipses and substitutions. Making sense of anaphora means figuring out their antecedents—i.e., what they refer to in specific situations. In cases where the antecedent isn't immediately obvious, the most straightforward strategy for finding it is to look earlier in the text for possible candidates, replace the anaphoric device with one of the possibilities, and check if the resulting interpretation makes sense. For example, consider "Our cats like to chase mice, bat them across the floor, pick them up in their mouths and carry them around, drop them back down, and generally torment them. For all that, they never kill them." The two pronouns in the second sentence, "they" and "them," have two possible antecedents in the first sentence: "the cats" and "the mice." Substituting in different combinations yields "For all that, the cats never kill the mice" and "For all that, the mice never kill the cats." Once both these possibilities are on the table, choosing between them is straightforward.

After modeling this strategy, teachers might give students paragraphs with the anaphoric devices bold-faced or underlined. Initially at least, teachers might list three possible antecedents to choose from: an inappropriate choice, one that is appropriate within the sentence but not within the context of the broader narrative, and one that is appropriate for both the sentence and the narrative. For example, in "Jack banged the shovel against the wall and dented it," "it" can't refer to "Jack," but could refer either to the shovel or to the wall. But in the context of a broader stretch of discourse that also includes a subsequent sentence like "Now the first thing Wendy and Danny saw whenever they entered the front room was an indentation in the drywall," it becomes clear that "it" probably refers to the wall.

Echoing this last tactic are the pronouns exercises found in DI's reading comprehension workbooks. These present pairs of sentences like "He set a ladder against the wall and broke it. He had to buy a new ladder," where there are two possible antecedents for "it," and "When she added ice cubes to the glasses of hot tea, they broke. The tea ran all over the counter," where there are two possible antecedents for "they" (Engelmann & Hanner, 2008, p. 335) Students are prompted to provide two possible meanings for the first sentence and then to decide, based on the second sentence, which one is the intended meaning.

Supporting these anaphoric device interventions are studies showing that students with autism are able to make appropriate connections within texts—and thereby move beyond mechanical reading to reading for meaning—when their attention is called to relevant details.

Indeed, there may be other discourse elements to which it is fruitful to direct the attention of readers with autism. Certain key words, like "both," "alike," "same," and "and," for example, signal that the text is highlighting similarities, while others, like "unlike," "different," and "but" signal that the text is making contrasts. One study that focused readers' attention on key words like these reported success in helping individuals with autism better understand science texts (Carnahan & Williamson, 2013).

Meta-cognitive approaches

We turn now to approaches that address specific cognitive weaknesses affecting reading comprehension, particularly in autism. As we've discussed, these include weaknesses in Theory of Mind, big-picture thinking, background knowledge, and several aspects of executive functioning: attention, working memory, complex information processing, and metacognition. We'll begin with metacognition.

Metacognition is what underlies the self-monitoring and error-repair strategies that, as we've seen throughout this chapter, are regularly deployed by successful readers, but not by many individuals with autism. Autistic readers often do not read for meaning or notice their comprehension errors and attempt to repair them by rereading. The studies we just alluded to in connection with anaphoric device interventions, however, suggest that autistic readers may be able to fix some of their errors—for example, errors with pronouns and homophones—when their attention is called to the relevant details. Teaching autistic readers to monitor their own reading might, therefore, enable them to repair comprehension mistakes on their own. Some interventions accordingly aim to improve reading comprehension in the autistic population by targeting metacognitive skills like self-monitoring.

Indeed, several of the strategies we've already reviewed have boosting self-monitoring skills as one of their hoped-for side effects. One is question generating, which gives the child a more active role in the reading process. Another is the reciprocal questioning intervention that has motivated students to go beyond "mechanical reading" without comprehension. A third is the pronoun interpretation exercises, which prompt students to pause and consider alternative text meanings. A fourth is sentence prediction—making predictions about hidden sentences within a paragraph—which may prompt students to notice when they've misunderstood the text. A fifth is making predictions prior to reading based on titles and headers, which may prime readers to notice discrepancies between their predictions and the actual text content once they start engaging with it.

One strategy for fostering metacognition that we have not yet explored is the TWA (Think-While-After) approach. TWA is a variant of what is called "self-regulated strategy development," an approach used with students with disabilities that is backed by more than 25 years of research. When used with struggling readers, it has proven more effective than the reciprocal questioning strategy we discussed earlier (Howorth et al., 2016).

TWA begins with pre-reading questions: questions about the author's purpose, what the child already knows on the subject, and what he wants to know. During reading, the teacher prompts students to monitor their reading speed and adjust it according to text complexity, link their prior knowledge to new information presented in the text, and reread when confused. Teachers also prompt students to reread the passage and highlight the main idea in pink, the details in green, and the nonessential text in orange. After they finish reading, teachers prompt them to identify the main idea, summarize the details, and state what they've learned. Teachers also have students create checklists, using their own words, for the steps of the TWA strategy.

One study of TWA (Howorth et al., 2016) showed significant improvements in students' performance on comprehension questions. Two weeks after the training, given new passages to read and no explicit prompts to use TWA, students had maintained these improvements. Moreover, they expressed satisfaction with the intervention, seeming to appreciate the structure it imposed on the reading process. Especially appealing to the students were the systematic rules for highlighting. As we'll discuss further in the next chapter, individuals with autism often thirst for structure and systematic rules.

Graphic organizers

Another family of strategies for improving reading comprehension in autism are graphic organizers. Graphic organizers are visual displays that depict the relationships between facts, concepts, and ideas. Common examples are tree diagrams, Venn diagrams, and flow charts. In Chapter 3, we explored how each of these can be used to teach basic concepts, but they can also support reading comprehension. Also useful for reading comprehension are concept diagrams, which provide visual linkages showing how a text's ideas and concepts are interrelated and how they connect to the main idea; and story maps, which provide visual representations of the main elements of a story (characters, time, place, beginning, middle, and end).

Graphic organizers potentially address several reading-related weaknesses in autism. They can address big-picture thinking challenges by helping readers visualize the text and its main points as a whole. They can address challenges with properly integrating one's own knowledge into the reading process by providing readers with spaces in which to fill in this knowledge and visualize its connections to the text. They can address challenges with complex information processing by helping readers visualize the text's organizational structure, making the text easier to process and subsequent comprehension questions easier to answer. They can address problems with attention and working memory by representing key events and concepts in a clear, compact, and static visual format. And they can address perspective-taking challenges by helping readers visualize how different traits are associated with different characters, as well as the characters' differing points of view. Taken together, all this potentially helps individuals with autism comprehend and retain the text's key content and conceptual or narrative flow.

Several studies report efficacy of graphic organizers in boosting reading comprehension and retention, particularly when these are used in conjunction with other strategies like teacher-guided questions, Direction Instruction, systematic prompting, reciprocal questioning, and highlighting key words (Bethune & Wood, 2013; Carnahan & Williamson, 2013; Williamson, Carnahan, Birri, & Swoboda, 2015).

Linguistic strategies

Extended discourse, of course, is essentially a linguistic phenomenon—one in which meaning interacts with linguistic structure. In general, for example, the subject(s) of the first sentence of a paragraph is generally its topic, and the subjects of the component sentences are often either repetitions of this topic or related subtopics. Thus, "Anne tricked Sally into thinking that the marble was in the basket" is about Anne, and "Sally was tricked by Anne into thinking that the marble was in the basket" is about Sally. In a paragraph about Anne, the first formulation is better; in a paragraph about Sally, the second one is more appropriate.

Meanwhile, the final phrases of sentences and the final sentences of paragraphs indicate what, within the given topic, the writer is emphasizing. Thus, "Sally thought the marble was in the basket, but Anne moved it to the box" emphasizes the new location of the marble, while "Although Anne moved the marble to the box, Sally thought the marble was in the basket" emphasizes Sally's misconception.

Teaching these principles to autistic children, who, as we're observing, depend a great deal on structure, may help them organize their reading process. Learning to look for the author's current topic or subtopic in the first sentences of paragraphs and in the subjects of sentences, and his intended emphasis in the endings of sentences and paragraphs, offers a framework for attending to the meanings of sentences and paragraphs.

Another linguistic strategy involves "unpacking" certain linguistic structures that are prevalent in written discourse. Expository writing, as we discussed earlier, often compresses meaning into complex noun phrases with ambiguous meanings. As we've also noted, students with autism may be capable of resolving ambiguities when their attention is drawn to the relevant details. To draw their attention to the ambiguities of complex noun phrases, we might have them explore the multiple ways in which these can be expanded into more explicit phrases and sentences. For example, phrases of the form The X of the Y can mean either:

- The X that happened to the Y.
- The X that the Y caused.

After teaching students this formula, we might give them phrases like "the flooding of the dam" and prompt them to say or write out the two alternatives: the flooding that happened to the dam or the flooding that the dam caused. We can then ask them to consider which one makes the most sense in the broader context of the discourse and/or the real world.

Some simple noun phrases—particularly noun–noun combinations—also allow multiple interpretations. For example, "government control" can mean either "control by the government" or "control of the government." Here, too, we can ask students to consider and write out the two alternatives and reflect on which one makes the most sense in context.

A similar strategy can disambiguate constructions involving appositives— those phrases set off by parentheses, commas, hyphens or colons, discussed earlier in the context of these examples:

- Some piano teachers prefer to teach novices: people who haven't yet developed bad keyboard habits.
- Some piano teachers prefer to teach novices: people who are insecure about their pedagogical skills.

Students can be prompted to consider which of the noun phrases in the main sentences ("some piano teachers" or "novices") makes the most sense as the thing being modified by the appositive (as either not having developed bad keyboard habits or being insecure about their pedagogical skills).

In order to decide between competing interpretations like these, however, it is often helpful, as we noted earlier, to have acquired some relevant background knowledge—e.g., about the effect of dams on water flow, or about whether governments are more likely to control or be controlled, or about the kinds of things that are likely to concern piano teachers).

Background knowledge

As we discussed earlier, two background knowledge challenges are common in autism. One is that students may lack the background knowledge, particularly the social knowledge, necessary to make sense of what they read. The other is that even when autistic individuals have the requisite knowledge, they often fail to integrate it into the text.

The latter challenge is potentially addressed by some of the metacognitive and graphic organizer interventions discussed above. Beyond this, the teacher might explicitly guide students in calling up their existing knowledge and connecting it to the text. One framework for doing so is the KWL Method (What we Know, what we Want to know, what we Learned) in which teachers have students fill out K-W-L charts before reading. Students might also brainstorm about elements in their lives that are related to those in the reading passage. Teachers, however, need to ensure that these elements are truly relevant. Activating irrelevant details may impede comprehension, especially, as we've discussed, in students with autism.

As for deficits in background knowledge, teachers should determine ahead of time what information and vocabulary a given text requires, assess students for this knowledge, and then teach it as needed. Doing so before the student starts engaging with the text is essential: We want to do all we can, before she starts reading, to reduce her memory load and prepare her to focus, with minimal interruptions, on the text itself.

Certain types of vocabulary—vocabulary that expresses social and emotional concepts—and certain types of texts and narratives—especially highly social texts or texts that assume large amounts of incidental cultural knowledge—may require a great deal of pre-teaching. Consider, for example, what sorts of linguistic meanings and background knowledge teachers may need to pre-teach in order to prepare a student for this opening passage of *From the Mixed-Up Files of Mrs. Basil E. Frankweiler*:

Claudia knew that she could never pull off the old-fashioned kind of running away. That is, running away in the heat of anger with a knapsack on her back. She didn't like discomfort; even picnics were untidy and inconvenient: all those insects and the sun melting the icing on the cupcakes. Therefore, she decided that her leaving home would not be just running from somewhere but would be running to somewhere. To a large place, a comfortable place, an indoor place, and preferably a beautiful place. And that's why she decided upon the Metropolitan Museum of Art in New York City.

She planned very carefully; she saved her allowance and she chose her companion. She chose Jamie, the second youngest of her three younger brothers. He could be counted on to be quiet, and now and then he was good for a laugh. Besides, he was rich; unlike most boys his age, he had never even begun collecting baseball cards. He saved almost every penny he got. (Konigsburg, 1967, pp. 5–6)

Among the things that this passage assumes readers already know are some basic facts about the Metropolitan Museum of Art; some basic cultural knowledge (about the stereotypical ingredients of running away from home; about stereotypical picnics; about allowances; about collecting baseball cards); and, finally, the meanings of the idiomatic expressions "pull off," "heat of anger," "count on," "keep quiet," and "good for a laugh," most of which express concepts that tap into social and psychological knowledge.

What we know about efficacy

The half-dozen reviews we've cited of interventions for reading comprehension are consistent in their conclusions. The most effective interventions are question generation, reciprocal questioning, explicit instruction, Direct Instruction, inference training, main idea identification, exercises in pronoun interpretation, and graphic organizers. This tallies with two general observations about individuals with autism: their frequent dependence on explicit instruction and prompting, and their tendency to default to mechanical reading processes in the absence of external reminders to focus on meaning and integrate relevant elements of background knowledge.

What the studies do not address, however, are broader questions relating to long-term efficacy. Some interventions simply focus on improving students' comprehension of a given text; others look at whether the intervention carries over to improved comprehension of new texts, generally just a few weeks after the intervention concludes. In some cases only some of the skills were maintained at these follow-up evaluations. The most important question, ultimately, is whether students learn strategies that they can independently apply to novel passages of discourse over the long term, and here many uncertainties remain.

Two additional caveats are in order. First, there are a number of comprehension challenges that these interventions do not fully address— particularly those relating to deficits in social knowledge and difficulties with pragmatics: difficulties, that is, with the many subtle metaphors, ironies, and indirect uses of language that pervade all sorts of discourse. Second, the various interventions tend to be most effective with children at the higher functioning end of the autism spectrum.

Extended discourse and writing skills

Discourse comprehension is arguably the most urgent linguistic prerequisite for K12 education. Across all academic subjects, understanding what your teacher and your textbooks say is essential for learning. Only in certain subject areas is it also important to be able to produce extended discourse. Yet this, too, is a major challenge in autism. Many autistic students struggle to construct coherent descriptions, explanations, and narratives.

While there is a great deal more research on text comprehension than on text production, some of the comprehension interventions also include strategies that address writing. DI's reading comprehension workbooks, for instance, contain several varieties of writing exercises. These include "sentence combining" exercises where students are given two short sentences and asked to combine them using certain words—e.g., "and," "but," "who," "which," or "because." In addition, there are exercises that ask students to produce the directions required for constructing a given diagram (e.g., "Draw a triangle, then draw a square under the triangle, and then draw a vertical line from the top of the triangle to the bottom of the square").

In addition, the same sentence structure rules that we proposed as a framework for reading—i.e., about topics going in subject position and what's being emphasized going in final position—can also be used to guide writing.

Finally, graphic organizers—particularly concept maps and story maps—can assist students with autism in the construction of their own expository and narrative discourse.

We'll delve more deeply into these finer points of writing in the next chapter, where we address the various challenges of K12 education.

References

Bethune, K. S., & Wood, C. L. (2013). Effects of wh-question graphic organizers on reading comprehension skills of students with autism spectrum disorders. *Education and Training in Autism and Developmental Disabilities*, 48(2), 236–244.

Carnahan, C. R., & Williamson, P. S. (2013). Does compare-contrast text structure help students with autism spectrum disorder comprehend science text? *Exceptional Children*, 79(3), 347–363. https://doi.org/10.1177/001440291307900302

Engelmann S., & Hanner, S. (2008). *Corrective reading comprehension C: Concept applications workbook*. McGraw Hill.

Flores, M. M., & Ganz, J. B. (2007). Effectiveness of direct instruction for teaching statement inference, use of facts, and analogies to students with developmental disabilities and reading delays. *Focus on Autism and Other Developmental Disabilities*, 22(4), 244–251. https://doi.org/10.1177/10883576070220040601

Ganz, J. B., & Flores, M. M. (2009). The effectiveness of direct instruction for teaching language to children with autism spectrum disorders: Identifying materials. *Journal of Autism and Developmental Disorders*, 39(1), 75–83. https://doi.org/10.1007/s10803-008-0602-6

Grindle, C., Kurzeja, O., Tyler, E., Saville, M., Hughes, J. C., Hastings, R. P., & Brown, F. J. (2020). Teaching children with autism reading comprehension skills using online reading instruction: Preliminary evaluation of Headsprout Reading Comprehension®. *Journal of International Special Needs Education, 30*, 1–12. https://doi.org/10.9782/17-00008

Howorth, S., Lopata, C., Thomeer, M., & Rodgers, J. (2016). Effects of the TWA Strategy on expository reading comprehension of students with autism. *British Journal of Special Education, 43*(1), 39–59. https://doi.org/10.1111/1467-8578.12122

Johnson, K., & Street, E. M. (2012). From the laboratory to the field and back again: Morningside Academy's 32 years of improving students' academic performance. *The Behavior Analyst Today, 13*(1), 20–40. http://dx.doi.org/10.1037/h0100715

Knight, V. F., Wood, C. L., Spooner, F., Browder, D. M., & O'Brien, C. P. (2014). An exploratory study using science eTexts with students with autism spectrum disorder. *Focus on Autism and Other Developmental Disabilities, 30*(2), 1–14. https://doi.org/10.1177/1088357614559214

Konigsburg, E. L. (1967). *From the mixed-up files of Mrs. Basil E. Frankweiler* (pp. 5–6). Athenaeum.

Loukusa, S., Mäkinen, L., Kuusikko-Gauffin, S., Ebeling, H., & Leinonen, E. (2018). Assessing social-pragmatic inferencing skills in children with autism spectrum disorder. *Journal of Communication Disorders, 73*, 91–105. https://doi.org/10.1016/j.jcomdis.2018.01.006

Nally, A., Holloway, J., Lydon, H., Lydon, H. & Healy, O. (2021). A randomized controlled trial of Headsprout on the reading outcomes in children with autism using parents as facilitators. *Behavior Analysis Practice*, 14, 944–957. https://doi.org/10.1007/s40617-021-00597-1

Nelson Head, C., Flores, M. M., & Shippen, M. E. (2018). Effects of direct instruction on reading comprehension for individuals with autism or developmental disabilities. *Education and Training in Autism and Developmental Disabilities*, 53(2), 176–191.

Ostrolenk, A., Forgeot d'Arc, B., Jelenic, P., Samson, F., & Mottron, L. (2017). Hyperlexia: Systematic review, neurocognitive modelling, and outcome. *Neuroscience and Biobehavioral Reviews, 79*, 134–149. https://doi.org/10.1016/j.neubiorev.2017.04.029

Robbins, J. K., & Layng, T. V. J. (2010). *Fluent thinking skills: A generative approach 2nd Ed*. P.E.E.R International.

Williams, C., Wright, B., Callaghan, G., & Coughlan, B. (2002). Do children with autism learn to read more readily by computer assisted instruction or traditional book methods? A pilot study. *Autism: The International Journal of Research and Practice, 6,* 71–91. https://doi.org/10.1177/1362361302006001006

Williamson, P., Carnahan, C. R., Birri, N., & Swoboda, C. (2015). Improving comprehension of narrative using character event maps for high school students with autism spectrum disorder. *The Journal of Special Education, 49*(1), 28–38. https://doi.org/10.1177/0022466914521301

Yuill, N. M., & Oakhill, J. (1988). Effects of inference awareness training on poor reading comprehension. *Applied Cognitive Psychology, 2,* 33–45. https://doi.org/10.1002/acp.2350020105

CHAPTER 6

FROM ABA TO DI: WHAT THE EVIDENCE-BASED AUTISM THERAPIES TELL US ABOUT WHAT WORKS IN THE CLASSROOM

The interventions we've focused on up till now have primarily targeted language-based difficulties—vocabulary, sentence-level comprehension and production, discourse-level comprehension, and (briefly) discourse-level production. Except when discussing reading and writing, we focused on skills that help prepare students *for* K12 education—as opposed to skills that students develop *during* K12 education. In addition, most of the interventions we reviewed are best suited to settings outside of regular education classrooms—i.e., in homes, clinics, or—if in school settings—in "pullout sessions" with speech-language pathologists or reading/literacy specialists.

In this chapter we turn to challenges that arise during academic instruction—whether in K12 classrooms or homeschooling environments. As with the last two chapters, the children we have in mind here, in terms of their linguistic and cognitive skills, are relatively high functioning. That is, they are children who will spend at least some of their classroom or homeschooling hours engaging with academic subjects—Language Arts, math, social studies, and/or science. In addition, as in earlier chapters, what we cover here will be applicable to parents, autism specialists, and regular classroom teachers.

Unlike in earlier chapters, however, different people reading this book will face significantly different constraints on how much of what we recommend they can execute. If you are a parent who is homeschooling (whether full time or part-time) and/or providing out-of-school tutoring, you are free to implement, to the extent you think appropriate, each one of this chapter's instructional recommendations. If, however, you are a classroom teacher—whether an autistic support teacher or a teacher whose classroom includes students with autism—you have far less flexibility. This is particularly so if you teach in a public school with a mandated curriculum and testing requirements. Similarly constrained are the majority of parents who aren't primarily homeschooling their kids. With these two stakeholders in mind, therefore, this chapter offers not just recommendations, but also critiques of those trends in K12 education that adversely affect students with autism. This critique will give you not only a sense of what problems to look out for, but also a basis for advocating for the various accommodations and instructional strategies recommended later on in the chapter.

We begin with a look at how autistic students fare in K12 schools and what sorts of challenges they face as a result of their autism-related idiosyncrasies. We then identify various K12 practices that, given these challenges, are especially problematic for students with autism. Finally, we suggest ways to better accommodate these students and optimize their academic success.

School performance

Looking at academic achievement in the autism population, we find a high degree of variability. Partly, this reflects the variability, across the autism spectrum, in overall intellectual functioning. But this can't be the whole story. Some individuals with autism perform better than expected based on their IQ scores, while others perform worse than expected.

Indeed, there are additional factors besides intellectual impairment that affect academic achievement—many of them directly related to autism. These include the attention issues, social challenges, language challenges, and weak central coherence limitations that we've discussed at length in earlier chapters. They also include the issues with executive function and complex information processing that we first broached in the last chapter.

Consider attention. Individuals with autism, as we've seen, are easily distracted away from people and what they say—e.g., their teachers and classmates—by environmental stimuli—e.g., the classroom's visual clutter, and/or the sounds of rustling papers and moving chairs. They may have "sticky attention": difficulty disengaging from one activity and switching to another in a timely fashion. Relatedly, they may struggle to switch attention back and forth between speakers to fully follow class discussions.

In the social arena, students with autism, engaging less frequently in joint attention behaviors, are less likely to automatically attend to the same things that their teachers and classmates are attending to. They are also less apt to engage with their peers and, even when they do engage, are less successful in their interactions.

In the linguistic arena, any impairments in vocabulary, sentence, and discourse comprehension will affect a student's comprehension of the language of the classroom and, most importantly, the language of instruction. These impairments, as we saw in the last chapter, apply equally to written language and are further impaired by weak central coherence, executive function deficits, and complex information processing difficulties. Difficulties with expressive language, meanwhile, may impair oral and written responses.

Executive function deficits may also impede a child's organizational skills, such that he struggles to keep track of his belongings. He may struggle, as well, with activities and assignments that involve multistep directions and multiple steps to execute.

Compounding this are the complex information processing difficulties that, as we noted in the last chapter, underlie that "thirst for structure" that is so common in the autistic population. As tasks and material encompass more detail, more wide-ranging material, and more moving parts, students with autism are disproportionately impaired—unless these materials are structured or organized for them.

As far as classroom-based complex information demands go, the most obvious examples are assignments involving large numbers of disorganized facts and/or multiple information sources. But complex motor movements—e.g., penmanship and drawing—also involve complex information processing. As the high functioning autistic adult

Stephen Shore explains in *Beyond the Wall: Personal Experiences with Autism (2nd ed.)*:

> I have always wondered how I can have the fine-motor control to take apart a watch's gears while my drawing and penmanship when writing in script is so poor. Perhaps it is because the structure is inherent within the watch innards themselves, whereas when writing or drawing in freehand, I am forced to provide the structure. Even though I am well aware of my difficulties in penmanship and drawing, having to provide that structure from within myself makes it impossible for me to do these activities well. (Shore, 2003)

Similarly, complex information processing difficulties make it hard for individuals with autism to come up with their own rules—as opposed to following existing rules—and to apply familiar concepts to new situations.

Certain writing assignments that arise in K12—namely, summaries, narratives, and descriptions—also run up against autism-specific challenges. Detail focus and weak central coherence make it hard to extract gist, and therefore hard to write summaries. Weak central coherence and complex information processing difficulties make it hard to organize facts and ideas into consistent wholes. Difficulty putting himself in the readers' shoes can cause an autistic student to provide insufficient descriptions, explanations, elaborations, and background information, and to leave out the kinds of connections and transitions that make texts coherent to readers. Difficulty putting herself in the shoes of the other characters, meanwhile, may cause her narratives to lack what some call a "landscape of consciousness." Her narratives, that is, may contain few emotion words, little psychosocial content, and infrequent attributions of thoughts, feelings, and internal motivations to the people she's writing about.

For some students, additionally, diminished knowledge of common cultural events and artifacts, including the cultural artifact of narration itself, can lead to an under-awareness of what a narrative is in the first place: an inability, that is, to conceive of narrations as sequences of coherent events. Lack of basic cultural knowledge can also lead to narratives and descriptions that lack a principled hierarchical organization from general to specific, with objects and events depicted at appropriate levels of abstraction. For example, one autistic boy, asked to say what happens when people eat at restaurants, reported details specific to his own personal restaurant outings: "Fish 'n ' chips . . . They had beans, sausage and pie for dinner."

Potentially the strongest subjects for individuals with autism are those most removed from their autism-related challenges: subjects that are less language intensive, that do not require mentalizing about other people, that do not involve complex motor control or complex masses of unorganized information, and that instead are more grounded in structure and explicit, systematic rules. The most obvious candidates are math and science, but there's also drafting or technical drawing (as opposed to open-ended art projects), music theory (as opposed to open-ended composing), and music performance (as opposed to musical improvisation). Even within language-intensive subjects, some are significantly more accessible than others—for example, essay writing (as opposed to less structured "creative" writing); sequential, fact-intensive history (as opposed to social studies); grammar, including the grammar of other languages (as opposed to open-ended communicating); and playing a part in a play (as opposed to improvising).

And yet, even within these areas, we find great variability across the autistic population, with different students excelling in different tasks. Naturally, some of this variability reflects the natural range of talents and interests across individuals both on and off the autism spectrum. But there is one other key factor affecting how individuals with autism perform in K12 classrooms: namely, the classrooms themselves. How different classroom pedagogies, curricula, and expectations interact with the strengths and weaknesses of students with autism will be the focus of the remainder of this chapter.

The dominant paradigm for 21st century classrooms

Since well before the turn of the century, a certain paradigm for classroom instruction has increasingly permeated K12 schools, particularly those schools that are held up as models. Known alternatively as "progressive education" or "Constructivism," buttressed as we'll see by the Common Core Standards, it is grounded in the following principles:

- Child-centered experiential learning
- Cooperative learning
- Real-world relevance
- Project-based learning
- Metacognition
- Writing and communicating across the curriculum
- Educating the whole child

The principle of child-centered, experiential learning holds that children learn best when they direct their own learning and make their own discoveries. Particularly in early elementary school classes, learning, retention, and conceptual understanding are said to be optimized in the context of hands-on activities—e.g., drawing pictures; counting objects; stacking, bundling, and building; cutting things into pieces; and pasting them back together. Often, especially in elementary school, this child-centered learning is reflected in the classroom seating arrangements. Instead of desks oriented in rows to the front of the classroom, we find desks pushed together into "pods." This puts students more directly in contact with one another than with their teacher.

As for the teacher, he is no longer the traditional "sage on the stage," but the "guide on the side." Instead of spending most of his time standing in front, addressing the class as a whole, and writing things out on the blackboard or whiteboard, he walks around the classroom and facilitates students as they explore and discover. He may still occasionally take center stage, for example, to introduce new material or procedures, but this explicit teaching is minimized to short (10–15 minute) "mini-lessons" and mainly serves to get the ball rolling.

Closely related to child-centered learning, the principle of cooperative learning holds that children learn better when engaging with their peers—exploring and discovering things together, bouncing ideas off one another, explaining things to one another, cooperating on strategies, and agreeing on solutions—than when working independently.

The principle of real-world relevance, meanwhile, is based on two premises. First, students are most engaged in what they learn when it relates to their personal lives. Second, learning is most meaningful when it's embedded in the real world. This real-world embeddedness also informs today's notions of mastery: To fully master a given concept, it is said, a student needs to be able to apply it to novel, real-life scenarios.

The principle of project-based learning is, in part, a corollary of child-centered discovery learning. But it also harks back to nineteenth-century education reformer John Dewey, who argued that children are most motivated to learn when pursuing topics of their own choosing (ideally in collaboration with others).

The Constructivist principle of metacognition goes beyond the metacognitive self-monitoring strategies we discussed in Chapter 5 as interventions for reading comprehension. For Constructivists, metacognition enhances learning in general. Metacognitive reflection, or reflecting on your learning, is, purportedly, a key way to deepen your understanding and to demonstrate it to others. Constructivism assumes that metacognition, though it happens inside people's heads, is fundamentally a verbal phenomenon. Students, accordingly, are expected to be able to transcribe their meta-cognitive processes into oral or written words. In this way they purportedly make these internal processes visible to teachers and classmates.

A close cousin of metacognition, therefore, is writing/communicating across the curriculum. Communicating your thinking processes and your knowledge is, purportedly, not only an important metacognitive skill, but also an important life skill. It is a skill, therefore, that students must practice by communicating their learning to teachers and classmates—whether it's about math, science, or, say, project-based research.

The principle of the whole child, finally, holds that social and emotional development is as important as cognitive and academic development. Classroom practices should therefore foster the former as much as the latter, and classroom expectations should include social and behavioral norms.

Many of these principles and practices—especially those relating to group learning, real-life relevance, and communication skills—have been encoded in the official standards that have guided US classrooms since 2010. These are the Common Core State Standards, a set of standards and goals intended for all K12 schools across all 50 states that are designed to ensure, in the words of the Common Core standards "About" page, that all US students are "graduating high school prepared for college, career, and life."

In the next sections, we'll review various ways that each of these principles and practices poses problems for students with autism.

Problems with child-centered learning

The child-centered learning paradigm, opposed as it is to traditional, teacher-centered instruction, should recall the contrast we drew in Chapter 3 between the two competing frameworks for autism therapy: Floortime and ABA. Floortime is child-centered and unstructured. Learning opportunities arise incidentally, depending on the child's focus and interests. ABA is therapist-centered and highly systematic, following a specific regimen of subskill-by-subskill instruction.

As we noted, ABA is by far the more successful therapy, with Floortime's efficacy limited to interventions in which it's used in combination with ABA. Child-centered learning, thus, is ill-suited to children with autism for the same reason that Floortime has turned out to be: Autistic children tend not to acquire skills and knowledge incidentally through the natural environment. They depend, instead, on direct, systematic instruction.

Child-centered learning also fails autistic students in its lack of structure. Children, left to their own devices, are ill-equipped to grasp the overarching organizational structure of new material that they're in the process of learning. Nor do they naturally organize their activities and objects of attention so as to optimize learning, practice, and mastery. Whether they're exploring how to add numbers or how to read words, what they learn and practice, even when they are most focused and motivated, depends on what they stumble across or what happens to attract their attention. Their learning is accordingly haphazard, ad hoc, and disorganized.

How well child-centered learning serves students in general is one question. As for students with autism, let's recall Stephen Shore's words about how poorly his skills develop when "I am forced to provide the structure." Only in teacher-directed environments do students receive systematic instruction and practice, whether in phonics or arithmetic; only teacher-directed environments can guarantee the organization upon which students with autism depend.

Then there's the hands-on component. Hands-on discovery classrooms are cluttered with materials, simultaneous activities, and attendant noise. For many autistic kids, these distractions impede learning; for some, the sensory overload is downright aversive.

We should note that in many K12 classrooms, child-centered learning is implemented only partially. This is due, among other things, to the various practical challenges involved and because child-centered learning is not a Common Core priority. Nonetheless, elements of child-centered learning have still permeated many classrooms, particularly in elementary schools, with hands-on activities replacing many pen and paper activities, and with students encouraged to devise their own strategies for doing math problems and their own ways to spell words.

Problems with project-based learning

One specific manifestation of child-centered learning is the open-ended project. Open-ended projects tap into several autism-specific weaknesses. First, they often require students to track down and integrate large amounts of information from multiple sources. Second, there's no guarantee that the information found in these various sources is written at a level that is accessible to autistic readers. Third, many projects culminate in oral presentations, and grading rubrics often include "presentation skills" like oral language skills and eye contact—key areas of weakness in autism. On top of all this, many projects are designed for groups, thus raising some of the concerns that we will discuss, below, in connection with cooperative learning.

Problems with cooperative learning

To students with autism, cooperative group learning poses some of the same problems as child-centered discovery. Even though cooperative groups are relatively small (often just 2–5 students) their activities are inevitably less structured than whole-class activities that are led by a teacher. In addition, multiple simultaneous group conversations around the classroom may distract autistic students from what's going on within their designated group. Beyond this, they may struggle to follow the group conversation, to jump in at the right moments, and to express themselves clearly.

But the biggest problems for autistic students are the social challenges. Teachers can't monitor multiple groups simultaneously, and socially awkward interactions may provoke subtle forms of shunning and bullying. Unfortunately, students with autism are generally less subtle in their responses to being bullied and more easily manipulated by their groupmates. Therefore, adding insult to injury, they are often the ones who end up getting in trouble when group work goes awry. Even in the best-case scenarios, however, as research on the social preferences in autism has suggested, autistic students generally prefer to work on their own.

Problems with real-life relevance and real-world application

The emphasis on real-life relevance has already shown itself to be problematic in the context of reading comprehension. Individuals with autism often have difficulty suppressing irrelevant details from their personal lives. Making things relevant, therefore, potentially distracts autistic students away from what's being taught and/or distorts what they learn. For example, if a teacher tries to make a lesson about nocturnal animals relevant to students' lives by asking them about their own sleeping habits, a student with autism may be distracted with thoughts about a recent dream he had, or may end up thinking that "nocturnal" means sleeping.

Beyond this, many assignments strive for relevance by referencing the types of knowledge that are often deficient in autism—i.e., basic cultural knowledge and other common, everyday sorts of background knowledge. Thus, social studies assignments may assume that students know about neighborhoods or the stereotypical activities and events that occur in parks and playgrounds, while math problems may assume they know, say, about parties and restaurants.

Real-life relevance has even permeated fiction, with literature and creative writing assignments geared towards realistic, contemporary fiction featuring the kinds of regular, school-aged characters that most students relate to. The more culturally naïve autistic student is, once again, at a disadvantage. She may lack the social and cultural knowledge to make sense of The Fault in Our Stars (Green, 2012) and, when asked to write her own story, may produce something that teachers consider insufficiently realistic. Well before today's special emphasis on realism, writings by autistic students already provoked dismay. Steven Shore reports on how his teacher dismissed as "babyish" a story he wrote about pets that "that alternated between existing as cats and puppies" and "sold for $47,000 each."

In general, given the knowledge deficits in autism, what makes an assignment more accessible to students in general often makes it less accessible to students with autism. A truly level playing field, in contrast, would have all students reading and writing fantasy fiction, science fiction, or fiction set in faraway times and places.

Then there are the cognitive challenges of real-life relevance. As autism researchers have noted, autistic individuals excel at decontextualized learning: at learning concepts, e.g., about arithmetic, that are abstracted away from specific environments, e.g., grocery stores. Grounding concepts in real-life situations makes them less accessible to students with autism. In addition, as we noted at the beginning of this chapter, autistic students struggle to apply the concepts they've learned to novel situations. While this may be a worthy goal for all students, it may not be a realistic one for students with autism—unless we come up with systematic, step-by-step strategies for getting them there.

Problems with metacognition and communicating across the curriculum

In practice, promoting metacognition means having students reflect on their learning and express their reflections in words. Students with autism, however, may lack the necessary language skills, particularly when it comes to cognitive vocabulary like "think," "remember," and "imagine." Moreover, even if they've completed a task successfully or learned a new skill, they may not have engaged in anything resembling verbal reflection while doing so. Nor are they necessarily capable of engaging in such reflection after the fact. Indeed, one of the most famous individuals with autism, the highly verbal Temple Grandin, tells us that she thinks mostly not in words, but in pictures. To explain to us how she designs cattle-handling equipment, she reports, she has to translate her visual imagery into words—something that may be well beyond the skills of many students with autism.

Deficient verbal skills can also impede writing/communicating across the curriculum. While autistic students may have no trouble doing math and science, they may struggle to communicate *about* math and science.

Communication goals that tap into autism-specific weaknesses also figure prominently in the Common Core standards. Below are some excerpts of the Speaking and Listening standards for seventh-grade English and Language Arts. Notice how many of these tap into the various socio-communicative weaknesses in autism:

- "Initiate and participate effectively in a range of collaborative discussions (one-on-one, in groups, and teacher-led) with diverse partners on … topics, texts, and issues, building on others' ideas and expressing their own clearly and persuasively."
- "Follow agreed-upon rules for discussions (e.g., listening to others with care, speaking one at a time about the topics and texts under discussion)."
- "Build on others' talk in conversations by responding to the comments of others through multiple exchanges."
- "[U]se appropriate eye contact, adequate volume, and clear pronunciation."
- "Adapt speech to a variety of contexts and tasks"
- "Respond thoughtfully to diverse perspectives"
- "Evaluate a speaker's point of view… assessing the stance, premises, links among ideas, word choice, points of emphasis, and tone used."

http://www.corestandards.org/ELA-Literacy/SL/

As with real-life concept application, these are noble goals. But, again, it is unclear whether it's reasonable to expect autistic students to reach them—at least until someone figures out a roadmap for getting them there.

Yet, well before such goals were codified, expectations for class participation have long dogged individuals with autism—tapping as they do into their expressive language difficulties, their difficulties following conversations, particularly group conversations, and their difficulties jumping in at appropriate moments and saying appropriate things.

Problems with non-academic expectations

A final set of challenges come from the last principle we listed under Constructivism: "Educating the whole child." This means going beyond cognitive and academic skills to other developmental skills. In classroom practice, these other developmental skills are, primarily, organizational skills, social skills, and age-appropriate behaviors.

The organizational expectations of K12 classes have increased substantially in recent decades. We see this, for example, in open-ended projects, whose demands we discussed above. We see it, as well, in other assignments that ask students to research answers to questions using multiple sources—research that growing Internet access has made increasingly feasible, but that also poses organizational challenges, particularly to students with autism.

Besides the expansion of research-based assignments, there are two additional reasons why organizational demands have increased. One is that more and more classes, particularly in social studies, have eschewed a single textbook in favor of readings from multiple sources, including from primary source documents. Much of this is printed out and stapled together into multiple bundles that sometimes come apart over time. For students with autism especially, these are, physically speaking, more difficult to keep track of than a single textbook—and, cognitively speaking, more difficult to integrate into a coherent understanding of whatever the current topic is.

At a much more basic level, the simple act of turning in homework has, for many autistic students, become a much bigger organizational hurdle than it used to be. A generation or two ago, teachers walked around, paused at each desk, and waited for each student to hand them their homework. Now students are expected to remember, upon entering the classroom, to remove their homework from their increasingly cluttered backpacks and place it in the classroom's designated drop-off location. Most students routinely manage to do this, but for some students with autism, it is a major challenge in executive functioning. Despite repeated reminders from their parents as they head off to school, their homework may be several days late before they finally remember to turn it in.

The organizational demands of turning homework in on time, of course, are not to be confused with the organizational demands of getting it done on time—a challenge that long predates the emphasis on "the whole child."

Besides their difficulties working in cooperative groups, students with autism are prone to numerous social blunders. Among the higher functioning autistic students, one of the most common errors is bluntly correcting their classmates or teachers.

Autistic students may also struggle with the socio-behavioral rules of the classroom. Many such rules—for example, rules about keeping one's hands off the teacher's desk and away from other people's belongings—aren't explicitly spelled out. Nor do they generally need to be: They are the kinds of "common sense" rules that most children pick up incidentally. But autistic children, as we've seen, miss out on many incidental learning opportunities—particularly for sociocultural knowledge. They depend therefore on explicit instruction in rules and norms. Unfortunately, it can be hard for those who might provide this instruction—say their parents and therapists—to anticipate and successfully teach ahead of time all the rules and norms that might come up.

An autistic student, therefore, may break a "common sense" classroom rule without even knowing it exists. The teacher, meanwhile, may be insufficiently direct in correcting him. Today's teachers are expected to be affirming and encouraging rather than critical. But saying "Tommy, how would you feel if I touched the stuff on your desk?" rather than "Tommy, you are not allowed to touch the stuff on my desk" may not get the point across to a student with autism. Tommy may continue to break rules, and the more he does, the more defiant he appears.

Deepening this impression of defiance is the fact that individuals with autism often have trouble making sense of the teacher's directions. Even basic requests may pose comprehension challenges. As the high functioning autistic author Daniel Tammet reports in his book *Born on a Blue Day*:

> I would get into trouble in class if a teacher thought I was being unresponsive, when in fact I had not realized that they were expecting me to give an answer. For example, he would say: "Seven times nine" while looking at me, and of course I knew that the answer was sixty-three, but I did not realize that I was

expected to say the answer out loud to the class. It was only when the teacher repeated his question explicitly as "What is seven times nine?" that I gave the answer. (2007, p. 76)

Further impeding an autistic student's timely and appropriate responses to questions and requests is the slow reaction time that often comes with autism—that "sticky attention" that can make it hard for him to disengage from one attentional focus and switch over to another. In the case of multistep directions, he may flounder—and aggravate his teacher—even further.

Besides coming across as blunt, defiant, and unresponsive, autistic students can also look like they're willfully not attending. That's because they are much more distractible than other students are, and because they can be distracted by sights and sounds that aren't apparent to others. These attention problems are aggravated by their difficulties sustaining attention over time, as well as by any difficulty they may have making sense of their teacher's explanations or following class discussions. Tuning out, after all, is a natural response to not comprehending.

And so, unfortunately, are problem behaviors. When a student can't follow what's going on around him, he easily gets bored. Boredom, in many children, is a recipe for acting up—for anything from squirming and fidgeting to behavior that is downright disruptive.

Collectively, all this—the social inappropriateness, the apparent defiance and lack of cooperation, the apparently deliberate failure to attend, and the disruptive behavior—can make a child look much more immature and behaviorally challenged than he would be under different circumstances and in different sorts of classrooms.

Problems with class assessment standards

All these factors, in turn, can lower a student's grades. Modern-day assessment standards, reflecting "the whole child," often incorporate such considerations as motivation, effort, initiative, cooperation, maturity, and behavior. Sloppy handwriting—a common issue in autism, perhaps due to the complex motor demands—often aggravates things further.

So does late homework. One parent on an autism listserv asks:

Is it fair to deduct from his grade for work being turned in late? To me that also seems to be punishing him for a disability. I think his report card should reflect his organizational challenges (under "work habits," or something), but his grades in science and social studies should be reflections of his performance in science and social studies, not his organizational issues.

Indeed, these organizational and behavioral expectations lower grades that are already adversely affected by the social demands, the challenges of relevance-based assignments, and the emphasis across the entire curriculum on language and communication.

Grades that underrate a child's academic abilities, of course, make it less likely for him to receive appropriately challenging material. Lack of sufficient challenge, in turn, can lead to further boredom and disengagement—and so to a potentially vicious cycle.

Problems with reading assignments

We now take a closer look at two academic areas that recent trends have made significantly less accessible to students with autism: reading and math. First, we'll address the challenges of reading assignments, particularly in the upper grades.

These challenges go beyond the reading issues we covered in the last chapter and the additional challenges we discussed in this chapter in reference to "relevant" readings. Besides all this, there are the Common Core reading guidelines for English and Language Arts. These mandate, for all but the most intellectually challenged high school students, some works by Shakespeare. They also list other works as "exemplary"—i.e., as representing what level of literary challenge students should be getting in which grade. Among the exemplary texts for eighth grade is *Tom Sawyer*, which includes the following sentence:

> Inspired by the splendor of his own act, he took without an outcry the most merciless flaying that even Mr. Dobbins had ever administered; and also received with indifference the added cruelty of a command to remain two hours after school should be dismissed—for he knew who would wait for him outside till his captivity was done, and not count the tedious time as loss, either. (Twain, 2005, p. 124)

The Common Core guidelines thus impose on nearly all secondary school students—all but the most intellectually challenged 1%-2%—a level of literary challenge that far exceeds the linguistic capabilities of many students with autism.

Compared to *Tom Sawyer* and Shakespeare, secondary school textbooks are far more accessible. But even in textbook-based classes like science and social studies, new obstacles to reading comprehension have surfaced. As we noted earlier, many teachers incorporate readings from multiple sources rather than relying on just the textbook. Some of these texts, particularly primary source documents, may require greater amounts of background knowledge and higher level reading skills than grade-level textbooks do.

Problems with Progressive Math

While reading-intensive classes are among the least accessible for many students with autism, math is one of the most accessible—precisely because it isn't based in language. Math is also systematic, rule-governed, and removed from the messy, real-world circumstances that can baffle children with autism.

But Reform Math, now more commonly known as Progressive Math, has changed all that. Dating back to the 1990s, Reform Math includes such programs as *Everyday Mathematics* (McGraw Hill), *Investigations in Number, Data, and Space* (Scott Foresman), *Eureka Math* (Great Minds), *Bridges in Mathematics* (The Math Learning Center), *enVision Math 2.0* (Pearson/Scott Foresman), *Connected Mathematics* (Prentice Hall), *My Math* (Carter & McGraw-Hill Education), *Illustrative Math* (Illustrative Mathematics), and *College Preparatory Mathematics* (CPM Educational Program). Though updated in the 2010s to reflect the Common Core math guidelines, Reform Math has long embraced the Constructivist principles we discussed earlier: discovery learning, cooperative learning, real-life relevance, meta-cognitive reflection, and verbal communication.

In addition, backed by the Common Core standards, what we'll henceforth call Progressive Math prioritizes "conceptual" over "procedural" understanding. This means that students shouldn't get in the habit of applying mathematical procedures (e.g., the standard algorithms for adding whole numbers or fractions) before they understand how and why these procedures work—and, moreover, are able to demonstrate this understanding to others.

What all this means is less explicit, systematic, teacher-directed instruction of abstract, formal rules, and more child-directed experimentation with ad hoc, problem-specific tactics. General rules for arithmetic, like carrying from the ones place to the tens place, borrowing from the tens place to the ones place, and the multiple steps of multi-digit multiplication and long division, are often delayed until the fourth grade or later. Instead, students are encouraged to come up with multiple ways to solve specific problems, as we see in these Progressive Math exercises:

> Solve each problem in three different ways. Using a calculator can be one way. Make notes about how you solved the problems. Be sure that others can understand what you did.
>
> 1. $42 + 36 + 18 =$
>   First way:
>   Second way:
>   Third way:
> 1. $57 + 3 + 56 =$
>   First way:
>   Second way:
>   Third way:
> 1. $125 + 53 + 27$
>   First way:
>   Second way:
>   Third way: (*Investigations in Number, Data and Space, Combining and Comparing*, p. 57.)

Thus, instead of practicing a general algorithm over and over again on a bunch of different problems, students are solving a smaller number of problems over and over again using a bunch of different strategies. This means less of the kind of skills practice that autistic individuals depend on—i.e., the systematic drills that characterize successful autism interventions like ABA.

In addition, students are often expected to solve problems not by straight-up pen and paper computation, but via concrete materials like Cuisenaire Rods and number boards, and concrete methods like drawing pictures and arranging objects:

> Make a picture of 100 of the same thing. You might draw 100 things. Or you might glue 100 of something small onto a sheet of paper. Arrange the 100 things in equal groups. Make it easy to see that you have 100 things on your paper. (*Investigations in Number, Data, and Space, Landmarks in the Hundreds*, p. 39)

To students with autism, this introduces all kinds of distractions that shift their attention away from the actual math.

Also upstaging the more math-focused problems that consist simply of numbers and mathematical symbols are "real-world" problems. These tend to contain many more words than the word problems of 40 years ago, and to assume sociocultural background knowledge that many autistic students lack. Here is an exercise that my autistic son brought home one day when he was in third grade that assumes familiarity with promotions, logos, and advertisements:

> A Mexican restaurant sells tacos for $1.50. As part of their special "Taco Thursday" promotion, if you wear a T-shirt printed with the restaurant logo that advertises "Taco Thursday," you can buy the tacos for $1.25 each. The shirt costs $12.99. Should you buy a shirt? Will you really save money on the tacos? What other factors are there?
>
> Teacher Created Resources, *More Brain Puzzlers* (2002, p. 192)

Notice how that final, open-ended question is mostly about the messy, real-world aspects of the scenario—do you really want to buy so many tacos? How do you feel about wearing a promotional T-shirt?—and not about its numerical content.

Besides the reading comprehension challenges of language-intensive word problems, there are the writing challenges of explaining one's answers—often a requirement for full credit. Indeed, in some exercises and test questions, correct but unexplained answers earn the same amount of partial credit as incorrect but explained answers. Partial credit also goes to explanations deemed incomplete, as we see in some of the grading guidelines for Common Core-based tests. Within these guidelines, sample student explanations are excerpted and rated for completeness. Consider this comparison by Maryland's Test Guidelines of explanations in a test question about clock time. The question asks where, on an analog clock, you should draw the minute hand for 7:20.

This explanation is considered complete:

> I figured it out by counting
> by 5's I start at the 1
> and count 1 is 5 2 is 10 3 is 15
> 4 is 20 so that is how I
> figure it out.

This explanation, in contrast, is considered incomplete:

> you count buy 5's.

As the Guidelines explain, the second student has not discussed the relevance of counting by 5's.

Even if an autistic test taker has the linguistic skills of the first student, he may lack the socio-communicative awareness to realize that he's expected to spell out why his strategy is relevant.

Tapping further into social awareness, some explanations require perspective-taking skills. Consider, for example, this exercise, which requires a third grader to put herself into the shoes of a second grader:

> Some people think 1 and 1/4 is a larger share than 1 and 1/3. Some people think 1 and 1/3 is a larger share than 1 and 1/4. Which share do you think is bigger? Write a letter to a second grader. Tell why you are right. Use drawings to explain your thinking. Remember, a second grader must understand what you write. (*Investigations in Number, Data, and Space, Fair Shares*, p. 29)

All of this—the reduction in structured, systematic instruction, the deemphasis on math as an abstract system, and the emphasis instead on real-world application, reading comprehension, and communicating about math— shortchanges students with autism. It distracts them from learning actual math and, potentially, significantly diminishes their interest in it.

We should note that math classes have long involved some applied math problems and some requests for explanations. It's just that these demands are more frequent—and for autistic students more prohibitive—than ever before.

Yet, within the long history of "explain your answer," we see problems for autistic students cropping up in the earliest literature on high functioning autism—what was then called Asperger's syndrome. One of Hans Asperger's autistic patients, when asked to explain his answer to a math problem, stated "I can't do this orally, only headily." As Asperger's syndrome expert Tony Attwood puts it:

> The child can provide the correct answer to a mathematical problem but not easily translate into speech the mental processes used to solve the problem. This can mystify teachers and lead to problems with tests when the person with Asperger's syndrome is unable to explain his or her methods on the test or exam paper. Attwood, 241)

Also relevant to today's trends is another of Attwood's observations:

> One of the learning-profile characteristics associated with Asperger's syndrome is a strong drive to seek certainty... The child or adult appears uncomfortable with any situation in which there is more than one right answer... At school, they tend to prefer subjects that provide certainty such as mathematics. (Attwood, 241)

As we've seen, however, this one-right-answer certainty no longer holds for today's math. Students are expected to produce multiple answers (via multiple strategies), and correct answers often aren't considered correct unless they include explanations that meet certain unspecified socio-communicative standards.

Thus, one of the aspects of math that most appeals to students with autism is no longer a feature of classroom math. More fundamentally, there's the actual math content. As the applied and verbal components of classroom math grow, the mathematical component has shrunk. Math curricula now include fewer multi-digit arithmetic problems, fewer fractions with "unfriendly" denominators, fewer mathematical steps required to solve problems, fewer algebra problems with multiple variables, and fewer abstract geometry proofs.

But it's the pure math—the abstract systems and procedures and deductive problem solving—that, for many students with autism, resonates the most. In addition, it's this kind of mathematical rigor that would best prepare them for the most promising types of careers that potentially await them—for example in engineering, data science, or even mathematics itself.

Tragically, parent reports suggest that a great many math-loving autistic children are floundering in Progressive Math classes. Once they're provided with alternative math programs, however, many of these kids rebound, rediscovering their love of math. We'll explore these alternative programs in the next section, where we turn to remedies for the many autism-unfriendly aspects of Constructivist, Common Core classrooms.

Educational alternatives and accommodations

In the following sections, we discuss various educational alternatives and accommodations that can help children with autism be more successful in today's classrooms. Different sections will be applicable to different members of our audience. If you are a regular education teacher who has autistic students in your classroom, or a parent who is advocating for a child in a general ed. classroom, the most relevant sections are those on differentiating instruction and providing accommodations. If you are a parent who is educating your child, at least partially, outside of school (whether via homeschooling or tutoring), or an autistic support teacher who is able to provide individualized instruction in your classroom, the most relevant sections are those on optimal programs and pedagogies.

Differentiating instruction

Differentiating instruction is another relatively new classroom priority. Ideally, differentiating instruction means providing different students with different learning options depending on their readiness levels, interests, and preferred ways of learning. In practice, differentiating instruction only goes so far: the Common Core standards, the Common Core-based accountability tests, and a host of school and school district requirements and practical considerations limit how much teachers can modify the curriculum and learning activities to suit the needs of each student. However, there are some relatively easy adjustments that teachers can make—and that parents can advocate for—to ameliorate some of the more extreme problems that today's classrooms pose to students with autism.

Perhaps the most obvious adjustment is to allow these students to work independently rather than in groups. As we've seen, classroom groups are confusing and potentially hostile learning environments. Proponents of group learning may argue that students with autism will miss out on social learning opportunities that they, especially, are in need of. But a much more promising social learning environment for autistic people is one that is specifically dedicated to social skills instruction, that provides them with the explicit feedback they need, and that protects against bullying. In other words: a small social skills group led by a trained social skills therapist. If the school can't offer such a thing, school counselors can refer students and their families to convenient and affordable options outside of school. (Generally, an autism diagnosis is enough for insurance to cover the costs).

Independent work has additional advantages. It allows for a more structured learning environment with fewer sensory distractions, and for lessons and assignments that more closely match the child's skills and interests. To leverage these possibilities, the teacher should locate a quiet corner of the classroom and pick materials (textbooks and workbooks) that offer explicit instruction and structured activities. She should, of course, check in with the child from time to time to assist him as needed.

Not all autistic students, however, are able or motivated to work independently and unsupervised for long periods. And, at least in some subjects, they may need more than just textbooks to instruct them.

Ideally, certain school personnel—reading/literacy specialists, classroom assistants, or classroom volunteers—can provide one-to-one tutoring as needed.

An alternative—or additional—option is computerized instruction. Khan academy, discussed in Chapter 3 in connection with pre-K skills, provides free interactive, computerized instruction in math, science, reading, history, and computer programming (often a great strength in autism), among other academic subjects.

Teachers can also differentiate instruction by modifying specific assignments. For example, they might give students who struggle with oral participation the option to submit contributions in writing, and students who struggle with oral presentations the option to submit written essays instead. Some people may object, arguing that autistic students, in particular, need practice with oral participation and presentation skills. Once again, however, the more optimal environment is a social skills group led by a trained social skills therapist.

One type of assignment that cries out for modification, given all the challenges in autism, are reading assignments—particularly those that align with the high literary standards of the Common Core. The only modifications that the Common Core guidelines mention for reading difficulties are accommodations like enlarged print and text-to-speech. However, as we discussed in the previous chapter, such accommodations do not address the core comprehension challenges in autism. Other options are alternative versions of the reading assignments themselves— for example, simplified texts like *No Fear Shakespeare*. However, given that much of what makes Shakespeare Shakespeare is the language, simplified Shakespeare may defeat the purpose. The same is true of other great works of challenging literature.

Other options, besides alternative *versions* of the reading assignments, are alternative readings. For example, while the rest of the class reads *Romeo and Juliet*, an autistic student might read *Fahrenheit 451*. Classroom teachers, however, may not have the freedom to differentiate instruction to such an extreme.

Perhaps in no other subject are the needed modifications more obvious, or easier to put into place, than in math. As we saw, one of the biggest challenges—and irritants—to students with autism is that requirement to explain their answers verbally. The alternative is simple. Swap out "Explain your answer" with "Show your work," and only ask students to write out their mathematical steps. As for problems that they can do in just one step, simply leave it at that.

But what about claims that metacognitive reflection is an important part of the learning process? As we noted earlier, however, it's not clear that autistic individuals, while doing math problems, engage in the kind of metacognition that translates into words. Perhaps a better way to enrich the mathematical understanding of students with autism—and to ensure that they truly understand the math—is to assign them more problems, including problems that are more mathematically challenging. In other words, instead of asking a student to explain his answer to a small number of simple addition problems, one might instead ask him to solve a larger number of more difficult addition problems.

What about the claim that communicating one's thinking is an important life skill? Indeed, communication skills in general count as important life skills—just as social skills do. But just as the optimal way to address social skills in autism are social skills groups with trained social skills therapists, the optimal way to address communication skills in autism is language therapy with trained language therapists.

Finally, what about those state math tests? A child who isn't in the habit of explaining her answers may underperform relative to her potential. Here, there are two questions to consider—for teachers and parents alike. To what degree is this kind of teaching to the test worth the effort and frustration? And is it likely to result in significantly improved scores that have tangible effects on the child's life?

The other big challenges in math relate to the curriculum. As we saw, Progressive Math texts are filled with linguistically demanding "real-life" word problems. The obvious solution is alternative textbooks that cover the same mathematical content in a less verbose, less applied context. Such textbooks include those published prior to the 1980s, and those from other countries that have been translated into English: Singapore Math and Russian Math in particular. Many of these texts are available, at relatively low cost, through Amazon.

These curricular modifications, while not nearly as extreme as swapping out *Fahrenheit 451* for *Romeo and Juliet,* may go beyond what some teachers are permitted to do in differentiating instruction. However, if the student is doing math on her own, it may be possible for teachers to quietly make these adjustments—especially if her parents are advocating for them. And, indeed, given how self-contained math is and how structured, systematic, and explicit the best math texts are, there's probably no other subject that is more suited to independent work.

Accommodations

Beyond alternative assignments, there are accommodations. Indeed, there are quite a number of accommodations that teachers can make, and that parents can advocate for, to better support students with autism.

Teachers can ameliorate sensory distractions by allowing their autistic students, when they're feeling unfocused, overwhelmed, or restless, to retreat to quiet places and engage in activities that absorb them.

Teachers can address attention issues by allowing students extra time to answer questions, respond to requests, and switch from one step or task to the next. When students look like they're not attending, teachers should recognize that one common indication of attention, namely direct eye contact, may not apply to individuals with autism—or be a reasonable expectation. In autism, as we've discussed, direct eye contact is often aversive. As far as learning goes, what matters is joint attention—attending to what your teachers and classmates are attending to. Teachers, therefore, should encourage their autistic students to look at the material being taught rather than insisting that they look at the person who is teaching it.

Teachers can address under-awareness of classroom rules and routines by laying them out explicitly, including via visual prompts like text and pictures—e.g., an "ask before using" label on the stapler, or a written schedule of the day's activities on the front wall. Many of these classroom prompts are routine, but, for many students with autism, there are rarely enough prompts. Especially crucial, as we've seen, are clear reminders about when and where to turn in homework. One promising model for autism-friendly classrooms is TEACCH, one of the more effective classroom teaching frameworks for special needs students (Mesibov, 2014). TEACCH involves strategies like maintaining a well-organized classroom and providing organizational supports like schedules of the day's activities to help students with challenges in executive function and attention. Also central to TEACCH is presenting information visually and/or through text so as to address challenges in attending to and retaining spoken directions. TEACCH thus makes liberal use of labels, picture schedules, and charts.

Related to under-awareness of rules is difficulty with indirect language. Teachers can address this by making their language direct and explicit—whether when making requests, asking questions, or giving directions. And, suppressing the instinct to be polite and affirming, they can give autistic students more direct feedback when they break rules or fail to follow directions—especially when these "infractions" are unintentional.

Teachers can address difficulties with class participation by periodically calling on autistic students directly. Giving them a specific question to answer and a specific moment to start talking helps bypass the challenge some students face in jumping in with appropriate remarks at the appropriate moments. Teachers can assist students further by giving them plenty of time to respond and helping them, as needed, to shape their words into relevant, coherent contributions.

Particularly in the upper grades, as material becomes more complex and teachers spend more extended time presenting it orally in front of the class, there are accommodations that they can provide—both before and after the fact. Beforehand, teachers can prime students with written previews of what they'll be covering and assigning, perhaps with key words highlighted and blanks for students to fill out while listening. Key words and blank-filling tasks may help students to focus their attention. Afterwards, teachers can give students lecture notes or power points so they can review what was covered and anything they may have missed.

As for reading challenges, some of the interventions we discussed in the previous chapter showed the efficacy of supports like graphic organizers, metacognitive checklists, and markers for color-coding different types of content. In addition, digitalized texts, which we discussed earlier as an intervention strategy, sometimes offer comprehension support—for example, by providing definitions or background information when users click on particular words or phrases. The latter is something we'll examine further in the next chapter in connection with assistive devices.

As we discussed in the last chapter, some reading difficulties arise simply because autistic readers default to mechanical reading or to a narrow focus on details. Recent studies suggest that people with autism are able to shift from piecemeal to global processing when explicitly told to do so. In general, then, teachers may be able to encourage meaningful reading simply by prompting students, now and then, to think about what they're reading and to focus on the text as a whole.

Teachers can also support writing assignments with explicit prompts. In his memoir, autistic adult Tim Page describes how, when asked to report on a class field trip to Boston, he produced this:

> Well, we went to Boston, Massachusetts through the town of Warrenville, Connecticut on Route 44A. It was pretty and there was a church that reminded me of pictures of Russia from our book that is published by Time-Life. We arrived in Boston at 9:17. At 11 we went on a big tour of Boston on Gray Line 43, made by the Superior Bus Company like School Bus Six, which goes down Hunting Lodge Road where Maria lives and then on to Separatist Road and then to South Eagleville before it comes to our school. We saw lots of good things like the Boston Massacre site. The tour ended at 1:05. Before I knew it we were going home. We went through Warrenville again but it was too dark to see much. A few days later it was Easter. We got a cuckoo clock. (2010, pp. 1–2)

Page's teacher found this report so inappropriate that she annotated it with "See me!" in red letters that broke through the paper. Had she told Page explicitly to write about the historic sites he saw once he got out of the bus, he might have produced something more to her liking.

In general, the moral of the story is that autistic students need clear directions, extra structure, and visual and organizational supports. This applies equally to classroom rules and to assignments—including the most organizationally challenging assignments of all, namely projects. Projects may require the gamut of organizational supports—checklists, timelines, graphic organizers—along with frequent check-ins by the teacher, multiple drafts, and explicit feedback at each stage of the process.

Tests and other assessments also cry out for accommodation. One study finds that over half of children with high-functioning autism have challenges with processing speed (Hedvall et al., 2013). Attention difficulties—sticky attention and distractibility—can lead to slower reaction times and problems sustaining attention. Difficulties processing and producing verbal information can also slow things down. To demonstrate their true abilities in the subject areas being assessed, therefore, autistic students may need extra time on tests. For longer assessments, they may also need occasional testing breaks. As far as math tests in particular go, a case can be made, as we did earlier, for exempting autistic students from explaining their answers and instead giving them a larger number of straight-up math questions.

Finally, when filling out report cards, teachers should take care not to downgrade autistic students for apparent inattention, perceived laziness, lack of cooperation, and behavior problems. As we discussed earlier, these are often not what they appear to be, but instead are functions of the diagnosis. The last thing teachers want to do is to downgrade a student for simply being autistic.

This relates to one final point. Patience is key. To foster patience in themselves, teachers (and parents) need to remember the various challenges that make it hard for autistic children to produce appropriate and timely responses: their various attention issues, their comprehension challenges, and their under-awareness of various "common-sense" social and behavioral expectations.

Optimal programs

We now turn to the options available to those who have direct control over academic programming—namely, parents who are educating their kids, at least partially, outside of school; and those classroom teachers, particularly special education teachers, who have the freedom to select specific programs for specific students.

We begin with reading comprehension. In the last chapter we showcased a reading program that has had remarkable success with special needs students in general and, some evidence shows, with autistic students in particular. The program in question is Direct Instruction (DI), specifically DI's multilevel *Comprehension Skills* series (Engelmann et al.,

1999). As we discussed earlier, DI uses a systematic, structured approach that is similar to ABA, and therefore similarly promising for autistic students.

DI's *Comprehension Skills* gradually takes readers beyond the basic comprehension skills we focused on earlier to higher levels of critical reading. Some exercises focus directly on reading. They ask students to infer from short passages what the author wants them to believe, what motivated a particular character, or the likely meaning of an unfamiliar word. Other close-reading tasks involve eliminating redundancies, identifying inconsistencies, locating evidence, finding irrelevant words, interpreting pronouns, and filling in tree diagrams based on the passage's content.

But beyond these reading-specific tasks, DI follows the premise that successful reading comprehension often depends on analytic skills. The *Comprehension Skills* series, therefore, also includes various sorts of logic and analytic thinking exercises. These ask students to determine what is relevant to what, what is evidence for what, what can be inferred from a particular rule, and which rules explain which details.

Some sets of exercises combine analytic thinking with close reading. Consider the analogies exercises, which present students with several similar analogies, for example (Engelmann et al., 1999, p. 316):

- An engine is to gas as a lightbulb is to electricity.
- An engine is to a car as a lightbulb is to a lamp.
- An engine is to metal what a lightbulb is to glass.

Students are asked to identify the kind of information on which each analogy is based—e.g., what each object is made of, where you find each object, what makes each object run, or what category each object belongs to.

Higher level strands of *Comprehension Skills* turn to argumentation. Here students are asked to draw conclusions from evidence, identify common logical fallacies, find and fix contradictions, and solve various logic puzzles. More advanced exercises have students tackle logical possibilities ("maybe") in addition to logical certainties. Students are also asked to identify which fact best explains which statement, to identify good versus bad sources of information, and to distinguish statements of fact from statements about what merely ought to be true.

Collectively, DI's logic and argumentation exercises may help students become more careful, critical readers—especially of expository writing and academic textbooks, if not of *Romeo and Juliet*.

What, then, about the great works of literature?

The problem is that a big part of what makes most works great is their social and psychological complexity. As we've seen, autistic students often struggle to make sense of psychosocial texts. In some cases, therefore, prioritizing great literature may not be realistic. On one hand, we don't want to deprive students of readings that may broaden their horizons; on the other, we want to ensure that readings are accessible and rewarding.

In general, as many first-person accounts of autism affirm, nonfiction is more accessible and rewarding than fiction. Especially accessible and enjoyable, of course, are nonfiction texts on high-interest topics. As we saw in the last chapter, when students were given texts related to their perseverative interests, some of the reading interventions became more effective. Among other benefits, texts that tap interests may motivate autistic readers to be more attentive to meaning. Potentially, prolonged practice with high-interest texts may foster reading habits that carry over into texts of lesser interest.

Within fiction, first-person accounts suggest that science fiction works are often the most accessible and appealing, particularly when they avoid heavy servings of psychosocial material. Fantasy fiction may be similarly engaging. Both science fiction and fantasy fiction have one additional advantage: They generally don't draw on everyday background knowledge.

Some autism specialists advocate serial books: book (or story) series with recurring characters, settings, and basic plot formulas, along with a consistent base of made-up background information. Such series range from *The Magic Treehouse* books to *Harry Potter* to *Sherlock Holmes*. However much guidance an autistic reader may need with the first book or story of the series, she may be able to read each succeeding installment with increasing independence. Potentially here, too, she may develop reading habits that carry over to other genres.

In an ideal world, decisions about what a particular autistic student reads should be based, first and foremost, on a careful assessment of his overall comprehension skills, his background knowledge, his psycho-social awareness, his interests and motivations, and just how far it is reasonable to push him, at any given moment, in broadening his literary, worldly, and psychosocial horizons.

The same is true of writing assignments. For many autistic students, essays about specific interests are a better starting point than realistic fiction. For many, creative writing may never be a reasonable priority. Some students may find it insufficiently meaningful and motivating. Others may still be struggling with forms of written communication that are more relevant to daily living, like filling out forms and composing email messages.

As for writing mechanics, a good place to start is with the writing exercises of DI's *Comprehension Skills* and the topic-first, emphasis-last rules that we discussed at the end of the last chapter. DI's exercises target increasingly advanced writing skills. They include sentence-combining exercises (with a variety of connecting devices, including "however" and "although"), editing exercises (fixing errors in punctuation and verb agreement; eliminating redundancies), and simile-writing exercises (e.g., "Tell how trees and houses are the same. Now write a simile").

As for the topic-first, emphasis-last rules, these can serve as the basis for sentence-revision strategies. That is, we can teach ways to revise sentences that get the intended topic and intended emphasis into just the right places. Six common techniques are:

1. Moving modifier phrases to different places in the sentence—e.g., "At the last minute, she changed her mind" versus "She changed her mind at the last minute."

2. Active versus passive voice—e.g., "The president vetoed the spending bill" vs. "The spending bill was vetoed by the president."

3. Switching the positions of objects—e.g., "She gave a book on the history of trains to her youngest grandson" versus "She gave to her youngest grandson a book on the history of trains."

4. Clefting—e.g., "What she gave to her youngest grandson was a book on the history of trains" or "It was a book on the history of trains that she gave to her youngest grandson."

5. Extraposition—e.g., "Giving that book to her grandson was a good idea" versus "It was a good idea to give that book to her grandson."

6. Fronting—e.g., "She gave a book on the history of trains to her youngest grandson" versus "To her youngest grandson, she gave a book on the history of trains."

In the spirit of DI and also of Precision Teaching (PT) (see the next section), we can have students practice each of these strategies one at a time to mastery and fluency. Using the first sentence in example 2, we might ask students to use passive voice to move "the president" to the end of the sentence. Or, using the first sentence in example 6, we might ask them to use fronting to move "her youngest grandson" to the front.

While the above sentence-combining, editing, similes, and sentence-rearranging exercises are useful to all students, their formal, rule-governed character potentially appeals, especially, to students with autism.

Also presented in a structured, systematic way are DI's larger writing assignments. These include directions, explanations, and stories. Helping to structure the story writing assignments are detail-rich picture prompts, highly explicit verbal prompts, and lists of key words. For example, students might be shown a detailed picture of a rescue operation and asked to write a story that tells what happened before the picture, within the picture, and afterwards, using the words "lifeguard," "cliff," "beach," "lake," "swimming," and "suddenly." Thanks to all these prompts, what is still very much a creative writing assignment avoids the unstructured open-endedness that can overwhelm many students with autism—or lead them to produce bizarre, incomplete, off-track or off-task narratives.

Let's turn, now, to social studies, math, and science. For social studies, the best programming adjustment may be to replace it wholesale with straight-up history. Presenting world events in chronological order, with a greater emphasis on political, military, economic, and technological content than on social content, provides autistic students with greater structure and more accessible material. Included in this linear history, of course, should be structured facts about the lives of ordinary people at different times and places, the abuses they have suffered, and the rights they have fought for. Many straight-up history books provide precisely this type of content. One history series popular with homeschoolers is Susan Wise Bauer's *Story of the World* (Peace Hill Press, various) and *History of the World* series (W.W. Norton, various).

As for the less-historical aspects of social studies—civics and current events—these can also be taught in a more structured, rule-based way. Civics can focus on structural and procedural phenomena like the levels and branches of government, the rules for primary and general elections, and the workings of the criminal justice and judicial systems. Current events, capitalizing on the advantages we discussed above in reference to serial reading, can center on daily readings of the front-page articles in a given local and/or national newspaper.

For math programming, we have already suggested alternatives to today's Progressive Math books: Singapore Math, Russian Math, and American math texts published prior to the 1980s. As for science, some contemporary texts contain potentially distracting material on real-life application and social relevance, but these sections can easily be skipped over. Some science texts are more straightforwardly scientific—particularly Advanced Placement texts.

Optimal pedagogies

Let's turn from optimal programs to optimal pedagogies. As we've already suggested, the most promising of these use ABA-like procedures—direct, systematic, subskill-by-subskill instruction. This promise, indeed, is part of what informed our selection of optimal programs—which included a number of programs straight out of DI.

In many ways, DI's teaching protocols are a classroom-based variant of ABA. Instead of working one-on-one with an individual child, the teacher instructs the class as a whole. DI involves the same basic procedures as ABA: prompting, eliciting responses, and modeling corrections as needed. The difference is that what's elicited aren't individual responses from students, but choral responses from the class. Thus, the teacher models corrections not just for incorrect responses, but also for non-unison responses. The general protocol is what's called "model-lead-test": the teacher models the response, then leads the students in reproducing it ("Now let's say it together"), and then tests their ability to produce it, collectively, on their own ("Now you do it").

One of DI's priorities is maximizing efficiency. This is accomplished in part via "general case" strategies: strategies that, as some DI proponents put it, "use[] the smallest number of examples to produce the largest amounts of learning" (Binder & Watkins, 2013, p. 75). For example, when teaching a particular category, say, "mammal," DI favors exemplars with lots of unrelated features (humans, rats, dolphins, and bats) so that the shared, essential features stand out more. To further underscore what's essential, DI contrasts examples with carefully chosen non-examples. That is, it favors non-examples (robots, rat-sized frogs, sharks, and bat-sized birds) that share lots of irrelevant features with the examples. This "eggs and neggs" (examples and non-examples) strategy helps speed up category learning and generalization.

Another DI strategy for generalization is systematically shifting the academic tasks along several distinct dimensions: from prompt to no prompt, from simple to complex, and from intensive sessions of repeated drills or "massed practice" (to encourage acquisition) to practice broken up into shorter sessions over a longer time period, or "distributed practice" (to facilitate retention).

A recent review suggests that DI may be effective in teaching academic content to autistic students (Frampton et al., 2021). Among other things, its systematic methodology appears to meet that thirst for order and structure.

A variant of DI, used with both disadvantaged and special needs students, is Precision Teaching (PT). As we noted in the previous chapter, PT has had so much success that its main site, the Morningside Academy in Washington State, offers a money-back guarantee to the parents of any child who starts out more than two grade levels behind and doesn't advance at least two grade levels in one year. PT combines ABA's behaviorism and DI's classroom-based settings with the additional instructional goal of fluency: speed in accurate responding.

What counts as full fluency is the ability to do the task in question, whether it involves words or numbers, at just under the rate it takes to write the words or numbers when there's no additional task involved. A key component of PT, therefore, is timed tasks. In general, students do not move on to a new task until they're fluent in the prerequisite task(s). Thus, students don't write paragraphs until they can first write letters fluently, then spell words fluently, then combine simple sentences fluently into more complex ones and, finally, sequence sentences fluently.

In the case of new students who haven't experienced PT from the beginning, teachers conduct systematic assessments that examine both accuracy and speed. A teacher might discover, for example, that a pre-algebra student is slow to write numbers, or that there's a quadrant in the multiplication table where he isn't fully fluent. Before the student proceeds further into math, therefore, he first goes back and works on fluent number writing and fluency with the problematic part of the multiplication table.

Fluency building includes not just task speed, but also task complexity. PT, accordingly, gradually increases complexity until the tasks resemble those of daily life. Thus, unlike the word problems of Progressive Math, PT's math word problems only gradually add in more words and extraneous details.

Relatedly, the ultimate goal of PT is what's called "applying": specifically, applying concepts to new situations or performing tasks that haven't been explicitly trained. For example, after gradual, systematic training in faulty logic puzzles, followed by gradual, systematic training in identifying logical errors in written passages (training that continues until students are able to identify these errors at speeds that are just under their normal reading speeds), students might suddenly be asked to detect logic violations in a live debate. PT practitioners propose that a direct connection exists between 1) building fluency and automaticity and 2) retaining skills and applying them to novel, real-life situations. Indeed, some PT proponents have proposed that building up fluency may address the widespread difficulty that autistic students have with real-world concept application.

Finally, PT researchers have found that fluency helps ward off distractions. While the research has focused on ADHD, the results may hold for autism as well. Indeed, they may hold for all of us. The most likely moments for distractions to seep in, after all, are during our slow periods or lulls, as opposed to when we're "in the zone." Those of us who are most prone to distractions, including many individuals on the autism spectrum, are among the people who may benefit the most from fluency training.

In addition, whether we're zipping down a hill or zipping through a reading passage, speed is fun. Thus, in yet another benefit of PT's focus on fluency, the increasing speeds that students attain with the various tasks they're learning may be rewarding enough to serve as built-in reinforcements. Similarly rewarding, potentially, is the sense of progress that PT brings students as it explicitly, systematically advances them through rising levels of challenge.

As far as autism goes, the most important thing about PT is that it combines the structure and explicit instruction of ABA and DI with other tactics that may reduce distractibility and facilitate information processing and the application of concepts to novel, real-world situations. Thus, of all the programs out there, PT, while not specifically intended for this population, may nonetheless be especially suited to our students on the autism spectrum.

Conclusion

Our general takeaway is that what works in autism therapy tells us a lot about what works in education. What works in therapy, therefore, can guide those who have the ability to optimize a student's education, while giving those who have less control an evidence base for arguing for specific remediations and accommodations. Even if you are a teacher or parent dealing with the limitations imposed by classrooms, schools, school districts, and Common Core standards, there is much you can do to improve the learning environment for your autistic students.

The greatest needs in autism, as we've seen, are structure, explicit instruction, and a gradual, systematic introduction of complexity. Also essential—both for motivating our autistic students and for preparing them for their most promising future vocations—is ensuring that they have unfettered opportunities, not only to overcome their weaknesses, but also to develop their strengths.

References

Attwood, T. (2007/2008). *The complete guide to Asperger's syndrome* (p. 241). Jessica Kingsley.

Binder, C., & Watkins, C. L. (2013). Precision Teaching and Direct Instruction: Measurably superior instructional technology in schools. *Performance Improvement Quarterly*, 26(2), 73-115.

Carter, J. A., & McGraw-Hill Education (Firm). (2019). *My math.* Author.

Charles, R. I., Bay-Williams, J. M., Berry, R. Q., & Pearson/Scott Foresman. (2017). *EnVision Math 2.0*. Great Minds.

Cooper, J., Draper, C., Birdsall, L., Sallee, T., & CPM Educational Program. (2003). *College preparatory mathematics 4: Mathematical analysis*, (7th ed.). CPM Educational Program.

Eureka Math. (n.d.). Author.

Engelmann, S., Hanner, S., Osborn, S., & SRA/McGraw-Hill. (1999). *Comprehension skills* (p. 316). SRA/McGraw-Hill.

Frampton, S. E., Munk, G. T., Shillingsburg, L. A., & Shillingsburg, M. A. (2021). A systematic review and quality appraisal of applications of Direct Instruction with children with autism spectrum disorder. *Perspectives on Behavior Science, 44*(2-3), 245–266.

Green, J. (2012). *The fault in our stars*. Dutton.

Hedvall, Å., Fernell, E., Holm, A., Åsberg Johnels, J., Gillberg, C., & Billstedt, E. (2013). Autism, processing speed, and adaptive functioning in preschool children. *The Scientific World Journal*, 2013, 158263. https://doi.org/10.1155/2013/158263

Matassa, M., & Rubini, L. (2014). *Bridges in mathematics*. The Math Learning Center.

Mesibov, G. B. (2014). *TEACCH approach to autism spectrum disorders*. Springer.

Page, T. (2010). *Parallel play*. Anchor Books.

Russell, S. J., & Rubin, A. (1998). *Investigations in number, data, and space, landmarks in the hundreds: The number system* (p. 29). Dale Seymour.

Shore, S. (2003). *Beyond the wall: Personal experiences with autism* (2nd ed., p. 60). Autism Asperger Publishing Co.

Sparknotes. (n.d.). *No fear Shakespeare*. Author.

Tammet, D. (2007). *Born on a blue day: Inside the extraordinary mind of an autistic savant* (p. 76). Free Press.

Tierney, C. C. (1998). *Investigations in number, data, and space: Fair shares* (p. 29). Dale Seymour.

Twain, M. (2005). *The adventures of Tom Sawyer: Original illustrations* (p. 165). Literary Touchstone Edition.

CHAPTER 7

THE CHALLENGE OF MINIMALLY SPEAKING AUTISM: FACILITATED COMMUNICATION VERSUS EVIDENCE-BASED ASSISTANCE

A boy in his mid-teens sits in front of a tablet, his right index finger extended toward the keyboard, as people ask him questions about his autism. Slowly but regularly he types out the letters. One by one they line up on the screen into perfectly spelled sentences. First, I know I am intelligent. *Half a minute later,* until I learned to read and write people thought I had no mind. *Tap, tap, tap. The boy is calm, deliberate, rhythmic. His face is impassive. But sometimes, barely interrupting his typing, he turns towards his mother, who smiles and murmurs encouraging words. She is sitting on his right side, her hand on his shoulder, her eyes glued to the keyboard. Sometimes the boy glances off briefly to the left, but the letters keep coming, tap, tap, tap.* I realized that letters would liberate my mind.

Seven years ago, the boy, long diagnosed with severe autism, was completely non-verbal. Even after years of intensive language therapies he couldn't speak or write or sign. Not even his mother—for all the long hours she spent, every day of the week, talking, gesturing, pointing things out, looking into his eyes—felt that she was breaking through and communicating anything. Only when they embarked on this method of slow, deliberate, index finger typing, with the emotional and physical support of a nearby facilitator (his devoted mother), did the language start emerging. Perfectly spelled words. Perfectly composed sentences. Ideas of astonishing awareness and insight. But most memorable of all was the very first message: I love you mom.

Throughout this book we have been treating autism as a deep disorder of social cognition—one in which increasing severity correlates with decreasing language. Deficits, beginning in early infancy, in attention to social stimuli like voices and faces limit one's linguistic immersion. Related deficits in joint attention (in attending to what speakers are looking at and referring to) limit one's ability to attach meaning to words. Ongoing deficits in social motivation limit social engagement, social insight, and the ability to communicate with others.

And yet this boy appears to defy all that. Nor is he alone. Around the world, there are thousands, perhaps tens of thousands of children diagnosed as severely autistic and as at most minimally verbal, who, once introduced to this or similar forms of facilitated communication, turn out to have been soaking up everything around them like sponges.

What they soak up includes not just overheard language, but also printed words. Somehow these kids have cracked the written code of English, with all its idiosyncratic spelling rules, combining letters into meaningful messages. How do they do it? Hyperlexia, that precocious interest in letters and ability to recognize whole words, can't be the full answer—disproportionately common though it is in autism (estimates, as we've noted earlier, range from 6% to 21%). Decoding words is not the same as understanding them. Indeed, hyperlexia often co-occurs with poor reading comprehension. Yet this boy, who discovered that *letters would liberate my mind*, must understand the words he is typing.

Are the proponents of Whole Language right after all? Is systematic phonics instruction largely unnecessary? Is it enough to be immersed in natural environments that are annotated with printed words? Can one really pick up written language through incidental exposure alone? Indeed, proponents of facilitated communication (FC) make precisely this argument. Rosemary Crossley, the first big promoter of FC in the English-speaking world, has observed that even a child with no interest in books will get a reading lesson every time she opens the refrigerator and sees all the food labels. Douglas Biklen, who introduced FC to the US, has stated that facilitated children learn to read in the same way that most of us do—that is, he states, by being immersed in a language-rich environment.

In this chapter, we shift away from the moderate to mildly autistic individuals we focused on in the last three chapters: those ready for sentence and discourse-level language instruction and inclusion in general ed. classrooms. Instead, we'll be focusing on individuals with more severe autism: those whose language skills, or at least whose speaking skills, are much more limited. With many of these individuals, standard language interventions have minimal success. There are, however, two sets of alternative intervention schemes specifically intended to enhance communication in severe autism. In this chapter, we'll discuss both approaches: FC and AAC (Augmentative and Alternative Communication). The one we'll begin with, FC, is an approach that, however much it defies what's known about autism, is something about which parents and practitioners are increasingly likely to hear highly compelling anecdotal accounts and expert endorsements.

FC round one: The initial rise and fall

FC emerged in Denmark in the 1960s. In the 1970s, Rosemary Crossley, then at the St. Nicholas Institution in Melbourne, Australia, promoted it there. In the late 1980s, it was exported to the US by Douglas Biklen, then a professor at Syracuse University and later the dean of its education school.

"Until I learned to read and write people thought I had no mind." Though not an autism expert, Biklen nonetheless felt compelled by the often sophisticated messages generated by FC to redefine autism. It could not possibly be the socio-cognitive disorder that autism experts had been claiming since the 1940s—and that we have been saying it is throughout this book. Instead, autism must be a disorder of "praxis," or of the ability to enact speech and other intentional, goal-directed movements. Autism, in other words, must amount to a sort of mind-body disconnect or "locked in" syndrome. And it must be for this reason, and this reason alone, that individuals with severe autism are unable, or only minimally able, to speak.

Where does FC fit in? First, index-finger typing is a much simpler motor activity than speech, handwriting, and ten-finger typing. Second, the physical contact provided by the facilitator helps the facilitated person gain some control over the typing—which, even when it is reduced to a single outstretched finger and back-and-forth arm movements, still poses challenges. Initially, the facilitator places her hand over or under the facilitatee's wrist or forearm, helps him to isolate his index finger, and pulls his hand back after each letter is typed so as to ensure that he takes enough time to make his next selection and doesn't perseverate on a particular letter. Occasionally the facilitator reminds the facilitatee of the message he is composing by reading back what he has typed thus far ("Until I learned to read?..."), or prompts him to stay on task with phrases like "Keep going" or "What's the next letter you want?" Beyond this, even when the facilitatee becomes skilled enough at index finger typing that the facilitator's arm support is no longer necessary, a hand on the thigh or shoulder keeps him calm and focused and gives him emotional support.

It's an often intimate relationship that develops over time, even when the facilitator is someone other than a parent. And every once in a while a facilitatee suddenly starts typing out messages that disclose serious trouble at home—messages all too consistent with the disturbing fact that severely disabled children, as many in the disability world are well aware, are at high risk for abuse in the home and elsewhere.

It was when the first allegations of parental abuse—of sexual abuse in particular—were elicited through FC, back in the early 1990s, that FC was first put on trial. The upshot took many by complete surprise: it was FC, and FC alone, that turned out to be the actual culprit. Fathers who had been convicted of abuse (and were often serving time in solitary confinement) were released. Children were returned to their homes. Families were reunited. The evidence against FC: two simple, empirical validity tests.

Designed by disability and communication expert Howard Shane and conducted by Shane during one of the sexual abuse trials, the two tests became the centerpiece of the PBS Frontline documentary *Prisoners of Silence* (1993). In one, the "double-blind" test, the facilitator and facilitatee, sitting side by side, are shown two series of pictures: one series for the facilitator, the other for the facilitatee. Each series is visible only to one person, such that neither the facilitator nor the facilitatee can see the images that are shown to the other. Sometimes the pictures are the same; sometimes they differ. The facilitator might see a flower while the facilitatee sees a key. After each viewing, the facilitatee is asked to type out, with facilitator support, what she saw.

In the second of these tests, the message-passing test, the facilitatee is escorted out of the room and given a simple object to inspect. With the object no longer in view, she is escorted back to her facilitator. Then she is asked to type out what she saw, again with facilitator support.

In the overwhelming majority of cases in which the facilitator did not see what the facilitatee saw and the facilitatee typed out an answer (with facilitator support), that answer expressed what the facilitator saw, not what the facilitatee saw: the flower, for example, rather than the key. This finding, which dozens of rigorous studies have replicated, is unequivocal evidence that the facilitators are controlling the messages. *I am intelligent; until I learned to read and write, people thought I had no mind; I realized that letters would liberate my mind; even I love you mom.* All the most rigorous experimental data indicates that these are not the words of the non-speaking autistic person, but of his facilitator.

But how is it possible that the facilitators are controlling the messages? Surely most of these people—many of them parents or individuals long dedicated to special education and communication rights—have the best of intentions. Surely the mother who facilitates that initial *I love you mom* isn't deliberately forcing out such a message: What meaning could it then possibly have for her? And how would merely touching her son's shoulder allow her to direct his index finger to specific letters?

Further research into the psychological underpinnings of FC suggests what is really going on. All forms of FC leave wide open the possibility of cueing. The index finger typing—as opposed to ten-finger typing—allows the facilitators to see which letters a single outstretched index finger is approaching, and to react accordingly. Through physical pressure (even if restricted to the shoulder), and/or keyboard movement, and/or auditory effects (voice inflection, breathing), and/or visual effects (body language), facilitators may convey cues to the facilitatee that subliminally signal which letters should be typed. In particular, the facilitator's body tends to relax as the facilitatee's finger approaches the desired letter, to tense once the finger reaches it, and to relax once the finger selects it.

All of this, or nearly all, is completely unintentional. First, it turns out that people who are observing someone search for a specific target or answer have great difficulty, when they know the solution, in suppressing the tell-tale signals of tension and relaxation—even when they consciously try to. Second, there's the "ideomotor illusion"—an illusion that makes us unaware that we ourselves are directing a subconsciously motivated action. Consider Ouija boards users, who unwittingly nudge the planchette towards certain letters; or dowsers, who unwittingly shift their so-called "divining rods" when dowsing for water or precious metals; or pendulum holders (in fact all of us are susceptible here), who, in reaction to certain questions, unwittingly influence the pendulum's direction of movement when it is surrounded by words like "yes," "no," and "maybe." Third, there is "action projection": the tendency to think that these subconscious actions of ours are emanating from someone or something else (spirits from Beyond; the tug of precious metals; the supernatural forces controlling the pendulum). Collectively, these three phenomena—our inability to suppress certain physical responses, our lack of awareness that we are performing them, and our certainty that they are coming from another source—explain how facilitators, unwittingly and often inevitably, guide letter selections while confident that their facilitatee is the one directing the messages.

In light of all the evidence against FC, numerous medical and disability agencies, to this day, have position papers against it. The American Academy of Pediatrics, for example, states that "[c]urrent scientific evidence does not support the use of facilitated communication in which a nonverbal individual is guided to communicate" (Hyman et al., 2020). The American Association on Intellectual and Developmental Disabilities states that "there is no scientific evidence supporting its validity, and there is considerable evidence that the messages are authored by the facilitator rather than by the individual with a disability" (American Association on Intellectual and Developmental Disabilities, 2019). And the American Speech-Language-Hearing Association states:

> Facilitated Communication (FC) is a discredited technique that should not be used. There is no scientific evidence of the validity of FC, and there is extensive scientific evidence - produced over several decades and across several countries - that messages

are authored by the "facilitator" rather than the person with a disability. Furthermore, there is extensive evidence of harms related to the use of FC. Information obtained through the use of FC should not be considered as the communication of the person with a disability. (ASHA, 2018).

FC has also been deemed ineffective by the American Academy of Child and Adolescent Psychiatry, the Association for Behavior Analysis International, the Association for Science in Autism Treatment, the International Society for Augmentative and Alternative Communication, the National Council on Severe Autism, and the National Institute for Health and Care Excellence, as well as by a number of similar organizations around the world.

One would think that the collective weight of the accumulated evidence against it and the opposition from major institutions must, surely, have spelled the end of FC. In fact, new variants have emerged in the last two decades that have made it more popular than ever.

Facilitated Communication redux: RPM, S2C, and "end-stage" Facilitated Communication

Her mother never touches her; she merely holds up a simple, laminated letterboard. As the girl's outstretched index finger touches letters, her mother calls them out; as the letters form words, the mother calls those out; as the words form phrases and then sentences, she calls these out as well. I could finally tell people how I really felt.

His father never touches him; he merely holds up an electronic keyboard. As the boy's outstretched index finger types out letters, they appear on the screen that sits on the table. When the boy finishes typing, he hits "play" and the words come out: I think that all non-speakers can do this.

Her mother never touches her; she merely sits next to her while she types on a stationary keyboard on the table. As she types, the words appear on the attached screen. My body does not do what I tell it to do.

These are what some of the more recent variants of FC look like. Often there is no physical contact; sometimes the facilitator simply sits nearby. What is going on, and how could there possibly be any cueing?

Some of these cases exemplify what we might call the "end stages" of old school, touch-based FC. Over years of working side by side, facilitators and facilitatees (however subconsciously) jointly develop ever more subtle cueing patterns. Cues may slowly evolve from the facilitator's support of the facilitatee's wrist or forearm to pressure on the shoulder, back, or thigh, to no contact at all. Instead, the facilitator may simply hold up the keyboard or sit next to the facilitatee.

Others of these cases exemplify new brands of FC: the Rapid Prompting Method (RPM) and Spelling to Communicate (S2C). RPM originated with Soma Mukhopadhyay, known as Soma, who initially developed the method for her nonspeaking autistic son Tito. Originally from India, Soma was invited to the US by the Cure Autism Now foundation via one of its co-founders, Portia Iversen. In the US, Soma further developed and promoted her method with Iversen's son and with nonspeaking autistic students at the Carousel School in Los Angeles. In 2005 Soma moved to Austin, Texas, where she founded an RPM center called the Halo-Soma Institute.

Later, a spinoff of RPM was developed by the speech-language pathologist Elizabeth Vosseller, who was initially trained by Soma but later expunged all references to RPM and renamed her method "Spelling to Communicate," "S2C" for short. Vosseller founded an S2C center in Virginia near Washington DC, which now has a satellite clinic in Pennsylvania near Philadelphia.

What distinguishes these two new brands of FC is that, even at their earliest stages, neither require physical contact between the facilitator (aka "helper," "assistant," or "communication partner") and the facilitatee. Instead, novice RPM facilitatees are prompted to point (either with an extended index finger or with a pencil) to one of two handwritten choices, while novice S2C facilitatees are prompted to point with their index finger to letters on three different letterboards that each display one third of the alphabet—a stage that RPM users also go through. Eventually, RPM and S2C facilitatees move on to a single letterboard and then, later on, to a held-up keyboard which in some cases eventually evolves into a stationary keyboard with the facilitator merely sitting or standing nearby.

The end-stages of both traditional FC and RPM/S2C, and even the earlier, held-up letterboard stages of RPM/S2C, appear to many observers to allow minimal cueing. Indeed, numerous autism experts, including several acclaimed neurologists, have become convinced that these variants are valid. In a 2003 article in the *New York Times Science Section* on Soma's son Tito, for example, Matthew Belmonte, a U.K.-based neurologist, is quoted as saying that "He [Tito] taps out intelligent, witty answers on a laptop with a voice synthesizer. No one is touching him. He communicates on his own." Also quoted is San Francisco neurologist Michael Merzenich: "Tito is for real. He unhesitatingly responds to factual questions about books that he has read or about experiences that he has had in detail and in high fidelity" (in Blakeslee, 2002).

Years later the late neurologist Oliver Sacks, quoted on the back cover of a 2011 memoir attributed to Tito (*The Mind Tree*) writes:

> [I]t has usually been assumed that deeply autistic people are scarcely capable of introspection or deep thought, let alone of poetic or metaphoric leaps of the imagination—or, if they are, that they are incapable of communicating these thoughts to us. Tito gives the lie to all these assumptions, and forces us to reconsider the conditions of the deeply autistic (in Mukhopadhyay, 2011).

Nor is Tito the only individual whose facilitation has garnered endorsements from experts. There is also Sue Rubin, diagnosed with autism and a chromosomal abnormality, who types on a held-up keyboard or with her facilitator (often her mother) sitting next to her. In a Washington Post article, eminent autism neurologist Margaret Bauman states: "I'm certainly convinced that what I've seen [Sue Rubin] do in front of me was her independent work. Her mom sits next to her. Sometimes Mom says, 'I don't understand that, do it over again.' It's painstakingly slow" (Mann, 2005).

Most recently, world-renowned autism expert Barry Prizant, after observing a group of autistic, minimally speaking RPM users, wrote a letter to the American Speech-Language-Hearing Association opposing its position statement on RPM, citing "surprisingly insightful" messages on letterboards. He adds:

In no, and I mean NO instances were they physically or gesturally directed to specific letter targets... I am aware of some claiming that the facilitator in such instances may be providing subtle cues, even unconsciously, but I did not observe any of that...

Might these experts—familiar as they are with autism in general, and autism neurology in particular—be right about these new variants of FC? Is the fact that there is no direct contact, and that the facilitator is often merely sitting nearby, enough to rule out the possibility of substantial facilitator influence over the typed-out messages?

Extraordinary claims and naked eyes

There are, in fact, several reasons for skepticism about all this—despite what these experts have said. First of all, there is the immediate phenomenon at hand: linguistically well-formed, socially insightful messages coming from individuals with severe autism, but only via index-finger typing in the presence of a facilitator. This, as we suggested earlier, requires a redefinition of autism away from the sociocognitive disorder that experts dating back to the 1940s have held it to be. Instead, autism must be, as Douglas Biklen proposed, some sort of disorder of intentional motor control. RPM promoters point to problems with initiating intentional actions and suppressing unintentional behaviors. S2C promoters single out problems with fine-motor control. These takes on autism, however, do not explain the early attentional and social motivation deficits that are backed up by decades of research. They do not explain why infants later diagnosed with autism look at objects more than at people and orient to environmental sounds more than to speech sounds. They do not explain why autistic toddlers point to things to request them but not to share them as objects of interest. Nor do they explain why pointing to letters, but not pointing to foods, would require the presence of a facilitator.

Second, there are questions about the purported language acquisition. How do these individuals, shortly after facilitation begins, start exhibiting such sophisticated linguistic skills? As we discussed earlier, experiments have shown that joint attention behaviors are critical to learning what words mean. How can individuals with severe autism, whose joint attention behaviors are commensurately limited, passively sponge up the meanings of words, phrases, and sentences?

Third, there are questions about the purported language disability. As it turns out, a number of facilitated individuals are able to pronounce, quite clearly, the names of letters of the alphabet, as well as whole words and phrases. Some individuals call out the letters as they type them; others can read what they type, sometimes quite fluently, but only after they've typed it. Others speak out words and phrases at odds with the words and phrases they're typing. In one troubling scene from the 2020 film *The Reason I Jump*, we see a girl undergoing S2C facilitation and purportedly typing (we cannot see what she types) a sophisticated sentence about finally being able to express herself, all the while crying out "No more! No more!" as if she's desperate to get up and do something else.

FC-proponents try to have it both ways. Speech that conforms to the typing (calling out the letters being typed; reading out the words after they're typed) is purportedly evidence that the facilitatee is the one directing her messages. (In fact, such speech shows merely that the person knows the names of letters and/or can decode words, and not that these letters and words weren't cued by her facilitator, or that she has any idea what they mean). As for speech that conflicts with the typed messages ("No more! No more!"), that speech, purportedly, is merely reflexive— i.e., unintentional and meaningless. *Please don't assume that every word I speak is what I intend to say. Making words with your mouth isn't the same as communication*: so claims the voiceover in the "No more! No more" scene in The Reason I Jump. The only criterion for determining whether speech is genuine or reflexive, apparently, is whether or not it conforms to the facilitated messages, which are assumed from the get-go to be authentic.

Another complication is the linguistic discrepancy between the simple phrases that many facilitated individuals are capable of speaking and the sophisticated language that they are only able to produce by typing. This discrepancy has forced FC-proponents to posit the existence of a language disorder that has never been attested anywhere in the clinical or empirical literature. That is, a disorder that combines intact pronunciation skills with complex syntax and conversation skills that emerge only during the much slower process of hunt and peck typing. While it's hard to prove that something doesn't exist, such a disorder is unlikely to ever turn up. In general, if one has the oral skills to pronounce words and the linguistic skills to type linguistically sophisticated responses, one ought to be able, without any prior typing, to pronounce those linguistically sophisticated responses as well.

Fourth, there is the question of literacy acquisition. How do these individuals pick up reading and spelling without explicit instruction? Most of them, because of their diagnoses, did not attend general language arts classes that might have included at least some basic instruction in phonics. Early FC proponents like Douglas Biklen and Rosemary Crossley, as we mentioned earlier, argue that children can learn to read simply by existing in print-rich environments. The actual research on reading, however, does not support them. Few children master the code of written English through incidental exposure alone. Most require direct, systematic instruction—a need that is reflected in America's ongoing reading crisis. Self-taught reading is something that, various estimates hold, no more than 5% of children actually pull off. Even if the rate of hyperlexia among facilitated individuals is at the high end of the 6%-21% estimated for people with autism (Ostrolenk et al., 2017), that leaves unexplained the purported decoding skills of over three quarters of the facilitated population. Furthermore, reading entails not just decoding, but also comprehension, and hyperlexia, as we've noted, often co-occurs with poor comprehension.

Finally, there is knowledge acquisition. Parent reports suggest that facilitated children, during all their years before facilitation, must have sponged up not only high levels of spoken and written English, but also a wealth of skills and knowledge. For example, shortly after being introduced to RPM by Soma, Portia Iversen's 10-year-old son, asked to define "galaxy," types out "group of stars." Two weeks after the 911 attacks, he typed to his uncle, a New York City resident, "Did you know anyone who died?" When asked how he knew about 911, he typed "NPR." As for his math skills, he learned the multiplication tables from overhearing his sister recite them for homework.

Another boy, the subject of the recent memoir *Underestimated*, though showing no prior math skills, demonstrated via S2C that he already knew basic arithmetic so well that he was able to quickly progress through algebra to calculus. (His facilitator for calculus also happened to be his calculus tutor). The boy also reportedly learned Spanish by observing his brother and sister practice Spanish in front of him.

Another young woman, the subject of another recent memoir (*I Have Been Buried Under Years of Dust*), managed, shortly after becoming a fluent index-finger typist via touch-based FC, to type out messages that showed a detailed knowledge of London:

> We were astounded as she told us details of the city. She pictured Big Ben and the soldiers with enormous hats, she knew about the River Thames, and that tall red buses filled the streets. She was fascinated by Lady Di and knew all about her and her tragic death. We didn't know where all this information had come from. We'd never told her anything about London. She told us she'd learned about it from watching the news; she'd been five at the time that Lady Di died. (Gilpeer & Grodin, 2021, p. 195)

Another parent reports that his son learned physics by overhearing the proceedings of a high school physics class through the cafeteria wall.

Not only does all this passive acquisition of knowledge and skills contradict what is known about attention, social engagement, and information processing in autism, but it also overstates two broader phenomena. One is what people in general are able to learn about the world from TV, radio, and overheard conversations without the basic background knowledge provided by regular education classes and back-and-forth conversations with knowledgeable informants. The other is what skills can be learned merely by overhearing people practice them. To make sense of a news report on 911, for example, one would have to know, at the very least, something about the World Trade Center, passenger jets, hijacking, terrorism, and Al-Qaeda. And to learn multi-digit arithmetic, one would need to practice doing it.

The main explanation that FC proponents have offered for the acquisition by autistic FC users of grade-level or above grade-level skills and knowledge through simple osmosis is simply this: that these individuals are not only free of the various socio-cognitive impairments long associated with autism, but preternaturally attentive, sponge-like in their absorption of information, and/or brilliant.

The extraordinary claims that FC, RPM, and S2C proponents have made about the nature of autism and about the astounding intellectual feats of facilitated individuals give us plenty of reasons for skepticism. Nor can these reasons be overruled by eye-witness experiences: for example, viewing subtle FC up close and finding ourselves (just as the various convinced autism experts did) unable to explain how the facilitators could possibly cue their facilitatees' letter choices. In and of itself, what our naked eyes seem to tell us is no reason to dismiss, out of hand, all that has long been established about autism and learning. Consider, as a different example, what has long been established about whether objects like rabbits can appear and disappear out of thin air or turn into doves. The fact that we cannot explain what our eyes seem to tell us during a live magic show does not—and should not—leave us believing in magic.

As we will see below, however, there are known explanations for the apparent magic of even the subtlest variants of facilitated communication.

Clever Hans

Once upon a time there was a magical horse from Germany named Clever Hans. Clever Hans could correctly answer math questions by tapping out the answers with his hoof. Ask him what seven plus twelve is in either oral or written German, and he would tap his hoof nineteen times. Ask him what the date of the following Friday would be if the eighth of the month falls on a Tuesday, and he would tap his hoof eleven times. Hans could also multiply, divide, work with fractions, and spell. In 1904, he was profiled in *The New York Times*.

A formal investigation in 1907 by psychologist Oskar Pfungst demonstrated that Hans was not actually performing these calculations. Instead, he was responding to unwitting cues from his questioner. As the horse's taps approached the correct answer, the questioner's posture would show an increase in tension; once the horse had tapped the correct number of times, the questioner's body would relax. Precisely these patterns of tension and relaxation, as we noted earlier, are ways in which facilitators can unwittingly, even inevitably, cue their facilitatees. Indeed, what came to be known as the "Clever Hans Effect" was later replicated in humans in an experiment that included Pfungst himself: Pfungst asked people to concentrate on particular numbers while he tapped out the answers with his right hand. A reversion of their downward head positions back to their original positions, before they had started concentrating on the number, told him when to stop tapping. What's special about the Clever Hans Effect is that the tension and relaxation cues are visual: They do not involve direct physical contact.

No one is touching him. He communicates on his own. The implicit assumption of the various neurologists and autism experts who have endorsed the more subtle variants of FC is that an absence of physical contact rules out facilitator cueing. Barry Prizant cites, in addition, an absence of gestures directing the facilitatees to specific letters. He adds that, since autistic individuals have difficulty interpreting body language, they wouldn't be susceptible to subtle body-language cues. But having trouble *interpreting* body language—which, as we discussed in Chapter 1, is an issue in autism, especially with facial expressions—doesn't make someone immune to subconscious cueing from body language. Others have claimed that non-tactile cueing would entail a distinct cue for each of the 26 letters of the alphabet and require the facilitatee to detect, decode, and act upon each cue: a complex, cumbersome process riddled with opportunities for error. But, as we saw with Clever Hans and as we will see again later, non-tactile cueing does not require 26 distinct cues and generally facilitates, rather than complicates, the process of letter selection.

What, then, are the possibilities for cueing without touching in the more subtle versions of FC? Let's return, first, to end-stage traditional FC. As we noted earlier, over years of working together, facilitator–facilitatee partnerships can evolve toward ever-more-subtle cues. In addition, over time the pair may have produced certain specific messages—for example, common requests or responses to frequently asked questions—so often that it takes few cues for the facilitator to set their letter sequences into motion. Finally, many of today's word processing programs include word prediction software that is far more sophisticated than that on our iPhones and iPads: more sophisticated both in the appropriateness of the words it predicts, and in how accurately it reflects the typing habits of particular users. As soon as users start typing, words pop up that are often just right for the message under construction and that users can select with just one click. This means that ever fewer cues are needed— especially for messages that resemble prior output. Thus, over time, and especially if there's help from word prediction, visual cues from body language akin to those that cued Clever Hans may be all that facilitators need to (unwittingly) generate messages.

As for the new brands of FC, which even in their earliest stages don't require touch, FC critics have noted that these raise the same sorts of concerns about facilitator control as traditional FC does. The only difference is this: While in touch-based FC the facilitator manipulates the person's body, in RPM/S2C she manipulates the device. Indeed, videos of RPM and S2C show letterboard movement to be more or less constant, especially movement that shifts the target letter closer to the facilitatee's extended index finger. But beyond this, there are other opportunities for cueing that are specific to RPM and S2C, and each of these is susceptible to the same ideomotor and action project effects that we discussed earlier in connection with traditional, touch-based FC.

At the earliest stages of RPM, when the facilitator simply holds up two possible answers to a question and prompts the facilitatee to choose between them, the facilitator can nudge up the initial 50-50 chance of a correct response by holding the correct choice closer to the facilitatee's pointing hand. At the three-letterboard stage—which is also the first stage of S2C—the facilitator can influence the letter selections, in part, by deciding which letterboard to pick up—a decision that, curiously, is not entrusted to the facilitatee. Throughout the various stages, the timing and intonation of the oral prompts—"Keep going," "You can do it"—may also influence selections.

Except in the final stages of S2C/RPM, when users are considered ready to graduate from a letterboard to a keyboard, the facilitator has two other opportunities to influence messages: opportunities that don't arise with traditional FC. This is because the letterboard, a low-tech laminated page, doesn't record the letters the user points to by displaying them on a screen. It is therefore up to the facilitator to keep track of and record the user's letter choices—generally by writing them down on a piece of paper or by saying out loud the words and phrases they spell. Before the spelling is complete, it is natural for the facilitators to keep track of the letter sequences by calling out each letter as it's selected. But this letter-calling routine opens up the possibility of (unwittingly) calling out a letter before it is actually chosen. Prematurely calling out a letter, of course, can cue the facilitatee to select it.

Another opportunity for facilitator control comes from the fact that the facilitator often needs to make judgments about when a letter choice was made and which letter was chosen. Is a particular hand movement a deliberate pointing gesture that should be recorded, or an incidental movement that should be ignored? Is the index finger closer to the "C" or the "D"? In cases like these, the facilitator may (however unwittingly) ignore some of the facilitatee's selections or call out letters that the index finger didn't actually get close to. Still another opportunity for facilitator control comes from her ability to whisk away the letterboard to prevent a selection or to terminate a message. This has the same effect on the facilitated message as the wrist-holding facilitator's action, in touch-based facilitation, of pulling back the facilitatee's hand to prevent an erroneous selection.

All of these facilitator-controlled, message-directing tactics—letterboard movements that bring fingers closer to target letters, prompting and premature calling out of letters, premature pulling away of the letterboard, questionable decisions about letter selections—can be seen in action in the various online videos of RPM and S2C. In fact, these tactics are so routine that it's clear how RPM and S2C practitioners are able, for the most part, to dispense with the direct physical contact that defined classic FC.

But touch is still an option, and in some RPM videos one can observe facilitators touching facilitatees, while in other videos, physical contact may be occurring just outside the frame. Another cueing option is for the facilitator to cue letter selections by moving her free hand in the direction of the next letter. Oral cues for specific words are also possible: we see this with Soma and Tito, where Soma, always within visual or auditory range, can often be heard articulating the starting syllable of the next word right after she repeats the word Tito has just finished writing or typing. Once users graduate to keyboards, the potency of these various cues can be boosted, as we discussed above, by word prediction software.

In general, so long as the facilitator is within visual and auditory range of the facilitatee and can see when the facilitatee is approaching the desired letter or the most appropriate predicted word, the situation is ripe for cueing. Indeed, in all the videos of all the variants of FC in which both the facilitator's face and the facilitatee's typing actions are visible, these two conditions are clearly met. The facilitator is near the facilitatee, her eyes are glued to the keyboard, and the facilitatee is typing with an isolated index finger such that, unlike with ten-finger typing, the facilitator can clearly see which letter he is about to type.

And, indeed, even in the examples that FC-proponents cite of people graduating from FC to what they consider to be full independence, precisely these ingredients are all still in place. This is true, for example, of all the FC veterans cited by Douglas Biklen, the founder of US-based FC. As Biklen himself freely admits, even those who speak what they type after they type it are still only able to engage in back and forth conversations when typing on a keyboard with a single index finger and with their facilitator sitting right next to them. There is no unequivocal evidence, throughout all the FC literature, of anyone who wasn't already able to type independently when she started out with FC, and who gets to the point of typing out messages that 1) are as sophisticated as her facilitated messages and 2) don't require a designated facilitator to sit beside her and watch her pick out the letters.

What about the empirical evidence for or against RPM and S2C?

Don't test.

Back in the 1990s, when FC was first subjected to empirical testing, it was, as we discussed, roundly debunked. It helped, back then, that many practitioners were genuinely curious about whether it worked. Since then, attitudes have changed, and promoters of FC and its new variants have come up with various reasons why facilitator–facilitatee pairs should never be subjected to rigorous double-blind and message-passing tests.

The big one is anxiety. Purportedly, the prospect of having their communicative capabilities questioned and tested by people who are, at best, skeptical and perhaps downright hostile makes facilitatees so anxious that they frequently experience difficulties with word retrieval and are unable to answer simple questions about pictures. Compounding this anxiety is "stereotype threat,": worry about confirming a negative stereotype about one's group, in this case, negative stereotypes about the capabilities of minimally speaking individuals with autism.

The other claim is that more valid, naturalistic tests of FC have already been done and have established that FC is valid. But these "qualitative" tests, compared to the more rigorous tests that have debunked FC, all have serious design flaws. As some researchers have pointed out, there is a negative, or inverse, correlation between how rigorous a study is and how much evidence it finds for FC.

The result is that, while there are anecdotes about unpublished double-blind/message-passing tests (some of which clearly indicate facilitator influence), there are no published double-blind/message-passing tests that either support or invalidate RPM and S2C. One RPM study (Chen et al., 2012) did find that gazing toward the letterboard did not improve the accuracy of the facilitatee's responses. Though the study's authors do not acknowledge it, their finding suggests that the facilitatees were not the ones directing the messages. Indeed, this study brings up one more reason for skepticism that we haven't yet mentioned: the fact that, while the facilitator's eyes are glued to the keyboard, the facilitatee's eyes are sometimes looking away.

FC proponents have handled the eye-gaze problem in two ways. Some claim, without evidence, that non-speaking autistic individuals have highly developed peripheral vision, such that they can see where they are pointing even when they appear to be looking elsewhere. Others have attempted to show that, more often than not, facilitatees are in fact looking at letters before they point to them (anticipatory gazing). The latter was the conclusion drawn in a 2020 study of S2C facilitatees (Jaswal et al., 2020). Their data indicated that participants gazed anticipatorily at latter targets at rates significantly above chance. Such data, however, does not tell us much about intentional looking, let alone about intentional communicating.

First, it is unclear whether the rates of anticipatory gazing are anywhere near the rates that would be found in individuals engaged in unfacilitated typing (individuals, that is, whose intentional communication is not in doubt). Second, consistent with what's routine in RPM and S2C, the study's videos show letterboards moving in ways that shift the target letter towards the facilitatee's extended index finger. This raises the question of whether, in cases where anticipatory gazing did occur, participants were gazing at letters intentionally, or only because the letters had shifted into their lines of sight. Third, even if the participants were intentionally looking at letters, it remains unclear whether this was part of a conscious message-authoring process. In one of the three videos, we can hear the facilitator calling out letters before the participant gazed at them. This participant may have intentionally looked at letters only in response to the facilitator's letter calling. In other cases, participants' gaze patterns may have reflected their familiarity with common letter patterns learned over years of S2C. (The letter "t," for example, is often followed by the letter "h.")

True message authorship is much more than looking and pointing intentionally at letter sequences, even if those letter sequences happen to produce meaningful phrases. Compared to the kinds of double-blind and message-passing tests done in the most rigorous studies, experiments like this one give us little reliable information.

Given the absence of meaningful empirical support for RPM and S2C and the susceptibility of RPM and S2C to facilitator influence, many of the same organizations that have position statements against traditional FC also have position statements against these newer brands. For example, the American Association on Intellectual and Developmental Disabilities states: "In the case of RPM, there is lack of scientific evidence for its validity, and concerns about message authorship similar to those for FC have been raised." And the American Speech-Language-Hearing Association states:

> It is the position of the American Speech-Language-Hearing Association (ASHA) that use of the Rapid Prompting Method (RPM) is not recommended because of prompt dependency and the lack of scientific validity. Furthermore, information obtained through the use of RPM should not be assumed to be the communication of the person with a disability.

While neither of these organizations mentions S2C, S2C is similar enough in its methodology and lack of empirical validity that a warning against RPM is, for all intents and purposes, also a warning against S2C. One organization that does explicitly warn against S2C along with RPM is the National Council on Severe Autism.

These warnings, however, haven't stopped neurologists and autism experts from endorsing RPM and S2C, let alone inspired them to publicly change their minds. Nor as we'll see below, have these warnings arrested the spread of S2C and RPM into the popular media and clinical practice.

The broader culture and clinical practice

Across the US, beyond the headquarters for FC, RPM, and S2C—the Inclusion and Communication Initiative in Syracuse, New York; Halo-Soma in Austin, Texas; and Growing Kids Therapy Center in Herndon, Virginia—there are at least 24 organizations around the US, among them schools and clinics serving autistic children, that are devoted to various forms of FC.

In addition, multiple autism institutions implicitly endorse FC. The Autism Self Advocacy Network (ASAN), for example, has had facilitated individuals on its board. The Autism National Committee has a pro-FC position paper. The Doug Flutie Jr. Autism Foundation has donated $70,000 to 11 schools and organizations to support their use and development of I-Pad technologies for FC. And the Autism Society of America has featured interviews of facilitated individuals conducted by its president. Among broader disability organizations, TASH (an advocacy organization for people with severe disabilities) has gone so far as to endorse FC as a human right.

Reflecting this last stance, several disability studies journals—*Disability, Handicap, & Society; Disability and Society;* and, especially, *Disability Studies Quarterly*—have published pro-FC articles. Indeed, the dominant disability rights take on FC is that questioning FC means questioning the communicative competence of facilitatees, and that opposing FC deprives facilitatees of their voices. Accordingly, among the disability studies articles is one that characterizes FC skepticism as hate speech. Rather than question FC, we are to "presume competence"—a maxim, popular in the disability rights world, that dates back to Douglas Biklen and that essentially entails accepting FC on faith.

Institutions of higher education have also embraced FC. The first was Syracuse University, home of Douglas Biklen's Facilitated Communication Institute, now the Inclusion and Communication Initiatives. Within the last decade, other universities have hosted pro-FC talks, offered courses, or provided resources: the University of Virginia, the MIT Media Lab, MIT's Simons Initiative on Autism and the Brain, California Lutheran University, Pennsylvania State University, and the University of New Hampshire. Others have recently enrolled and even granted degrees to facilitated individuals: the College of Liberal Studies at the University of Pennsylvania, Harvard Extension School, Tulane University, U.C. Berkeley, and, with Phi Betta Kappa honors, Oberlin College.

At the governmental level, the State of Vermont funds FC as an adult service, and the US Department of Health and Human Services Interagency Autism Coordinating Committee includes a non-speaking individual who is probably facilitated (videos show him typing with an extended finger on a keyboard with someone partially visible next to him). Other high-profile organizations include the United Nations, which for its 2019 World Autism Awareness Day featured several FC users and promoters, as well as a video about RPM by Soma, RPM's founder.

Then there is the mainstream media. Both local and national newspapers have published profiles of facilitated individuals. These date back to the 2003 *New York Times Science Section* piece about Tito and RPM. Tito, reporter Sandra Blakeslee stated, "writes eloquently and independently, on pads or his laptop, about what it feels like to be locked inside an autistic body and mind." Blakeslee also described how Soma's second RPM client, Portia Iversen's son, "broke out of his muteness." (Blakeslee, 2002, p. 1)

In 2013, the *LA Times* published a profile of another of Soma's clients entitled "In the 'Silent Prison' of Autism, Ido Kedar Speaks Out" (Curwen, 2013). In 2018, the *Wall Street Journal* ran an op-ed attributed to Kedar that claims that RPM "liberated" him: "I have always understood speech. I have insight and I'm intelligent. I just couldn't demonstrate this in my [remedial] drills because my body didn't enable me to speak or move the way I wished" (Kedar, 2018).

In 2020, the *Chicago Tribune* published a profile of yet another RPM user, a 17-year-old boy who purportedly acquired language and other skills by incidental reading (e.g., of street signs) and listening (e.g., to his father helping his sister with homework). "No one touches Mitchell's arms or hands or moves his board as he spells," the reporter assures us (Fazio, 2020).

Also in 2020, *USA Today* published an article entitled "Kids with autism learn to speak with hands, by spelling to communicate" (Kim, 2020). The capsule review beneath the headline echoes the redefinition of autism espoused by FC promoters: "Many think of autism as a behavioral disorder, but it's a movement sensory disorder."

Of all the mainstream newspapers, the one that has published the greatest number of pro-FC articles is the *Washington Post*. In 2016 it profiled an RPM facilitatee who purportedly wrote a letter explaining autism (Colby, 2016). In 2017 it published an article about parents advocating for RPM in their children's schools, describing it as a "novel communication technique" that leads to breakthroughs for people with autism (Chandler, 2017). Also in 2017 it published a follow-up op-ed, attributed to a 13-year-old facilitatee, that asserts that typing via RPM and FC gives individuals a "voice" (Reis, 2017). In 2020, it published an interview with an RPM user about the Covid pandemic (Sitz, 2020). The accompanying video shows cueing via the facilitator's letterboard movements and voice, and the facilitatee occasionally covering his eyes while typing. Finally, in 2021 the Post published an interview with a facilitated young woman and her mother, taking at face value the mother's claims about FC's efficacy and the words generated by her daughter via FC (Miller, 2021).

As for mainstream online media, both the *Huffington Post* and CBSNews. com have profiled facilitated individuals. So has mainstream television. In 2003, Soma, Tito, and RPM were featured on CBS's 60 Minutes. In 2004, CNN began airing a short film it co-produced, *Autism Is a World*, featuring the facilitated Sue Rubin (Cable & Margulies, 2004) In 2009, ABC's 20/20 profiled a non-speaking young woman, Carly Fleischmann, who was purportedly "unlocked" by typing. Fleischmann, who has interviewed various celebrities on her YouTube channel via button clicks that play canned questions and responses, has also appeared with Steven Colbert and Jon Stewart. Her first appearance was on *Stewart's Night of Too Many Stars* (Cooperman & Neihausen, 2019) in a live session that didn't go as expected; her second appearance, in a prerecorded session that went more smoothly, was on *The Late Show* with Stephen Colbert (Lenker, 2017; The Late Show with Stephen Colbert, 2018). Even PBS, the same broadcaster that aired the FC-debunking *Prisoners of Silence* in 1993, is now promoting FC, broadcasting *Deej*, a movie about a facilitated young man going through the college application process and attending Oberlin (Rooy, 2017).

Numerous books and movies, many of which have landed major publishers or distributors as well as reviews in major newspapers, also promote FC. Besides those already mentioned, there are the parent memoirs *Strange Son* (Portia Iversen's memoir), *I Am in Here, I*

Am Intelligent, Reasonable People, and *Underestimated,* and memoirs attributed to facilitated individuals like *How can I Talk if My Lips Don't Move* (attributed to Tito), *Ido in Autismland* (attributed to Ido Kedar), *Lucy's Story* (attributed to one of Douglas Biklen's informants), and *The Reason I Jump* (the memoir, as opposed to the subsequent movie, attributed to a non-speaking, autistic Japanese boy and translated into English by *Cloud Atlas* novelist David Mitchell).

Movies that uncritically present individuals with autism using FC, many of them garnering favorable reviews in major news outlets, include *Autism: The Musical* (Regan, 2007); *A Mother's Courage,* narrated by Kate Winslet, with original music by Bjork (Friðriksson, 2009); *Wretches and Jabberers* (Wurzburg, 2010; *I want To Say,* which showcases a variant of FC that involves guiding the child's hand with a stick (Lilienfeld, 2015); *Far from the Tree* (Dretzin, 2017), which profiles children with a variety of differences, with a facilitated boy as its only exemplar of autism; and, most recently, *The Reason I Jump* (Rothwell, 2020), inspired by the book of the same name. This last film, despite the troubling scene, mentioned earlier, in which a young woman's oral protests of "No more! No more!" are ignored, received rave reviews from the *Wall Street Journal* (Morgenstern, 2021) and other major newspapers around the world and won five major awards: the British Independent Film Awards, Denver International Film Festival, and Valladolid International Film Festival, all for best documentary; the Sundance Film Festival (world cinema, best documentary); and the Vancouver International Film Festival (impact award).

Even Apple has implicitly endorsed FC as a legitimate communication method: A video promoting its iPad ("Dillan's Voice") shows a teenage boy using the iPad via RPM.

The common denominator of the various news stories, documentaries, and memoirs are the extraordinary abilities that FC purportedly unlocks from individuals thought to be severely intellectually impaired. A huge part of the appeal of these pieces, therefore, are the feel-good, miracle narratives they recount. Indeed, one newspaper editor responded to criticism of a pro-FC story by explaining that the paper is looking for feel-good stories, not downers.

But there's another reason why these accounts have resonated, perhaps as never before, throughout contemporary American society. This has to do with a new paradigm for disability that is increasingly popular, particularly in academia and K12 education: a "social model" of disability, as opposed to the traditional "medical model." The social model says that we shouldn't view disability as a disease to be treated and possibly cured. Rather, we should see disability for what it truly is: a social construct. People are disabled only when society is insufficiently open, sympathetic, and accommodating. Furthermore, the differences that underlie the social construct of disability—from mobility differences to sensory differences to attention differences to social differences—are aspects of human diversity that we should celebrate rather than normalize. Severely autistic, non-verbal individuals pose a severe challenge for the social model—a challenge that is readily eliminated by recasting these individuals as intellectually intact or superior.

Perhaps partly as a result of all this pro-FC messaging, significant percentages of autism practitioners—speech-language pathologists, ABA therapists, Floortime therapists, teachers, and autism parents—have, over the last two decades, embraced various forms of FC. The Floortime Center in Bethesda has an RPM specialist on staff. A recent survey of special education teachers finds significant numbers using both touch-based FC and RPM/S2C—at rates that rival their use of evidence-based therapies like PECS and TEACCH.

Among autism parents, surveys report varying percentages who say they've used FC, with around 10% as the high. However, the rate among "eligible" parents may be considerably higher. For one thing, only around a third of the autism population is minimally verbal enough to include tempting candidates for FC, and not all of these individuals are compliant enough to put up with it. For another, the surveys may have omitted parents who use RPM or S2C, many of whom don't consider these methods as types of FC. In the course of informal interviews of several dozen autism parents conducted by the author in 2018–2019, it emerged that around one third to one half of the parents representing this subpopulation were considering, or were already using, one or another form of FC.

Why FC resonates in K12 education, and why it shouldn't

One reason why FC-related tenets like the social model of disability and the maxim to presume competence resonate so powerfully in the education world is how deeply they validate today's expectations for student learning. Students are increasingly expected to follow a curriculum that is calibrated only to what grade they are in and not to their academic readiness—an expectation that the Common Core State Standards have helped to codify. In addition, since students are rarely held back a grade, what grade they're in almost always reflects how old they are, which makes their age the main determinant of what they're supposed to learn. Even students with serious intellectual disabilities— the 1%–2% who are exempted from the standard Common Core-aligned accountability tests—are still expected to follow a curriculum based on modified Common Core goals. And they, too, are required to take tests that are based on the Common Core—albeit modified tests that provide alternative ways to "demonstrate understanding."

This means that minimally verbal and non-verbal autistic students, who generally spend most of their time in autistic support classrooms because of difficulties accessing regular K12 education, are expected nonetheless to meet learning goals in language arts, math, science, and social studies. The pressure is on to somehow facilitate their ability to demonstrate—or at least to appear to demonstrate—understanding, particularly on the modified Common Core-based school accountability tests. More generally, the pressure is on to somehow help minimally/nonverbal students be—or at least appear to be—academically successful in activities that are often far beyond their capabilities.

How, then, might one prompt a nonverbal, severely autistic student to, say, fill out a diagram of the food pyramid or answer questions about a short, illustrated passage on Martin Luther King?

Teachers report using a number of strategies to help such students demonstrate, or ostensibly demonstrate, understanding and academic success. A few of these are officially sanctioned, for example, by guidelines for testing accommodations. The bulk of them are ad hoc and expedient. They include 1) reducing the number of problems on assignments and tests; 2) transforming assignments and test questions that solicit multi-word or multi-sentence responses into single-word fill-in-the-blanks prompts or multiple-choice questions; 3) reducing the number of multiple choices from four down to three or two; 4) reducing the number of words in questions and reading passages and replacing words, where possible, with pictures; 5) reading the questions and passages to the child; 6) replacing pictures with 3D objects; 7) acting out the reading passages; 8) giving students a pass-fail option, whenever possible, on assignments and tests; and 9) making liberal use of classroom aides and therapeutic support staff, whose assistance—explaining the assignment, keeping the student on task—often blurs into heavy prompting and doing much of the work themselves.

This last tactic is, of course, an eerie echo of facilitator influence. Nor is classroom assistance from well-meaning aides the only factor that gives rise to FC-like phenomena in classrooms with severely autistic, nonverbal students. Consider what happens when a student fundamentally doesn't understand the assignment or test question, even when words are replaced with pictures and pictures are replaced with objects. Perhaps he doesn't even understand that he's being asked to respond to a question or to complete an assignment; perhaps he doesn't even know what a question is. In such circumstances, even reducing the answer options to two multiple choices or two held-up objects will not elicit a meaningful response. In these cases, teachers report sometimes simply prompting the student to point to one of the two choices, and if he doesn't oblige, holding up the choices in front of his hands. Eventually, hopefully, there is something resembling a selection; the teacher records it and then moves on. Many teachers confide that this procedure is essentially meaningless, even downright demoralizing, but that, when it comes to the mandatory testing, they have little choice but to go through the motions.

Related to the assumption that all students are capable of demonstrating understanding of Common Core-related content regardless of their intellectual profiles is the assumption that most skills can be acquired incidentally, without explicit instruction. Indeed, much of today's educational discourse is less about teaching students knowledge and skills and more about giving them access to learning opportunities. The implication is that much is already there, within the student, and merely needs a rich, nurturing environment in which to germinate. It follows that—as many teachers are trained to believe—incidental, hands-on, child-centered discovery is the best way to learn. This notion, as we've observed elsewhere, is akin both to the unstructured Floortime framework for autism therapy and to the Whole Language take on literacy acquisition espoused by FC-proponents (both of these approaches lacking efficacy). Conversely, educators are often trained to believe that direct, structured, systematic instruction in basic skills and facts—akin to ABA therapy—is not only unnecessary but cognitively and emotionally injurious.

Collectively, all this implies that even the most severely autistic students are capable of accessing at least modified versions of the general curriculum based only on how old they are and without any direct instruction that is tailored to their cognitive readiness. Not surprisingly, this is something that few people who spend significant time working directly with severely autistic students actually believe. And yet, if they are part of the K12 system, they are generally expected to act upon it.

With autism in particular, what we might charitably call wishful thinking about incidental, child-centered learning is especially unfounded. As we've discussed repeatedly, autistic children are especially dependent on structure and on direct, systematic instruction, and it is in part these things that make the most effective therapies—ABA, Direct Instruction, Precision Teaching—as effective as they are.

Where the most severely autistic students are concerned, these therapies have another key ingredient: namely, their built-in safeguards against unintentional cueing. If the ABA therapist, during her "touch cookie" and "touch doll" trials, begins by holding up the cookie and the doll, she knows that she needs to transition as quickly as possible to placing these objects on a stationary surface. She also knows to focus her eyes on the student's face or hands so that she doesn't accidentally signal with her eyes which object is the target. These protocols, reflecting an appreciation of just how powerful body-language cues can be, help ensure that the skills that emerge from ABA training are actual and independent, and not meaningless responses to subconscious cueing.

Yet another ingredient that makes evidence-based therapies and teaching strategies like ABA, Direct Instruction, and Precision Teaching as successful as they are is that they carefully assess students' skills, subskill by subskill. Teachers and therapists assess what a student is capable of doing on his own, fully independently, and then meet him precisely where he is. In other words, they emphatically do not presume competence—at least when it concerns what students already know.

The *presume competence* maxim does contain a grain of truth. Arguably, it is both reasonable and productive to begin by presuming that people, no matter how disabled, are competent—competent, that is, in the sense of capable of learning. But for FC's disability rights proponents, presuming competence means much more. Given the levels of literacy and the troves of knowledge that facilitated messages often display shortly after facilitation begins, presuming competence means presuming not just that severely autistic, nonspeaking individuals have the potential to learn, but that they have already learned enough material on their own that they are operating at or above grade level. This, of course, is perfectly aligned with what Common Core proponents and others in the education establishment would prefer to believe about everyone.

But there is a downside, for all students, to overestimating competence. Most of us depend on teachers and systematic instruction, and that instruction is accessible only when tailored to our actual level of mastered skills—not to some fantasized level of competence. FC, together with *presume competence*, thus deprives autistic individuals not only of their voices, but also of access to real learning at their actual levels of readiness, not to mention pathways to life skills and independent living. (Common Core-based educational strategies have similar, if milder, effects).

The challenge is that, where severe autism is concerned, the emergence of actual skills under ABA, in comparison with imagined skills under FC, takes considerably longer, if in fact these skills emerge at all. Indeed, progress may sometimes be slow enough to drive parents to FC. A more promising approach is to seek out ways to bypass some of the deficits of nonspeaking and minimally speaking autism—particularly those involving communication.

Alternatives: ABA, AAC, and assistive devices

How do we bypass the communication deficits in nonspeaking autism? The first step is to grasp the scope of these deficits. As is frequently pointed out, both by FC-proponents and by others, nonspeaking is not the same as nonverbal. Language includes not just speech, but sign language and written language. A deaf child may not be able to speak, but she may be able to express herself fluently in sign. Stephen Hawking communicated in written words, twitching his cheek to control a cursor that selected specific words. Others whose motor problems similarly impede speech—for example some individuals with cerebral palsy—may also communicate through text-producing devices.

But in autism in particular, minimally/nonspeaking correlates quite closely with minimally/nonverbal. This is because autism is not, as FC-proponents have claimed, a motor disorder, but, as we've discussed throughout this book, a disorder of social cognition. The same deficits that impede speech acquisition—not tuning into voices and faces, not engaging in joint attention behaviors, not engaging in social interactions—also affect language acquisition more generally. Some autistic individuals do tune into visual signs and symbols, including letters. The more hyperlexic of these individuals may learn to associate certain letter patterns with certain objects or pictures. But these language-learning opportunities are limited to situations in which the written word is clearly linked to something that depicts its meaning—as with labels on food packaging. Words used to label, however, represent only a tiny fraction of written language and do not provide access into language as a whole. There are no clear labels for abstract nouns like "friendship"; for most verbs, pronouns, and function words; or for the different verb tenses. If a child hasn't learned the meaning of the spoken word "friendship" or the spoken verb ending "ing," he has no way to figure out, on his own, the meaning of the written word "friendship" or the written ending "ing."

In short, in autism, minimally speaking and nonspeaking generally entail minimally verbal and nonverbal. In addition, given how autism severity is largely a function of how much a person tunes in to social stimuli, minimally-to-non-speaking/minimally-to-non-verbal generally correlates with severe autism.

That's not to say that nonspeaking, severely autistic children don't have a number of intact cognitive skills. Many are quite adept at sorting objects by category, completing jigsaw puzzles, doing arithmetic as complex as long division, and memorizing long lists of items by rote. Some are able to independently type out key words and phrases, for example while browsing YouTube—a preferred pastime for many of these children. But they nonetheless are severely impaired in those activities that require substantial verbal abilities, like reading, soaking up knowledge about the world, and typing out sentences with sophisticated vocabulary and syntax. And while evidence-based therapies like ABA can help some of these children acquire some language, many of them remain extremely limited.

The most obvious way to bypass the linguistic deficits in severe autism is through alternative, non-linguistic modes of communication. Over the last few decades, a variety of what are called Augmentative and Alternative Communication (AAC) tools have been developed. Generally speaking, AAC denotes any form of communication that supplements or substitutes for speech. AAC includes two approaches that we discussed in Chapter Three as strategies for language instruction: the Picture Exchange Communication Systems (PECS; Bondy & Frost, 1985) and sign language. Both PECS and sign language, of course, can also serve as media for communication. But for severely autistic children, PECS is by far the more promising.

The problem with sign language is that, while it is more visible than speech and easier to imitate, it is a full-blown language that includes abstract linguistic elements like tense, embedded clauses, and if–then statements. Some of these are encoded using facial expressions and postural shifts that autistic children may miss. Indeed, the tendency in autism not to tune into faces and social interactions is likely to limit sign language acquisition in the same way that it limits speech acquisition. Second, sign, like speech, is fleeting: Signs come and go just like spoken words do. Sign language therefore raises the same attention issues that speech does. Third, most people know few to no signs, making sign language difficult to fully embed in daily life. Some severely autistic children are able to learn a small number of individual, basic signs (e.g., "yes," "no," "more," "food"), but research comparing sign language to other forms of AAC has found sign language to be comparatively less effective.

For those who struggle with the abstractions of symbolic language, picture-based systems like PECS are far more accessible. On one hand, only the most concrete word meanings can be clearly captured with pictures, and even these, as we discussed earlier, may be hard to depict in ways that aren't overly specific (should the picture of the apple be red or green?). But to the extent that depictions do their job, they bypass the difficulties that severely autistic children have attaching meanings to words. Clear enough pictures convey meanings directly, without words.

The most basic picture-based system is PECS. PECS, as we saw in Chapter Three, involves choosing and assembling together laminated, Velcro-backed labels that contain drawings, icons, photographs, and, in some cases, words, and then handing the assembled labels (typically affixed to a Velcro-backed message bar) to one's communication partner. These labels are kept in a PECS book: a spiral notebook with Velcro-backed strips on each page, which can be organized by category or function (e.g., "food," "clothing," and "school"). PECS has the advantage of deploying concrete, readily manipulable materials in a concrete communication process: the PECS user walks up to her communication partner and literally hands the message to him. The communication partner can, of course, reply via his own PECS messages. Messages may range from requests like "I want juice" to statements (perhaps in answer to questions) like "Boy in red truck," or, if the PECS book includes labels for linguistic items like articles and copula verbs, "The boy is in the red truck." For children who are minimally verbal, of course, the linguistic elements of PECS may not be meaningful or accessible; the same may be true of more abstract icons like those for "yes" and "no."

The third common form of AAC, the one most frequently used in severe autism, is one we have not yet discussed. It is, essentially, a high-tech, screen-based version of PECS, but with electronic speech. The tool is a "speech generating device" (SGD) or "talker." Users construct messages by navigating through picture grids and clicking on pictures, which then appear in a "message bar" at the top of the screen. Once a message is complete, the user clicks on a button that reads it out loud. As with PECS, the user's communication partner often communicates back to him the same way.

High-tech, screen-based AAC systems have several advantages over PECS. They are generally more efficient: Finding a particular picture often involves just a couple of taps on labeled category folders and subfolders (e.g., "food," "clothing," "school") that open up grids of specific pictures, as opposed to paging through a PECS book. Second, instead of having to walk over to one's communication partner to deliver the message, high-tech AAC's speech generation allows messages to be delivered at a distance. Third, while PECS books quickly become unwieldy as new pictures/icons/vocabulary items are added, high-tech AAC programs readily store many thousands of such items. Fourth and finally, as we noted in Chapter Three in connection with computerized language learning programs, some AAC users show a clear preference for high-tech, computerized AAC screens over lower-tech forms of communication.

A large number of specific high-tech AAC programs are available. Among the most popular are GoTalk, Proloquo2Go, TouchChat, and LAMP Words for Life. These vary, in particular, in their levels of complexity: how many picture/icon/word items per screen; how many separate screens to navigate through; how numerous and how sophisticated the items; and whether or not the program offers grammatical function words (e.g., "and" and "the") and alternative word forms (e.g., singular vs. plural nouns and different verb tenses). Some programs offer multiple linguistic levels. In addition, most programs, as with PECS, include written labels above the pictures, and some allow text-only modes in which users select words rather than pictures/icons.

High-tech AAC, thus, can serve a range of different users: from those who are only ready for basic picture/icons and basic messages or have difficulty navigating through multiple screens, to those who can keep track of how multiple screens are organized and are ready for more complex messages. These programs are thus potentially accessible to a variety of non-verbal and minimally-verbal individuals with autism.

AAC programs potentially boost communication in two ways. One is by giving minimally verbal students a means to express themselves. The other is by boosting their communication skills. Indeed, there is potential for high-tech AAC, just as we saw with PECS, to serve as a tool for language instruction. Over time, a more basic user can have additional pictures, icons, and linguistic elements added to his screen. Eventually, the user may learn to associate the pictures he selects with both the speech sounds that the device outputs when he clicks on them, and the words that label these pictures, helping him attach meanings to words. Then, as he assembles longer messages ("I want juice"; "I see dog"), he may start to internalize basic subject-verb-object order. Gradually, pictures/icons might be replaced with just words. In addition, most of these devices offer keyboard modes that let users type in words rather than select them. As users learn spelling and get better at typing, typing may turn out to be faster than navigating through screens and locating words in grids. Thus, over time, some users may gradually transition from selecting pictures to typing words—in other words, to full-fledged linguistic communication.

As part of the process, they might transition from AAC devices to "assistive programs." Assistive programs offer various types of assistance, but for autistic individuals and others with language impairments, the biggest assistance comes from word prediction—something we discussed earlier in connection with subtle FC. As we noted, the word prediction is much more sophisticated than what we see on our iPhones—offering more choices, more linguistically appropriate choices, and choices that more accurately adjust to the user's communication patterns. The reason why word prediction is assistive, of course, is that it lets novice typists and those with spelling difficulties input words more quickly and more accurately than they would otherwise be able to. In addition, to help users recognize the suggested words, some assistive programs annotate them with pictures.

It's important to emphasize, however, that many individuals with severe autism do not progress beyond basic AAC programs, and many are only able to use these programs to express basic wants and needs—e.g., "cookie," "juice," "outside." Nonetheless, multiple studies and research reviews show AAC programs to be effective in moving severely autistic individuals from purely behavioral expressions of wants and needs (reaching, grabbing, cries of distress) toward intentional communication (see, e.g., Ganz et al., 2017; Morin et al., 2018). They have also improved the ability of some individuals to respond to basic questions. For those who previously had no clear way to communicate their needs or to answer people's questions, therefore, AAC can enable significant breakthroughs.

We conclude on a note of caution. AAC programs and assistive devices have been proliferating in classrooms, clinics, and homes, and this proliferation raises several concerns. One is the effect on everyone's incentives—particularly those of students and teachers. In general, the more efficacious the technology appears to be, and the more the user appears to be doing on his own, the more this reduces the urgency of teaching and practicing the skills that the technology is replacing, augmenting or assisting—whether speech, handwriting, unassisted touch typing, or vocabulary and grammar. It is essential that augmentative, alternative, and assistive technology be treated only as such—namely, as augmentative, alternative, and assistive—and not as grounds for cutting back on teaching and practice. This is particularly important in today's education world, where there is so much pressure 1) to believe that academic achievement is possible without direct instruction, and 2) to put students through the motions of demonstrating understanding and achievement even where little understanding or achievement has actually occurred.

Therefore, regardless of how effectively the child's AAC or assistive device is facilitating his communication and his ability to complete his classroom assignments, an ongoing focus on language instruction is still crucial—even if that instruction is wholly or partially mediated through the AAC program (or assistive device) itself. If the child is using a program with limited vocabulary and no grammatical function words, the adults who work with her should look for opportunities to transition her to a more advanced program with more vocabulary and an option to type on a keyboard. If and when she makes this transition, she should be encouraged, when ready, to use the keyboard option as much as possible, since written communication—as opposed to picture/icon based communication—is more open-ended and more linguistically expressive.

Another issue relates back to intentional communication and authorship. The concern that arises with FC also arises, albeit in a much milder form, with AAC and assistive devices. To what degree is the child the intentional author of the messages that are being outputted by the communication program? Particularly when AAC communications are limited to basic wants and needs, answers to basic questions, or basic communicative routines, it can be unclear, when the child clicks out, say, "I want juice," or "I am fine," or "How are you?", whether he is intentionally combining words whose meanings and sequences he understands, or is instead being guided by a rote memorization of various associations between certain key words and button strokes, on one hand, and certain routines or consequences, on the other. In some cases, the child may appear more linguistically capable than he really is, and this may distort people's expectations, sometimes to his detriment.

Word prediction raises similar concerns. A person who struggles to come up with appropriate words or to put words together into grammatical sentences may be tempted to click on a word suggestion rather than to continue typing letter by letter—even if none of the suggestions corresponds to what he would have typed independently. Once again, it may be hard to discern the child's actual linguistic skills or what he truly intends to communicate.

To reduce these concerns, supervisors must ensure that users of AAC and assistive technologies aren't simply following rote routines or rotely clicking on word selections. Where possible, routines should be diversified, writing assignments should be based on careful assessments of the child's vocabulary and syntax skills, and supervisors and communication partners should play an active role in ensuring that the child is fully engaged when using her communication program.

At the same time, as the troubling story of FC reminds us, the child's aides and AAC partners should be vigilant about whether they themselves might be unwittingly influencing his messages—especially those who spend the most time with him and who, in a sometimes intense desire to be helpful and foster progress, might be tempted, however unconsciously and unintentionally, to lead him along.

References

American Association on Intellectual and Developmental Disabilities (2019). https://www.aaidd.org/news-policy/policy/position-statements/facilitated-communication-and-rapid-prompting-method?fbclid=IwAR2futUBpErm5Om eQfy6o393qRDGXq7OB0ayOTmWYLEqwLfiRf3p0kjcVYwA

American Speech-Language-Hearing Association (2018). ASHA Practice Policy, Facilitated Communication. https://www.asha.org/policy/ps2018-00352/

Blakeslee, S. (2002, November 19). A boy, a mother and a rare map of autism's world. *The New York Times*, Section F, p. 1.

Bondy, A., & Frost, L. (1985). *Picture Exchange Communication System* (PECS). Pyramid Educational Consultants.

Cable, N. N., & Margulies, J. (2004). *Autism is a world*. [Television broadcast]. CNN.

Chandler, M.A. (2017, February 28). Parents want to give their autistic children a voice in schools, but scientists call their technique 'false hope.' *Washington Post*. https://www.washingtonpost.com/local/social-issues/parents-of-autistic-children-are-pushing-schools-to-allow-controversial-communication-techniques/2017/02/28/1bd33da2-ed6a-11e6-9973-c5efb7ccfb0d_story.html

Colby, I. (2016, May 19). This nonspeaking teenager wrote an incredibly profound letter explaining autism. *Washington Post*. https://www.washingtonpost. com/news/inspired-life/wp/2016/05/19/this-non-speaking-teen-wrote-an-incredibly-profound-letter-to-police-about-autism/

Cooperman, K. & Neihausen, R. (2017, November 19). *The night of too many stars*. [Television broadcast.]. HBO.

Chen G. M., Yoder K. J., Ganzel B. L., Goodwin M. S. & Belmonte M. K. (2012). Harnessing repetitive behaviours to engage attention and learning in a novel therapy for autism: An exploratory analysis. *Frontiers in Psychology* (3):12. https://doi.org/10.3389/fpsyg.2012.00012

Curwen, T. (2013, December 21). In the 'silent prison' of autism, Ido Kedar speaks out. *Los Angeles Times*.

Dretzin, R. (Director). (2017). *Far from the tree* [Film]. Ark Media, Flux Films, Participant.

Fazio, M. (2020, January 6). 17-year-old Highland Park boy with nonverbal autism blogs to reach others like him. *Chicago Tribune*. https://www. chicagotribune.com/news/breaking/ct-teen-nonverbal-autism-spelling-blog-20200103-bhk5zwz35rbm5k4mkkwih4lxem-story.html

Frontline & WGBH Educational Foundation. (1993). *Prisoners of silence*. [Television broadcast]. PBS.

Friðriksson, F. (2009). *A mother's courage: Talking back to autism*. Frontier Filmworks, in association with Klikk Production.

Ganz, J. B., Morin, K. L., Foster, M. J., Vannest, K. J., Genç Tosun, D., Gregori, E. V., & Gerow, S. L. (2017). High-technology augmentative and alternative communication for individuals with intellectual and developmental disabilities and complex communication needs: A meta-analysis. *Augmentative and Alternative Communication*, 33(4), 224–238. https://doi.org/10.1080/07434618. 2017.1373855

Gilpeer, V., & Grodin, E. (2021). *I have been buried under years of dust: A memoir of autism and hope*. William Morrow.

Hyman, S. L., Levy, S. E., Myers, S. M., & Council on Children with Disabilities, Section on Developmental and Behavioral Pediatrics (2020). Identification, evaluation, and management of children with autism spectrum disorder. *Pediatrics, 145*(1), e20193447. https://doi.org/10.1542/peds.2019-3447

Jaswal, V. K., Wayne, A., & Golino, H. (2020). Eye-tracking reveals agency in assisted autistic communication. *Scientific Reports, 10*(1), 7882. https://doi.org/10.1038/s41598-020-64553-9

Kedar, I. (2018, September 23). I was born unable to speak, and a disputed treatment saved me. *Wall Street Journal.* https://www.wsj.com/articles/i-was-born-unable-to-speak-and-a-disputed-treatment-saved-me-1537723821

Kim, Y. (2020). Kids with autism learn to speak with hands, by spelling to communicate. *USA Today.* https://www.usatoday.com/videos/news/education/2020/01/02/people-autism-learn-speak-hands/2062752001/

Lenker, M. L. (2017, November 19) Jon Stewart gracefully highlights autism awareness when segment doesn't go as planned. *Entertainment Weekly.* https://ew.com/tv/2017/11/19/jon-stewart-autism-awareness-carly-fleischmann/

Lilienfeld, S. O., Marshall, J., Todd, J. T., & Shane, H. C. (2015). The persistence of fad interventions in the face of negative scientific evidence: Facilitated communication for autism as a case example. *Evidence-Based Communication Assessment and Intervention* 8(2). 62-101. https://doi.org/10.1080/17489539.2014.976332

Mann, L. B., (2005). Oscar Nominee: Documentary or Fiction? *Washington Post.* https://www.washingtonpost.com/archive/lifestyle/wellness/2005/02/22/oscar-nominee-documentary-or-fiction/f576a9ae-d062-4a68-9726-92a6d97efa0d/

Miller, Stuart. (2021, April 9). It took a woman with autism 25 years to find her voice. Now she's telling her story. *Washington Post.* https://www.washingtonpost.com/entertainment/books/it-took-a-woman-with-autism-25-years-to-find-her-voice-now-shes-telling-her-story/2021/04/07/22b5e316-97a4-11eb-a6d0-13d207aadb78_story.html?fbclid=IwAR15U0wY8HdCe0HInozJKFHPRDfBfVQaWC_jEzSu4hdari9bXFOjyvsG7Dw

Morgenstern, Joe (2021, January 7). 'The Reason I Jump' Review: Brightening the autism spectrum. *Wall Street Journal.* https://www.wsj.com/articles/the-reason-i-jump-review-brightening-the-autism-spectrum-11610058777

Morin, K. L., Ganz, J. B., Gregori, E. V., Foster, M. J., Gerow, S. L., Genç-Tosun, D., & Hong, E. R. (2018). A systematic quality review of high-tech AAC interventions as an evidence-based practice. *Augmentative and Alternative Communication*, 34(2), 104–117. https://doi.org/10.1080/07434618.2018.1458900

Mukhopadhyay, S. (2008). *Understanding autism through rapid prompting method.* Outskirts Press.

Mukhopadhyay, T. (2011). *The mind tree: A miraculous child breaks the silence of autism.* Arcade.

Ostrolenk, A., Forgeot d'Arc, B., Jelenic, P., Samson, F., & Mottron, L. (2017). Hyperlexia: Systematic review, neurocognitive modelling, and outcome. *Neuroscience and biobehavioral reviews, 79,* 134–149. https://doi.org/10.1016/j.neubiorev.2017.04.029

Reis, H. (2017, March 13). Those who doubt rapid prompting method should come meet me. *Washington Post.* https://www.washingtonpost.com/opinions/those-who-doubt-rapid-prompting-method-should-come-meet-me/2017/03/13/1d154f58-035d-11e7-9d14-9724d48f5666_story.html?fbclid=IwAR04mhOlhhEIBzeqL70g8wvok0HnB_LGZI4P3M6BDZI-wvAgOXIc3KDnrfE

Rooy, R. (Director). (2017). Deej [Film]. America Reframed, Season 5 Episode 14. Public Broadcasting Service.

Rothwell, J., (Producer) & Higashida, N. (Screenwriter), (2021). *The reason I jump.* [Motion picture]. Kino Lorber, Inc.

Sitz, L. (2020, April 2). What we can learn about this covid-19 time from a nonspeaking autistic teen. *Washington Post.* 4/2/2020. https://www.washingtonpost.com/lifestyle/2020/04/02/what-we-can-learn-about-this-covid-19-time-non-speaking-autistic-teen/

The Late Show with Stephen Colbert (2018, January 13). [Video file] https://www.facebook.com/colbertlateshow/videos/carly-fleischmann-gives-late-night-tv-a-try/1305664662911615/

Wurzburg, G. (Director). (2010). *Wretches and jabberers* [Film]. State of the Art, Inc.

CHAPTER 8
HARNESSING STRENGTHS TO ADDRESS WEAKNESSES

"I think there is too much emphasis on deficits and not enough emphasis on developing abilities." (Temple Grandin, *Thinking in Pictures*, p. 100).

This chapter focuses on the cognitive strengths of autism and how to leverage them to address or bypass weaknesses. While we've already broached this question in earlier chapters—in parts of our discussions of language, literacy, and academic instruction—here we'll take more of a strengths-centered approach. That is, we'll go through the various strengths that commonly occur with autism and explore ways to tap them to help autistic individuals compensate for weaknesses and/or lead happy, productive lives.

As we discussed in the previous chapter, even the most severely autistic individuals often show skills in categorization and sorting, in jigsaw puzzles, in numerical calculations, and/or in rote memorization. These last two are the kinds of skills that K12 professionals often dismiss as rote and mindless. Yet, however subconscious their underlying processes are, and however narrow these processes may appear to be, each is a skill that therapists, teachers, and even individuals with autism themselves can build upon.

Other autistic strengths are flipsides of autism's cognitive weaknesses. The flipside of difficulty seeing the big picture (weak central coherence) is an ability to focus on details and to disregard their broader context— along with any distortions or biases that may come along for the ride.

The flipside to difficulty shifting attention and attending to social stimuli is the ability to sustain deep focus in non-social areas of interest.

Also frequently found in autism is the ability to detect or create systematic patterns (systematizing), and the ability to work out deliberately through language and logic the various phenomena (particularly social phenomena) where intuition falls short.

In specific individuals, some of these skills may manifest early on in life as specific talents: hyperlexia (the precocious interest in letters and ability to recognize words), perfect pitch (the ability to identify musical notes out of context), and the ability to mimic other people's gestures and speaking patterns.

Over time other talents may emerge: in proofreading (spotting minute errors within long passages of dense print); in drafting; in photorealistic drawing and painting; in mechanics, computer programming, and mathematics; in music; in nonfiction writing; in foreign languages; and, even, in acting. Accomplished autistic adults include, among others, animal scientist and cattle-handling equipment designer Temple Grandin; sound engineer, auto mechanic, and all-round techie John Elder Robison; and numerical and linguistic savant Daniel Tammet, who notes, in reference to the flipside of weak central coherence:

> A side benefit of processing information in parts instead of holistically is that having a very good eye for detail, I proofread very well. On Sunday morning, reading pages of the day's newspaper at the table, I would annoy my parents no end by pointing out every grammatical and spelling error I found.
>
> (*Born on a Blue Day*, p. 41).

As for the more artistically inclined, accomplished autistic individuals include architectural artist Stephen Wiltshire; painter Jessica Park; writer and artist Gilles Tréhin; writer and music critic Tim Page; and actors Darryl Hannah, Dan Aykroyd, and Anthony Hopkins.

We should note that some of these individuals were not diagnosed until well into adulthood and that most (though not all) are at the mild end of the autism spectrum. Even the most mildly affected of these individuals, however, report autism-related challenges in key areas like social interaction and big-picture thinking. Some of them, furthermore, have written memoirs in which they showcase both these weaknesses and various autism-related strengths. Excerpts from these memoirs, therefore, will provide most of the source material for this chapter.

In the forthcoming sections we will survey, one by one, the various autistic strengths, discussing how each can best be leveraged in a strength-centered approach to autism.

Sorting, rote memorization, puzzles, and numerical skills

When it comes to sorting, rote memorization, puzzles, and numerical calculations, all these simple, often repetitive activities, limited though they may appear to be, have broader applications. First, they can be calming. Sorting objects by category, doing jigsaw puzzles, performing numerical calculations—each of these is a potentially absorbing pastime that can help distract people away from the external stimuli or internal sentiments that disturb them. Children can be taught to use these activities as strategies for emotional self-regulation.

Categorization skills can be leveraged for several additional purposes. They can be used to help a child learn word meanings—e.g., by having her sort objects or pictures into what is and isn't a ball, or a dog, or a plant. They can be used to enhance cognitive flexibility—specifically, the ability to switch back and forth between different criteria—when we have her, for example, sort cards (say from a SET deck) first by shape, then by color, then by number. This and other grouping activities may help her think beyond specific objects to more abstract features (from a specific red truck to redness), or to holistic combinations of specific features (mapping redness, small size, and truck shape to a picture of a small red truck).

Jigsaw puzzles can be chosen for specific content—as with number and letter puzzles, map puzzles, and puzzles of informational diagrams. As he does the puzzle, the child may incidentally take in its content. At the very least, it's hard to fit the pieces together without paying some attention to the visual details, such that a small amount of prompting may be all that is needed to direct his attention to the bigger picture.

Numerical calculation skills, discounted though they often are by K12 professionals, are both a foundation for, and a buy-in to, higher level math.

If a child perseverates on multi-digit addition problems or long division problems, good for him. Gradually we might introduce additional mathematical complications (decimals, fractions) or areas of application (calendars, money), helping the child expand both his mathematical range and his mathematically based conceptual understanding.

Rote memorization can also be leveraged. Consider Tim Page, the autistic writer and music critic. He reports having memorized, as a young boy, the names and dates of all the US presidents and their wives such that, on request, he could recite them in reverse chronological order. While rote memorization skills are widely dismissed in K12 education, they can, as we discussed earlier in connection with extended discourse and reading, seed stores of background knowledge that aid higher level comprehension and higher level thinking. If we take a child like the young Tim Page and gradually expand his knowledge base beyond presidents' names, dates, and spouses toward other events in US history, we can help him build a more meaningful foundation of historical knowledge. The same goes for topics in science—another common area of rote memorization in autism. A child who knows by heart the names of all the major moons of Jupiter might be encouraged to think about connections between their sizes, the shapes of their orbits, and how closely they orbit Jupiter. The ability to commit vast stores of facts to memory should be seen as an educational plus. The key is to encourage the child to keep expanding that knowledge and to organize it in meaningful ways.

Acquiring stores of knowledge potentially boosts broader life skills. Daniel Tammet, the numerical and linguistic savant, reports eventually acquiring a "database" of experiences that "I could reference in all manner of future situations." It gave him confidence, he reports "in my ability to cope with whatever life might bring to me." (2007, p. 142).

Systematizing

One way to encourage students to broaden their memorized knowledge is to tap into their propensity to systematize—to detect or create systematic patterns. We might take as a starting point the template (however narrow it might be) into which they've organized their current knowledge on a particular topic. We then gradually introduce new material that naturally connects to this template. For example, if a child has memorized the names and dates of all the US presidents in chronological order, we might help him overlay the chronology, bit by bit, with additional facts about each president: which state he was from; which political party; who his opponents were; which issues dominated the election; and, eventually, information about the broader circumstances of each presidential term—e.g., newly admitted states; economic issues; demographics; conflicts.

As we'll see below, some aspects of systematizing, particularly the tendency to seek out rules, can also be tapped to boost conversation skills.

Narrow interests and intense focus

Narrow interests and intense focus have several potential benefits. In Chapter 3, for example, we saw that one of the strategies for fostering moments of joint attention—moments in which we and the child are focusing on the same thing—is to join the child in her preferred activities. One way to capitalize on the narrow interests in autism, then, is to give the child opportunities to pursue these interests and then join her. This raises two challenges, however. First, the activity may consume all the child's attention, leaving none for us. Second, she may find us an unwelcome intruder. We might therefore set things up so that she can't avoid interacting with us: perhaps some of the key items are out of her reach or hard for her to manipulate on her own.

Allowing children to pursue their intense interests can also ameliorate their behaviors. As we noted earlier, a common source of behavior issues—including apparent laziness or defiance—is boredom. As techie and autistic advocate John Elder Robison reports in his memoir *Look Me in the Eye*:

> Rather than take a close and sympathetic look at me, it proved easier and less controversial for the professionals to say I was just lazy, or angry, or defiant. But none of those words led to a solution for my problems.
> (2008, p. 90).

Robison eventually became so disengaged that he dropped out of high school.

Intense interests, like rote activities, can also help a child calm down and stay calm. Once during one of my math-obsessed son's bouts of agitation, back in his early teens, I whipped out Gelfand's *Algebra* and we went through Pascal's Triangle. Step by mathematical step, his woes abated and his breathing slowed to deep, regular breaths. If there is mathematical mindfulness for the mathematically minded, perhaps there is engineering mindfulness for the engineering-minded, scientific mindfulness for the scientifically minded, and so forth.

But the benefits of intense focus extend far beyond these immediate effects. As animal scientist and autistic advocate Temple Grandin has written, instead of trying to "stamp out" autistic fixations, teachers should broaden and channel them:

> For example, if a child becomes infatuated with boats, then use boats to motivate him to read and do math. Read books about boats and do arithmetic problems calculating boat speed. Fixations provide great motivation.
>
> (1995, p. 100).

Grandin also cites seminal autism researcher Leo Kanner, one of the first medical professionals to identify autism. Kanner proposed that, for some autistic individuals, the path to success is channeling fixations into careers.

Channeling fixations, indeed, is what led to many of the successes reported in the various autobiographies. For example, here is Robison recounting the skills he developed through his interest in the electronics of musical sound effects:

> I worked hard to imagine the results of my designs, and I refined my thought process as I visualized a circuit, then built it for real, and compared my imagined results with the real results. Gradually, I become able to visualize the results of my designs with a fair degree of accuracy. My earlier problems with math texts stopped holding me back as I developed the ability to visualize and even hear the flow of sounds through my circuits.
>
> ...I somehow figured out how to visualize the complex calculus functions that describe the behavior of electronic circuits in time.

> For example, I saw the pure tones of a guitar going into a circuit, and I saw the modified wave—immeasurably more complex—coming out. I understood how changes in the circuit topology or component values would alter the waves. And, most remarkably, I developed the ability to translate those waves I saw in my mind into sounds...
>
> (2008, pp. 64–65).

Robison explicitly connects these skills, which ultimately landed him a series of jobs and finally a career, to the capacity for narrowly focused concentration that characterizes autism, in particular, what was then called "Asperger's syndrome":

> I've met other Aspergian people with savantlike abilities like mine. In my opinion, part of this ability—which I seem to have been born with—comes from my extraordinary powers of concentration. I have extremely sharp focus.
>
> (2008, p. 65).

These observations recall Malcolm Gladwell's discussion in *Outliers* about the role of intense practice—10,000 hours is Gladwell's number—in attaining complete mastery of complex skills. Robison's story—and the prospect of how things would have turned out had he not found ways to pursue his interests—also highlights the potential downside of prioritizing weaknesses over strengths. Neglecting a strength can have huge opportunity costs. While strengths and interests may be narrower in autism than elsewhere, the payoffs to pursuing them may be significantly higher—and may bring significantly greater gratification to all concerned.

Even at the level of basic skills, leveraging interests has payoffs. We see this with Grandin's experience learning to read. Her reading skills, she reports, took off only after her mother set aside children's beginner books and introduced books on topics that Grandin found interesting. Indeed, some of the reading interventions we discussed in Chapter 5 have turned out to be especially effective when used with high-interest texts.

Ultimately, of course, we want to broaden autistic interests. This is, admittedly, a challenge: Many of these interests are intense fixations. As Liane Holliday Willey reports in *Pretending to Be Normal*:

> I argued with my teachers when they tried to convince me to read something other than western lore, telling them it was my goal to read every book in the library on every western character I could find.
>
> (2014, p. 40).

How might a teacher broaden the range of books that a student like Willey is willing to read? As a first step, we might take a closer look at what she is reading. Might the content be broader than we realize? In addition, perhaps each next book, however much it overlaps in content with its predecessors, is still presenting her with new vocabulary, new examples of figurative language, novel sentence structures, and novel psychosocial phenomena—such that her linguistic comprehension and her social learning can continue to grow. If, however, she seems to have stalled, we might look for ways to connect Western lore, say, to related events in Western history or to related lore from elsewhere in the world. If she resists, we might remind ourselves that the library has only so many books on Western lore and tell her that once she exhausts them she must move on.

Hyperlexia

Many autistic children, unlike Willey, show little interest or even ability with respect to extended written prose of any sort. Given how much of the academic curriculum consists of written texts, this is a far more fundamental problem than Willey's fixation on Western lore. One potential first step involves leveraging a different sort of narrow interest, namely hyperlexia. Hyperlexia, recall, is a precocious interest in letters and a precocious ability to recognize printed words. Although not exclusive to autism, it is estimated to characterize anywhere from 6% to 21% of autistic children (Ostrolenk et al., 2017). Even though autistic hyperlexia is often not accompanied by comprehension and therefore risks being dismissed as merely rote, it can open a pathway to more meaningful engagement with written texts.

It can also open a pathway to language more generally, as we noted in Chapter 3. For hyperlexic kids, text may be a more engaging medium than speech. Beyond the attraction of letters, there is the fact that written words, unlike spoken words, stick around. At the same time, the production of written words—writing or typing them out—is dynamic and potentially eye-catching. Printing words slowly and clearly, Clara Park was able to keep her daughter in suspense and hold her attention—while also making sure that Jessy's eyes followed each word as it took shape. As we noted earlier, Park also used written language to highlight the more elusive features of word pronunciation, using specific letters to direct her daughter's attention to the consonant sounds that she tended to mispronounce or omit.

The challenge in using written language, particularly with those who are intensely interested in letters, is to ensure that the child doesn't just learn printed words as sequences of abstract symbols, which in hyperlexia is often the default. We must find ways help him attach meaning to the words—for example, by illustrating them with pictures, as Park did, or by using them to label objects around the house. These word-to-object and word-to-picture associations can potentially jumpstart an understanding of words as meaningful symbols.

Perfectionism

Another manifestation of the narrow, all-consuming focus in autism is an obsessive perfectionism. As Willey reports regarding her writing process:

> Sometimes, the care I give to words can throw me into an obsessive-compulsive ritual. I typically end up spending far too much time selecting which word to use and too much time reworking a sentence so that it looks and feels and sounds right. All this translates into a fixation that can bring my thought process to a halt. When I get like this, I cannot concentrate on anything else, not a thing, until I have found the perfect term or phrase I need. This tendency can make my experiences with the written word tedious, at least in terms of time and other missed opportunities, but never meaningless or futile.
> (2014, p. 36).

Never meaningless or futile. In Chapter 6, we discussed several obstacles students with autism often have to turning in work on time. One hurdle that we didn't mention is obsessive perfectionism. For some students, the urge to find the perfect word or phrase might outweigh the pressure to meet a deadline. Yet, despite the potential obstacles that such perfectionism presents, so long as it doesn't interfere with those deadlines that are truly important, it isn't something to discourage. After all, as much as real life expects timely completion, it also often expects thoroughness, flawlessness, and polish.

Mechanical strengths

Mechanical strengths show up in several of the autism autobiographies. These strengths may be side effects of detail focus and systematizing; they also bypass social weaknesses. Autistic individuals may well find it easier to figure out how mechanical devices work than how people work. They may sense that mechanical devices offer more accessible and gratifying answers to "how things work" questions than people do. This is what drove Stephen Shore to take apart watches, radios, and bicycles—by some point in high school scoring over the 99th percentile on a mechanical abilities test.

John Elder Robison goes further, citing machines as a satisfying substitute for people:

> Machines were never mean to me. They challenged me when I tried to figure them out. They never tricked me, and they never hurt my feelings. I was in charge of the machines. I liked that. I felt safe around them.
>
> (2008, p. 12).

Machines were what drove Robison's career as he progressed from taking things apart, to putting things together in a work area in his basement, to exploring sound engineering and designing guitars for the rock band KISS, to designing electronic games for Milton Bradley and, ultimately, to running his own automobile service and restoration company, a capstone career that allows him to deal with people entirely on his own terms.

While Robison left high school early and pursued these talents mostly on his own, his accomplishments illustrate the benefits of giving students opportunities to explore their talents at school. Had Robison's talents been recognized and encouraged there, he might not have dropped out.

Associative thinking

In tension with the systematizing and logical reasoning proclivities in autism is what some have observed as a tendency toward associative thinking—a thought process that sometimes overrides or substitutes for logic. One autistic man reportedly continued his usual laundry routine even after the dryer broke down, taking his still-wet clothes out of the dryer and putting them into his dresser. For him, the dresser step followed the dryer step not because it was the logical next step, but merely because it was the next step in a sequence of associations.

But associative thinking is not necessarily a weakness. Here is Temple Grandin on how her mind can wander

> ...from fence construction to a particular welding shop where I'd seen posts being cut and Old John, the welder, making gates... to a series of short scenes of building gates on several projects I've worked on... [to] having a good time listening to John and the construction crew tell war stories, such as the time the backhoe dug into a nest of rattlesnakes and the machine was abandoned for two weeks because everybody was afraid to go near it.
>
> (1995, p. 25).

And here is Daniel Tammet on the associative nature of his thought processes:

> I often found my mind wandering, in part because I remember so much of what I see and read and a chance word or name in the middle of a conversation can cause a floor of associations in my mind like a domino effect. Today, when I hear the name Ian a mental picture of someone I know with this name comes spontaneously into my head, without me having to think about it at all. Then the picture jumps to one of the Mini he drives, which in turn causes me to picture various scenes from the classic film *The Italian Job*.
>
> (2007, p. 75).

While associative thinking is problematic when it overrides important logical considerations—like what to do when your clothes are still wet—it may also help fuel creative brainstorming. Although the jury is out on the validity of so-called creativity tests, some of what these measure is the ability to move beyond logic and make other kinds of associations. Open-ended creative writing assignments, as we noted in Chapter 5, often present difficulties to autistic students. For those whose minds, like those of Grandin and Tammet, are prone to associative meanderings, we might provide a few starter words and invite them to free-associate.

Ability to use structure

In her memoir *Thinking in Pictures*, Grandin expresses indebtedness to teachers who ran what she calls "an old fashioned, highly structured classroom." (1995, p. 97). In earlier chapters we emphasized this need for structure. We cited it, specifically, in the context of structured therapies like Applied Behavioral Analysis (ABA), structured curricula like Direct Instruction and Precision Teaching, and structured approaches to reading like graphic organizers.

As *Thinking in Pictures* and other memoirs suggest, however, the need of autistic individuals for structure can evolve over time into an ability to create structures of their own. Consider, for example, Stephen Shore. Shore, recall from Chapter 6, has reflected in his memoir *Beyond the Wall* on how his poor motor control in penmanship contrasted with his ability to take apart a wristwatch:

> Perhaps it is because the structure is inherent within the watch innards themselves, whereas in writing or drawing in free-hand, I am forced to provide the structure… [H]aving to provide that structure from within myself makes it impossible for me to do these activities well.
>
> (2003, p. 60).

Noting later that clear, coherent structure gives him a framework for creativity, Shore reveals that he ultimately developed the ability to create that structure himself. Here's how he describes his notes for an information technology class:

> I took notes in a multilayered outline format using up to six different colored pens. For example, the main idea was in black, subtopics in red, divisions of those in green, and further

prose-based explanations in light blue. The levels of indentation combined with the different colors helped me to map and retain key information for the class.

(2003, p. 91).

Shore's strategies recall one of the reading interventions we discussed in Chapter 5: the TWA (Think While After) approach. Here, teachers prompt students to reread passages and highlight the main idea in pink, the details in green, and the nonessential text in orange. As we noted, a study involving students with autism found not only that TWA was effective in improving reading comprehension, but also that students enjoyed the systematic rules for highlighting, apparently appreciating the structure it imposed on the reading process.

In another of Shore's courses where the structure was "difficult to grasp," a course on qualitative research, Shore came up with a different structure-imposing technique:

Only after I spent several hours diagramming the process with geometric shapes and arrows did I gain a sense of where the different components of a qualitative study were placed and their relation to each other.

(2003, p. 91).

Others on the spectrum may also have it in them to meet their need for structure on their own. In Shore's case, the necessary skills emerged by college. For those who have a latent ability but have yet to fully develop and apply it, are there ways that teachers might speed up the process? One finding of the TWA study was that students continued to use the text-highlighting strategies even after the intervention ended, provided the necessary materials (the highlighters) were still available. This suggests that simple modeling plus materials may sometimes suffice. That is, teachers may need only to demonstrate such strategies as color-coded highlighting or annotating texts with geometric shapes and arrows, and to provide the necessary materials, in order for autistic students to adopt these as routine measures for creating the structures they depend on. Attaining the ability to address a key need on one's own, obviously, is an empowering accomplishment.

Ability to use rules for social and conversational interactions

One area that particularly cries out for structure, as far as individuals with autism are concerned, is the social sphere. As Temple Grandin puts it, in the absence of intuition "the proper behavior during all social interactions had to be learned by intellect" (1995, p. 95). Recalling what Stephen Shore reports with respect to unstructured phenomena in general, Grandin highlights the need for outside guidance in the social world. She stresses how she has depended on sympathetic teachers and mentors; how "[p]eople with autism desperately need guides to instruct and educate them so they will survive in the social jungle." But she also notes that her social interaction skills have improved with experience and makes clear that she has figured out ways to construct her own social guidelines:

> I rely on pure logic, like an expert computer program, to guide my behavior. I categorize rules according to their logical importance. It is a complex algorithmic decision-making tree. There is a process of using my intellect and logical decision-making for every social decision. Emotion does not guide my decision; it is pure computing.
>
> (1995, p. 103).

Other autistic adults have also reported learning to work out explicitly what comes naturally to most people, starting with the most basic interactions. Here is John Elder Robison:

> In Pittsburgh, I finally started learning how to make friends. I knew now that kids and dogs were different. I didn't try to pet kids anymore, or poke them with sticks. And at nine years of age, I had a life-changing revelation.
>
> I figured out how to talk to other children.
>
> I suddenly realized that when a kid said, "Look at my Tonka truck," he expected an answer that made sense in the context of what he had said. Here were some things I might have said prior to this revelation in response to "Look at my Tonka truck":

a) "I have a helicopter."

b) "I want some cookies."

c) "My mom is mad at me today."

d) "I rode a horse at the fair."

I was so used to living inside my own world that I answered with whatever I had been thinking…. All of a sudden, I realized that the response the kid was looking for, the correct answer, was

e) "That's a neat truck! Can I hold it?"

Even more important, I realized that responses A, B, C, and D would annoy the other kid.

(2008, p. 20).

Tammet similarly reports having to deliberately work out appropriate responses:

If a person says to you: "I'm not having a good day," I have learned that the speaker expects you to say something like: "Oh, really," and then to ask what it is that is causing the bad day.

(2007, p. 76).

Willey, too, has derived formulas for social exchanges, even for routine interactions with her husband:

Like other people make lists to remind themselves to pick up milk or get the mail, I make lists that tell me how to act. On my list are things like—*hold Tom's hand for five minutes every day; … say 'Excuse me' instead of 'I have to get out of here now!'; count to five before replying; hug Tom three times today.* When I review my list, I remember how I need to act.

(2014, p. 84).

In discussing the more complex situations he faced as an adult, Robison notes that he still sometimes gets into social trouble because his approach is logical while conversation, of course, often isn't. Robison went so far as to study computerized conversational agents that engage with humans— examining the logical pathways that these programs follow to produce suitable responses, and observing that the responses didn't always sound natural, even to him. While his own attempts show a thought process that is similarly logical, and while his responses aren't perfect, they are nonetheless not entirely off base:

> For example, last week my friend Laurie said, "One of my girlfriends is having an affair. And the guy rides a motorcycle just like yours."
>
> Laurie's statement posed a problem. Unlike most interactions, ours had not started with a question. Should I respond with an opinion about the statement? Or should I ask a question myself? ...
>
> ...
>
> I knew she wanted a relevant response—something connected to what she had just said, more than just "Oh.".... It occurred to me that what I needed to do was to keep gathering information until I could frame an intelligent conversation. The successful conversation computer programs did that. So I asked a question.
>
> "Which girlfriend is that?"
>
> Laurie looked surprised. "Why would you want to know that?" she said.
>
> (2008, p. 189–190).

Shore also deliberately worked out strategies for tricky conversations—for example, conversations in which his interlocutors baffle him with emotional reactions. To manage such scenarios, Shore has filed away handy formulas for simultaneously expressing concern and soliciting guidance on how to respond:

> Some phrases that I keep in my response repertoire for these situations include "What can I do to make you feel better about this?" or "Look, I sense that you have some strong feelings about _____. Can we talk about it?"
>
> (2003, p. 122).

Shore adds that, while this "algorithm" is helpful, it doesn't approach the facility that non-autistic people have with emotional interactions.

Conversation skills are a major target of autism therapies. But it's not clear that therapists and social curriculum developers are any better at codifying the slippery rules of conversational interactions than these higher functioning autistic individuals are. Indeed, even in the most explicit of the standard autism curricula we have reviewed, the ABA language curricula, the rules pertaining to conversation are superficial, formulaic, and limited. In addition, as Willey notes, much as she appreciates learning rules, people frequently break them:

> As long as things followed a set of rules, I could play along. Rules were—and are—great friends of mine. I like rules... Trouble is, rules change, and if they do not, people break them. With broken rules forcing cracks in my boundaries, I was left to develop my own. My rules were different than any I had memorized before.
>
> (2014, p. 43).

Indeed, the rules that higher functioning individuals come up with for themselves may be more meaningful, easier to follow, and more suited to their specific needs than much of what the rest of the world has come up with for them. In addition to trying to teach them rules, therefore, we might also encourage them to create rules of their own—in the same way that, as suggested earlier, we might encourage them to create their own organizational structures.

One person who doesn't report deriving his own social rules is the autistic writer and music critic Tim Page. Page was instead inspired, in stumbling across Emily Post's Etiquette, to adopt someone else's social rules. Here is what he has to say in his memoir *Parallel Play* about the book that "helped pull me into the human race":

> Post explained the world to me. *Etiquette* offered clearly stated reasons for gallantry, gentility, and scrupulousness—reasons that I could understand, respect, and implement. It suggested ways to inaugurate conversations without launching into a lecture, reminded me of the importance of listening as well as speaking, and convinced me that manners, properly understood, existed to make other people feel comfortable... My confusion and ferocity began to be disciplined into courtesy; I reveled in Post's guidance and absorbed her lessons.
>
> (2009, p. 74).

Page's experience shows us the importance of motivating rules by explaining why they're important. What made Page take Post's rules seriously was realizing that they're intended to make others feel comfortable. Someone else, of course, might need a different reason to follow social etiquette.

Another approach to social interaction is to explore what underlies it: human psychology. Shore reports that psychology courses helped him better understand people's behavior and body language:

> When I become aware of the meaning of "body language" or nonverbal communication through a psychology class, I become fascinated with this mode of communication. This is probably because I have to analyze it pretty closely to understand this facet of interaction. In an educational psychology course, I did an extensive empirical study on non-verbal communication around the campus… To this day I enjoy reading books on nonverbal communication.
>
> (2003, p. 90).

Grandin, similarly, reports that she had no idea that eye movements had meaning, and that people communicate feelings with their eyes, until she read a monograph on social behavior and autism by Simon Baron-Cohen (*Mindblindness*; 1997).

In nearly every other subject in the humanities and social sciences, key aspects of human behavior are assumed as common background knowledge. But psychology, particularly behavioral and social psychology, makes no such assumptions. Psychology classes potentially open opportunities for autistic individuals to unpack and systematize the factors that underlie social behavior. This, in turn, can help can them refine the various rules for interactions—whether these are rules learned from therapists or etiquette books, or rules they've come up with on their own.

Strengths in interacting with diverse people

From the energy that these autistic memoirists have put into behaving appropriately and understanding other people, we can sense an abiding desire for social connection. We sense this even in Willey, who writes that she never craved deep ties with others. Willey still strove to be friendly to acquaintances and passersby, reached out to fellow loners and misfits, and ultimately got married.

Robison is particularly emphatic:

> *I did not ever want to be alone.* And all those child psychologists who said "John prefers to play by himself" were dead wrong. I played by myself because I was a failure at playing with others. I was alone as a result of my own limitations, and being alone was one of the bitterest disappointments of my young life. The sting of those early failures followed me long into adulthood, even after I learned about Asperger's.
>
> (2008, p. 211).

How can we tap this social motivation and help alleviate the isolation and loneliness of individuals with autism? Some memoirs suggest some answers. Willey made overtures to fellow loners and misfits. Others have reached beyond their immediate peer groups to people of different ages and cultures. Immediate peer groups, which are often quite homogenous, tend to put autistic differences in sharper relief than groups with greater diversity. With people of different ages, cultures, and eccentricities, there are other gaps to bridge besides autism. There is also less assumed common background knowledge and more occasion for topics of conversation that are more structured and/or substantive than the informal chitchat that so challenges individuals on the spectrum. Tim Page, for example, reports being happier around older people. With one especially old woman he would talk for hours about what it was like growing up in the 1910s.

Older people are also less likely than peers to bully autistic individuals, more likely to appreciate their special interests, and more likely to be knowledgeable on topics that interest them. Shore, for example, writes:

> I have always found it easier to relate to people who are not of my age or culture. For example, during both elementary and middle school I got along much better with my sister's friends, who were about four years my senior than with kids of my own age. These people were much more interesting to me and didn't have a need

to bully. Certainly, I made friends with adults pretty easily too. This continued through junior and senior high school and in the workplace.

(2003, p. 83).

Shared interests are another basis for social connections. Grandin reports relating better to scientists and engineers, who, she says, are guided less than others are by emotion. In addition, there were the animals she worked with:

When I pressed my hand against the side of a steer, I could feel whether he was nervous, angry, or relaxed... Sometimes touching the cattle relaxed them, but it always brought me closer to the reality of their being.

(1995, p. 83).

For Robison, animals also provided companionship—a respite from loneliness. He reports feeling safe around animals, petting dogs at the park, and, once he had a dog of his own, making it his friend.

When autism interventions address social skills, they tend to emphasize interactions with peers. But these first-person testimonials suggest it might be fruitful to broaden the scope of social goals and opportunities beyond the immediate peer group. After all, once a person leaves school there's no reason why his immediate peers should dominate his social life. For autistic individuals, the more promising social companions are those offering interest-based interactions—whether they tap into Page's interest in the past, Shore's interest in other cultures, or Grandin's interests in science and engineering and in people who share her scientific and engineering mindset. This last point, shared mindsets, suggests one other potential connection: the potential connection between fellow autistics.

Strengths in more structured interactions

Another thing to bear in mind is that back-and-forth conversation, perhaps the area of greatest social weakness in autism, isn't the only way to interact. Indeed, as far as many autistic individuals are concerned, it may be the least satisfying option. Even Willey, who could follow conversations closely enough to detect grammatical errors and reply when expected to, "never came to hear what they were really saying. I never understood their vernacular... I was unable to read between the lines." (2014, p. 56).

Other types of interactions, ones that build on people's strengths, may be as much or more fulfilling. Willey, for example, discovered both a strength and a satisfaction in public speaking, routinely finishing in the top five percent in competitions. As she notes:

> Given a chance, I would much rather speak to a large group than I would to an individual or two. Small group conversations make my nerves feel like they are wearing stilts on an icy pavement. When I talk to other people, I have trouble following conversation transitions. I step on other people's words, stumbling ahead with my own thoughts, in almost every conversation I have. It was not like this when I performed monologues and oratories.
>
> (2014, p. 37).

For Willey, one-way communication was perfectly satisfying. After all, *all* communication involves connection. In addition, public speaking bypasses the difficulties she had making sense of other people's nonverbal signals:

> I never experienced apprehension or fear when I spoke in public... Maybe I enjoy speaking in front of a group because it is a one-way communication experience and, as such, something that is not affected by the complications of other people's body language and non-verbal styles.
>
> (2014, p. 37).

Wiley's preferred form of public speaking was that which allowed maximum preparation:

> Most of my public speaking fell under a category called radio and television. Basically, I would sit behind a microphone and read news copy I had written, to a panel of judges. When I competed in this context, I usually won or finished in second place. There is no question that this was my favorite thing to do...
>
> (2014, p. 37).

For Willey, these public speaking moments were also occasions to hone her own body language skills.

> I enjoyed methodically planning how I could make a script or poem more meaningful with facial expressions and eye contact and the wave of a hand or shift of my weight. It was like a puzzle I could piece together. Little did I realize it was also a wonderful way for me inadvertently to learn how to use my nonverbal communication skills...
>
> (2014, p. 37).

Presumably, having planned out and prepared what she is saying, Willey has more cognitive bandwidth for considering what to do with her body.

As for conversations, when Willey is able to participate most adeptly, it's when her contributions are "the kind of quick retorts that sounded more like a monologue I had snared from drama class, than a two-way conversation." (2014, p. 41).

Page reports a similar discrepancy between comfort in formal public speaking venues and discomfort in open-ended conversations:

> I suffer little stage fright when it comes to public speaking or appearances on radio or television—I've got these particular acts figured out—but unstructured participation in social gatherings remains agonizing, unless I know exactly what is expected from me. It would be easier for me to improvise an epic poem before a sellout crowd at Madison Square Garden than to approach an attractive stranger across the room and strike up a conversation.
>
> (2009, p. 176).

Part of what's key here is a sense of control. In a back-and-forth conversation, no speaker has unilateral power, and little can be anticipated and prepared for ahead of time. If, as both Willey and Page suggest, public speaking is so much more comfortable and socially satisfying than informal conversation, then we should offer such opportunities to others with high-functioning autism.

A related possibility is debate. Debate has the virtue of being more interactive, but it is also highly structured and allows—indeed, expects—a great deal of planning and preparation.

Back when he was a young boy, Page discovered another way to take social charge—namely, by recruiting classmates to participate in an activity that simultaneously appealed to them, tapped into his interests, and put him in the director's chair:

> In the sixth grade… I found a way to both indulge my interest in silent movies and exert direct social control over my classmates. I saved up the five dollars necessary to buy fifty feet of 8mm film, then borrowed my father's ancient Revere home-making camera…
>
> …
>
> [E]very third or fourth Saturday was consecrated to film-making, and I would invite both friends from the neighborhood and people with whom I wanted to become friends, with potential stardom as my come-on. It is a rare preteen who doesn't fantasize, at least on occasion, about becoming a movie personality and that's what I was offering in my own, localized way. I controlled the camera, I composed the script, I chose the actors, I barked the orders, I edited the film, and I invited everybody back to the house a couple of weeks later, for screening and a cast party.
>
> (2009, pp. 56-57).

Ventures like these are not generally included among the social strategies and social activities suggested to individuals with autism. Yet they, too, provide opportunities for social connection and social growth. While Page's ideas and interests are unique to him, there may be other projects that both tap autistic interests and invite collaboration—projects in which individuals with autism can play leading roles while still attracting participants who are willing to submit to their directions. Possibilities include engineering projects, science projects, or large-scale art projects like set design.

The general takeaway is this: Even if the social needs of most people are best satisfied through back-and-forth conversations with peers, it may be that, for individuals on the autism spectrum, these other types of interactions, more one-sided and formal though they are, are both more realistic and more satisfying. Therefore, even as we work to help these individuals improve their conversational and peer interactions, we should make sure they have access to alternative ways of connecting.

Detail focus and social mimicry

Perhaps one of the most surprising facts about the accomplished autistic individuals we've cited in this chapter is that three of them are actors. Doesn't acting largely involve convincing depictions of social interactions? One route to such depictions, however, is precise mimicry of social behavior. And mimicry, tapping as it does into talent for picking up details, is an area in which some autistic individuals excel.

Willey, for example, was a meticulous observer of social interactions:

> I became very aware of the smallest and most subtle aspects of my peers' movements. I took note of how they threw their long hair over their shoulders, or tucked their bangs behind their ears... I mentally recorded the way they used their eyes, how they would open them wide when they spoke loud and animated, or how they would cast them downwards if they spoke quietly or slowly. I was captivated with the way their hands moved when they spoke, how they would bend them into shapes that looked like little buildings or twirl them about as if the hands were the message. I watched people like a scientist watches an experiment.
>
> (2014, p. 42).

When attempting to fit in, Willey would channel her observations into a "sophisticated form of echolalia." Identifying the person she was most taken with,

> I would watch them intently, carefully marking their traits, until almost as easily as if I had turned on a light, I would turn their personality on in me. I can change my mannerisms and my voice and my thoughts until I am confident they match the person I want to echo... [I]t worked to keep me connected and sometimes that was all that concerned me. It was simply more efficient for

me to use the kinds of behaviors other people used, than it was for me to try and create some of my own.

(2014, p. 71).

Mimicry, like monologues and movie directing, is not included in the social strategies routinely taught to individuals with autism. But for Willey it was a relatively accessible route to social connection. For others with similar skills, therefore, social mimicry might be something to encourage.

Mimicry skills may partly explain the success of professional autistic actors like Darryl Hannah, Dan Aykroyd, and Anthony Hopkins. But such skills, even at the high-functioning end of the spectrum, are far from universal. For example, Temple Grandin, while she reports a growing awareness of subtle rhythms of interaction, is unable to imitate these rhythms. Yet she has managed to adjust her own mannerisms after watching herself. She reports that "When I look at videotapes of some of my old lectures, I can see the things I did wrong, such as using odd voice patterns." (1995, p. 101). Video self-monitoring, indeed, has turned out to be an effective tool for tweaking social behavior. Here, too, the detail focus of autism may come in handy.

Autistic individuals, Grandin adds, need to be coached like actors in a play. For those whose mimicry skills are particularly strong, drama classes may bear fruit. Willey reports taking a class on dramatic arts and public speaking—a class in which she found the greatest acceptance among peers and that was also the genesis of her public speaking ventures. It inspired her to think of language in new ways—that is, she says, as more than just a tool for expressing needs. On the other hand, Willey wonders whether a more traditional theater class that required her to act as part of a group rather than performing solo monologues would have challenged her in even more productive ways.

Drama, tapping not just into mimicry but also into rote memorization skills, offers several potential benefits to individuals with autism. Once they've memorized their lines, they can, as Willey did in her public speaking ventures, concentrate on nonverbal behaviors like body language. They also get structured practice interacting with other characters—other *dramatis personae*. Even if the theatrical dialogues are completely scripted, as they generally are outside of improvisational theater, these dialogues typically model communicative behavior that is socially appropriate, at least in terms of conversational basics.

The capacity for logical empathy and principled morality

As we've seen, many of these autistic memoirists have compensated for their deficits in social intuition by extrapolating explicit rules. Some of these rules extend beyond conversational interactions and social routines to ethical ways to treat others. Both Robison and Tammet, for example, characterize themselves as being guided by "logical empathy" rather than by automatic, intuitive perspective taking. As Tammet puts it:

> My autism can sometimes make it difficult for me to understand how other people might think or feel in any given situation. For this reason, my moral values are based more on ideas that are logical, make sense to me and that I have thought through carefully, than on the ability to "walk in another person's shoes." I know to treat each person I meet with kindness and respect...
>
> (2007, p. 225).

What emerges is a behavior code that prioritizes equity, or treating everyone equally. Further cementing this code are two other tendencies in autism. First, there is the greater immunity to social pressures, including those that can cause non-autistic people, say, to treat someone they like or want to impress more favorably than someone they perceive as occupying a lower rung on a social hierarchy. Second, there is the ability to disregard broader context, that flipside of weak central coherence, which may insulate autistic individuals from the influences of societal stereotypes and prejudices. As Robison reports regarding the customers at his auto mechanics shop, "My inability to read body language or appearance meant—in an industry rife with discrimination—that I treated everyone the same." (2008, p. 214). All this recalls psychologist Paul Bloom's book *Against Empathy*. Bloom argues that, compared to emotional empathy—fickle and bias-prone as it is—universal, rational rules are a more ethical basis for behavior.

Diminished concern about other people's opinions is another plus for "autistic morality": We find, in even the most accomplished individuals, a refreshing absence of self-aggrandizement. These people got where they are not by schmoozing, backstabbing, and self-promotion, but by developing their talents through intense concentration and hard work. In addition, some are inclined, perhaps because of their autism, to direct some of their efforts toward ethical causes that extend, not just beyond the people they're closest to or most want to impress, but beyond people in general: causes, for example, concerning treatment of animals (Temple Grandin) or carbon emissions and climate (Greta Thunberg).

Another component of this "autistic morality" is an inclination toward honesty and directness. As Willey reports, despite how fickle most people are about honest opinions, she found it easy, "virtually all the time," to express hers:

> I was by far the most blunt and outspoken of our group, even when my friends suggested I had gone too far. I never knew how far was too far. Even now, I cannot find one reliable reason for keeping my thoughts to myself.
>
> (2014, p. 32).

Honesty, of course, has its downsides. But there are times when we all benefit from the existence of those who have the courage to speak out. One of the goals of social therapies is to train autistic individuals to suppress tactless observations and to be more polite and indirect in their criticisms. But we shouldn't discourage people from offering honest opinions where these are potentially productive—even in situations in which we ourselves might be afraid to speak our minds.

The ability to leverage language

Given all we've said throughout this book about the linguistic challenges of autism, it may seem odd to include language among the strengths. However, we've seen various indications in this chapter that, provided the hurdles to language acquisition are surmounted, at least to the point of mastery in vocabulary and syntax, language skills tend to be more effectively leveraged by autistic individuals, and for a greater variety of purposes, than they are by their non-autistic counterparts. That is because language, as many of these excerpts have suggested, serves as a medium for working out logically that which doesn't come intuitively.

Perhaps partly as a result of this, the intense interests of some autistic individuals include language. One of our autism memoirists—Tim Page—is a professional writer. Another—Daniel Tammet—is a linguistic savant who speaks eleven languages. Then there is Liane Holliday Willey, whose intense interests include words and linguistic rules:

> Linguistics and the act of speaking itself, have always been amongst my keenest interests... Words, and everything about them, hold my concentration like nothing else... On my over-stuffed bookshelf sit several thesauruses, a half dozen dictionaries... Language appeals to me because it lends itself to rules and precision even more often than it does to subjectivity.
>
> (2007, p. 35).

As we saw in an earlier excerpt, Willey's linguistic obsessions also include relentless editing and searching for the perfect words.

Precise words, besides satisfying linguistic obsessions, also address difficulties with nonverbal and indirect language. If a high-functioning autistic person doesn't understand the communicative intent behind "It's cold in here," a few additional words—"Can you please close the window"—are all that is needed.

As a medium for information, language also potentially addresses deficits in social awareness. It is often through language, especially through conversations about thoughts and feelings, that children learn about the mental lives and motivations of others. Stories, too, can be rich sources of information about other people's inner lives, including those of fictional characters. Both conversations and stories potentially boost children's perspective-taking skills. Questions like "How would you feel if...?" invite conversational participants to put themselves in other peoples' shoes. Stories often implicitly place listeners and readers in the shoes of their protagonists. Another verbal source on social phenomena, as we noted earlier, are psychology courses and psychology texts.

Language serves not just as a medium for information, however, but also as a scaffolding for thoughts. As we discussed in Chapter 1, it turns out that calculating other people's perspectives requires a certain degree of linguistic mastery—especially in syntax. We see this in false-belief tasks like the Sally–Anne test.

In the Sally–Anne test, recall, there are two puppets, Sally and Anne, and a marble used as a prop. The tester enacts the following scenario: Anne watches as Sally puts the marble in the basket. Sally leaves the room. Anne takes the marble out of the basket and puts it in the box. Sally comes back. Then comes the question: where will Sally look for the marble? To deduce that Sally will look in the basket we must detach ourselves from what we witnessed and calculate Sally's perspective—a perspective from which the marble's change of location was not visible. As we noted earlier, not only language-delayed individuals with autism, but also language-delayed deaf children (even if they're otherwise socially connected) have trouble calculating Sally's perspective. Once children acquire the necessary syntax skills, however, they're able to pass this and other false-belief tests.

But autistic children appear to depend more on language than their non-autistic counterparts do. To perform as well as others on false-belief tests, they typically need to attain significantly higher levels of linguistic mastery. While most non-autistic children can pass false-belief tests at a verbal mental age of five, a similar majority of autistic children do not pass them until they're over a verbal mental age of ten. This above-normal dependence on language, as we discussed in Chapter 1, suggests that autistic individuals are deducing Sally's perspective using mental processes that differ from those of their non-autistic counterparts. Researchers hypothesize that these processes involve deliberately reasoning through false-belief situations via language: "Sally was out of the room. That means she didn't see that Anne moved the marble. So, she'll think it's still where it was when she left the room." Just as with appropriate social responses in conversations, which for most people are intuitive but which for autistic individuals require conscious deliberation, so, too, with perspective-taking skills. And for such deliberation, language is crucial.

Higher functioning autistic individuals also depend on language—especially verbal, text-based language—for learning about the world and for making social connections. Emojis aside (and for some, emojis may be easier to interpret, or to memorize the meanings of, than facial expressions), text-based language does not include the nonverbal signals that elude autistic individuals. Because of this, books are often a preferred medium for learning, and text-based interactions a preferred medium for social interaction. As Grandin notes:

Problems that autistic people have with eye contact and awkward gestures are not visible on the Internet, and typewritten messages avoid many of the social problems of face-to-face contact. The Internet may be the best thing yet for improving an autistic person's social life.

(1995, p. 100).

Language, in a nutshell, is key to enabling autistic strengths in reasoning out logical rules; key to learning, including social learning; and key to having an online, text-based social life. But the ability to use language for these purposes depends on the ability to learn language. For the majority on the autism spectrum who do not master language on their own, the explicit instruction techniques we discussed in earlier chapters are essential. As per the strength-focused approach of this chapter, linguistic instruction, to the extent possible, should tap into autistic strengths. As we discussed in Chapter 5, one key aspect of language— namely, the systematic, rule-governed grammatical structures that form its backbone—readily lends itself to such strengths. The grammatical structures of language, furthermore, include structures that studies have identified as providing the mental scaffolding needed for reasoning through false-belief tasks (see, e.g., De Villiers, 2005 and Tager-Flusberg & Joseph, 2005).

The general promise of narrow interests, perfectionism, and powers of concentration

Among all the autistic strengths we have surveyed, the one that stands out in these personal accounts as possibly the most powerful of all—one that also figures prominently in the diagnostic criteria for autism— is the intense, narrow focus on specific interests. We conclude our survey, therefore, with a few reminders of just how powerful this particular autistic trait can be.

Here is John Elder Robison on his narrow, obsessive focus on engineering sound and lighting effects during a sold-out rock concert:

It's like magic, how it's all come together, though you don't think of it as magic because you understand how every single piece works and you know there's no magic involved. Just basic engineering principles. You've taken thousands of lifeless individual parts—lightbulbs, reflectors, circuit breakers, dimmer packs, power cables, clamps, and trusses—and turned them into a living thing. And you are its master.

...

Now that you're working, your concentration is so intense that you don't even hear the show... Instead, you're seeing each of those hundreds of lights as individuals, and it's all you can do to keep them following the music.

(2008, pp. 153–154).

Beyond allowing such "in the zone" satisfactions, Robison's capacity for intense, narrowly focused concentration was key to getting hired and earning a livelihood. Here he is on preparing for an interview for an electronic games job:

My Aspergian ability to focus and learn fast saved me. Between Sunday, when I read the ad, and the interview eight days later, I became a passable expert in digital design. My head was spinning, but I had absorbed the contents of three engineering texts from the Graduate Search Center library.

(2008, p. 177).

And here he is on landing what was ultimately the more satisfying job—now his career—of running an auto mechanics shop:

The thing that saved me was my technical skill, fueled by my Aspergian need to know all about topics that grabbed my attention. And cars certainly had my attention...

...

I had found a niche where many of my Aspergian traits actually benefited me. My compulsion to know everything about cars made me a great service person.

(2008, p. 214).

Tim Page shares similar reflections on his career:

I am also convinced that many of the things I've done were accomplished not despite my Asperger's syndrome but because of it. I'm sure that it's responsible, at least in part, for my powers of concentration, which permit me to absorb a congenial subject immediately, write an article in an afternoon or book in a summer, blotting out everyone and everything until the project is complete.

(2009, p. 178).

These accounts recall the words of Temple Grandin with which we opened this chapter: "I think there is too much emphasis on deficits and not enough emphasis on developing abilities." None of these individuals have fully overcome their deficits; all of them, however, are thriving on their strengths.

Caveats and takeaways

We have spent an entire chapter drawing largely on accounts written by those who are among the highest functioning autistic individuals out in the world today. While these accounts are our best source for first-hand testimonials about autistic strengths, it's important to acknowledge that these people are outliers. Most individuals with autism are not high functioning enough to leverage autistic strengths into anything approaching what these memoirists have accomplished. But that doesn't detract from the general message: namely, that there is much to be gained by leveraging strengths.

Thus, consider a child whose strongest cognitive skill at age 12 is the ability to sort objects by shape and color, which for him may bring deep satisfaction. That child can be encouraged to apply that skill to an ever-broadening range of objects and environments, and ultimately, perhaps, to some sort of vocational activity. A 15-year-old who perseverates on basic electronics may have the potential to develop the skills to disassemble laptops, printers, cellphones, and other appliances into their component parts—and thus to be hired by an electronics recycling company. And a 17-year-old who writes at a first-grade level may be able to learn enough written language to browse YouTube (a common source of entertainment for those on the autism spectrum) and/or to participate in online autism community groups.

We conclude this chapter with a half dozen takeaways:

- Our tendency to focus on weaknesses has the opportunity cost of neglecting strengths, including those with high payoffs.
- We should appreciate and take advantage of the positive effects on behavior and on emotional well-being of engaging in rote activities and pursuing narrow interests.
- We should encourage higher functioning individuals to come up with their own strategies for creating structure and their own rules for social interactions.
- We should broaden our focus on interactions with immediate peers and provide opportunities for interactions with older people, people from other backgrounds and cultures, and people with similar interests.
- We shouldn't prioritize back-and-forth, in-person social interactions over other forms of social connection (monologues; book writing; text-based, online interactions) that may be more accessible and bring people equal or greater satisfaction.
- Teaching language—oral and written—is a high priority not only for communication but also for enabling strategies that bypass social deficits, i.e., thinking things through deliberately through language and logic.
- Rote abilities, narrow interests, direct honesty, and dispassionate morality—often dismissed, discouraged, or under-appreciated—each has its virtues and potential benefits, both to individuals with autism, and, in some cases, to society at large.

References

Baron-Cohen, S. (1997). *Mindblindness: An essay on autism and theory of mind* (Rev. ed.). MIT Press.

de Villiers, P. A. (2005). The role of language in theory-of-mind Development: What deaf children tell us. In J. W. Astington & J. A. Baird (Eds.), *Why language matters for theory of mind* (pp. 266–297). Oxford University Press. https://doi.org/10.1093/acprof:oso/9780195159912.003.0013

Grandin, T. (1995). *Thinking in pictures and other reports from my life with autism* (pp. 25, 28, 32, 83, 95, 97, 100, 101, 103). Doubleday.

Ostrolenk, A., Forgeot d'Arc, B., Jelenic, P., Samson, F., & Mottron, L. (2017). Hyperlexia: Systematic review, neurocognitive modelling, and outcome. *Neuroscience and biobehavioral reviews, 79*, 134–149. https://doi.org/10.1016/j.neubiorev.2017.04.029

Page, T. (2009). *Parallel play: Growing up with undiagnosed Asperger's* (pp. 56–57, 74, 176, 178). Doubleday.

Robison, J. R. (2008). *Look me in the eye: My life with Asperger's* (Rev. ed., pp. 12, 20, 64–65, 90, 153–154, 177, 189–190, 211, 214). Three Rivers Press.

Shore, S. (2003). *Beyond the wall: Personal experiences with autism* (2nd ed., pp. 60, 83, 90–91, 122). Autism Asperger Publishing Co.

Tammet, D. (2007). *Born on a blue day: Inside the extraordinary mind of an autistic savant* (pp. 25, 41, 76, 142, 225). Free Press.

Tager-Flusberg H. & Joseph, R. M. (2005). How language facilitates the acquisition of false-belief understanding in children with autism. In J. Astington, J. W., & J. Baird (Eds.), Why language matters for theory of mind (pp. 298-318). Oxford University Press. https://doi.org/10.1093/acprof:oso/9780195159912.003.0014

Willey, L. H. (2014). *Pretending to be normal: Living with Asperger's syndrome* (pp. 32, 36, 37, 40–43, 56, 71, 84). Jessica Kingsley.

CHAPTER 9
IN SEARCH OF "DOUBLE EMPATHY" AND TRUE NEURODIVERSITY

In this final chapter, we take a broader look at both the communicative and educational needs of autistic individuals and the broader world in which these needs play out. Here, there are four key issues. First, there's the issue of mutual understanding between autistic individuals and those of us who interact with them. As we'll see, non-autistics also need to work on our empathy skills. Second, there's the issue of who is best positioned to advocate for autistic individuals. Who is our best source on the needs of the more vulnerable individuals who have difficulty speaking for themselves? Third, there's the issue of the reliability of the public messaging about the nature of autism and the needs of autistic individuals. We'll discuss which claims to be skeptical about and why. Finally, there's the issue of neurodiversity—the diversity within humanity of cognitive strengths, weaknesses, and idiosyncrasies—and, in particular, the neurodiversity of autism. Recapping the main points of the book, we'll conclude by discussing how best to direct our energies to address the neurodiverse educational needs of individuals across the autism spectrum.

Each of these issues harks back to the core socio-cognitive idiosyncrasies of autism and, in particular, to issues of empathy and perspective taking. As we'll see below, the empathy challenges in autism are more complex and multifaceted than we have so far let on.

Bridging the gap: The challenges of empathy between autistics and non-autistics

The empathy challenges in autism, significant and widely recognized as they are throughout the literature, are challenges we've brought up on multiple occasions. As seen in Chapter 1, autism does not entail a deficit in basic empathy—in the ability to feel other people's pain. But it does entail difficulties with automatic, intuitive perspective taking as seen, for example, in the Sally–Anne and other false-belief tests. What we haven't yet explored is how the ability to empathize with others is further complicated by issues of social awareness and interest.

In general, even high-functioning autistic people have difficulty relating to the preoccupations and priorities of their non-autistic counterparts— as many have reported in their autobiographical accounts. Particularly challenging are those preoccupations and priorities that are social in nature: chit-chat, gossip, romantic interests, social aspirations. Beyond these inherently social phenomena, there's fashion and pop culture. Not only are fashion and pop culture common topics of casual conversation; they're also largely a reflection of social awareness, social interest, and social affiliations. Lack of interest and lack of awareness go together, such that autistic individuals struggle to join in on or even make sense of much of daily conversation—as well as to empathize with the non-autistic perspectives of the conversational participants.

More fundamentally, many of the social emotions—jealousy, embarrassment, infatuation, vindictiveness—may be emotions that autistic individuals haven't experienced. If you're not socially tuned in enough to fully absorb how people are reacting to you, then you may never have had occasion to experience, say, embarrassment. If you've never felt embarrassed, how can you empathize with an embarrassed person? Similarly, if you've never been driven by a social goal like obtaining respect or acceptance, how can you empathize with someone who is?

Thus, beyond their difficulties with the accurate, intuitive perspective taking needed to calculate other people's knowledge, as in the Sally–Anne and other false-belief experiments, autistic individuals also struggle with empathy and perspective taking in situations where social emotions, social goals, or objects of social interest are concerned. But these second sorts of empathy difficulties—based as they are on non-autistic preoccupations and priorities—apply only when autistic individuals are attempting to empathize with non-autistic individuals.

This empathy barrier, moreover, goes both ways: Non-autistic people have trouble relating to many of the preoccupations and priorities of autistic people. As we noted in the previous chapter, non-autistic people often impose onto autistic people their own values and assumptions. What is a meaningful social interaction? What is a meaningful hobby? What is an emotionally calming activity? Non-autistic people may fail to recognize the potential social satisfactions of one-sided monologues and discussions with, say, older eccentric engineers; or the intellectual and emotional fulfillment of sorting objects, or manipulating circuitry, or memorizing and reciting facts. As we discussed in Chapter 6, non-autistic people often misread autistic students as lazy and/or defiant rather than confused and/or bored and/or overwhelmed. And they often assume that autistic students who have difficulty explaining things verbally do not understand the underlying academic concepts, particularly in math. In other words, non-autistic people often fail to put themselves into the shoes of autistic people.

Damian Milton, an autistic lecturer on intellectual and developmental disability at the University of Kent in England, has found evidence for empathy deficits in non-autistics towards autistics in the personal accounts of autistic people. Milton explains what he calls the "double empathy problem" this way: "When people with very different experiences of the world interact with one another, they will struggle to empathise [sic] with each other." Milton also cites research showing that "non-autistic people struggled to read the emotions of autistic participants, or form negative first impressions of autistic people" (Milton, 2018).

The research on emotion reading, however, is less decisive than Milton suggests. One of the studies he cites showed that non-autistic people have more trouble figuring out which types of situations elicit which types of emotional reactions in autistic vs. non-autistic subjects (Sheppard et al., 2016). But this outcome, perhaps, says more about how idiosyncratic the reactions of the autistic subjects may have been as compared with the more stereotypical reactions of the non-autistic subjects. For example, as we've noted, autistic individuals often focus on specific, non-social details rather than on more global, social aspects of scenes and situations. Their reaction to a scene of children at a playground may not be to the children's play, but to a missing rung in a ladder of a slide or to the fire-engine-red of the jungle gym. These kinds of reactions are hard to predict.

This raises a question that neither Milton nor the research addresses: How do autistic people perform at the same task? How good are they at figuring out other people's responses to specific situations? Do they perform better with responses from other autistic individuals than responses from non-autistic individuals; or do they, too, find responses from autistics more difficult to predict? In other words, how truly symmetrical is the double-empathy problem here?

Another study that Milton cites does compare non-autistic and autistic individuals on an empathy task (Edey et al., 2016). That task involved depicting emotions by moving around two triangles on a computer screen—treating them, say, as interacting characters. The study found that non-autistic people have more difficulty figuring out which emotions autistic people, as compared to non-autistic people, were depicting. It also found that the autistic participants were no better at figuring out the emotions depicted by the autistic triangle-movers than by the non-autistic triangle-movers. These outcomes, however, are consistent with other studies showing that autistic individuals tend to have more difficulty than non-autistic individuals do in both communicating and interpreting emotions.

When Milton turns to a second issue, namely, communication, he may be on firmer ground. Referencing "their unique communication styles," Milton suggests that autistic people have less difficulty communicating with one another than with non-autistic people. His suggestion is consistent with the challenges with figurative language and indirect language that we discussed at length in Chapter 5. Those who have trouble understanding non-literal language may also tend to avoid it in their own speech. Indeed, if we compare individuals with autism who have typical, age-appropriate language skills with their non-autistic counterparts, what we find is a difference in directness and formality. Autistic individuals tend to speak more explicitly and with a more formal vocabulary and tone; non-autistic individuals tend to use more slang and indirect language. To the extent that they avoid non-literal language, fellow high-functioning autistics with fluent language skills have an easier time understanding one another than they do understanding the majority of us who so often speak non-literally.

But the communication barrier is asymmetrical. This is because indirect language presents more socio-cognitive challenges to all of us than direct language does. When a speaker says, "It's cold in here" to someone standing next to an open window, what the speaker wants, however obvious it may be, is still less obvious than if she had said, "Please close the window." In general, it's easier for those who habitually use indirect language to understand those who habitually use direct language than vice versa. Therefore, while there may be some mutual communication difficulties between verbally fluent high-functioning autistic individuals and their non-autistic counterparts, the former will generally have more trouble understanding the latter than vice versa.

On the subject of language, Milton cites a study involving the game of telephone (Crompton et al., 2020). Here, the content to be relayed from one person to the next was a non-social story of a bear on a surreal adventure. Groups of eight participants were arranged into a sequence, or "chain," and each participant retold the story, one by one, to the next participant, out of earshot of the others. The study compared the results of three different chain types: chains consisting only of autistic participants; chains consisting only of non-autistic participants; and chains that alternated between non-autistic and autistic participants. As expected, in each iteration of the story, some of the details were lost. What was interesting, however, was how this varied by chain. In the autistic-only and non-autistic-only chains, there was a similar decline in the number of story details from one participant to the next. But in the mixed, non-autistic-autistic chains, there was a much steeper initial drop-off (Crompton et al., 2020).

While this study points to some sort of communication barrier between autistic and non-autistic individuals, however, its exact nature is unclear. For one thing, in the mixed chains, it was always a non-autistic participant who went first, and it was always at the very beginning, with the first two participants, that the steepest drop-off in story details occurred. Beyond these initial drop-offs, the loss of details in the mixed chains was similar to that of the autistic and the non-autistic chains. The authors hypothesize that additional factors may have come into play. For example, the initial, non-autistic participants may have recalled and/or shared fewer details due to anxiety about the pending need to interact with an autistic person or may have deliberately oversimplified the information for that person's perceived benefit. What's unclear is what would have happened in the mixed chains if autistic participants had gone first.

A second finding in the telephone study was that the autistic participants reported better mutual rapport in autistic-only chains than they did in the mixed chains. This recalls something we suggested in the previous chapter regarding an observation made by Temple Grandin: She enjoys being around like-minded people. In many cases, autistics get along better with fellow autistics than with non-autistics. This is not just because there are fewer barriers to communication and mutual empathy, but also because there are more shared interests, shared traits, and shared standards (or lack thereof) for social behavior. As Milton, in an interview with *Spectrum News*, states:

> Many adolescents with autism prefer to interact with autistic peers over non-autistic ones. And people with autism often build a greater sense of rapport and share more about themselves when conversing with others on the spectrum. One reason for this pattern may be that autistic people are less concerned with typical social norms, such as conversational reciprocity, and so don't mind as much when these rules are not followed. The principle of social compatibility may extend beyond autism diagnoses to autism traits. For example, the more similar two non-autistic people rate themselves on an autism trait assessment, the closer they rate their friendship. (https://www.spectrumnews.org/news/double-empathy-explained/)

Milton, however, takes this idea too far—especially when he adds that the social and communication challenges of autistic people fade away when they interact with fellow autistics. His sample, for one thing, is limited to higher functioning individuals: Those who have the linguistic skills to participate in the telephone study or to rate themselves on a trait assessment. However much their autistic traits may vary, those who are able to conduct an accurate self-assessment must share a solid command of certain psychosocial vocabulary items. And in qualifying for the telephone study, the participants, autistic and non-autistic alike, had normal IQs and age-appropriate language skills. Thus, what the data here tell us about the rapport between fellow autistics is, specifically, about the rapport between fellow high-functioning individuals, and not the rapport between individuals from across the entire autism spectrum.

Indeed, the reality of lower functioning autism is quite different—as is immediately apparent to anyone who visits an autistic support classroom or a social event geared towards those with moderate-to-severe autism. In general, if such individuals seek out anyone, it tends to be not their autistic peers, but the non-autistic adults. This is only natural, as the adults are generally more responsive than their peers are. But we find the same patterns even at events for older individuals that mix non-autistic and moderate-to-severely autistic peers. Here, the far greater socio-cognitive skills of the non-autistic participants allow them to have more successful interactions with the moderate-to-severely autistic participants than what is possible in autistic-on-autistic interactions between individuals with such significant levels of autism.

Beyond the socio-cognitive factors, we should add, there are behavioral factors. Autistic individuals often have sensory sensitivities that can cause them to be unusually distressed by behaviors that commonly occur in moderate-to-severe autism, especially behaviors involving sudden or persistent noises, sudden or persistent movements, intrusions on personal space, and meltdowns. In other words, autistic individuals, more than non-autistic individuals, often find it distressing to be in close sensory proximity to their moderate-to-severely autistic peers.

The other issue with Milton's double empathy conceit is that it leaves out cognitive perspective taking. Cognitive perspective taking, as in the Sally–Anne tests, has nothing to do with shared autism. Whether or not Sally has an autism diagnosis, she'll look for her marble in the basket. And sharing an autism diagnosis with Sally does not enhance a person's ability to predict that the basket is where Sally will assume the marble still is.

Finally, even among the higher functioning individuals who have no mutual language barriers, questions arise about how often interests will overlap enough for a satisfying and enduring rapport. As we know from the diagnostic criteria, interests in autism are typically narrow, and as we saw in the last chapter, they vary significantly from individual to individual. How interested will Grandin be in Willey's obsessions with words and editing, and Willey, vice versa, in Grandin's descriptions of cattle-handling equipment? How riveted will Robison be while Tammet talks about prime numbers and pi, and, vice versa, how entranced will Tammet be while Robison explains acoustic electronics and auto repair?

We should, of course, do what we can to encourage social relations among autistic individuals, particularly classmates and others who have daily opportunities for interaction. However, the most successful relations will tend to be limited to the small number of instances where both individuals have 1) good communication skills and 2) coinciding interests that they're open to sharing. Outside these very specific cases, it simply isn't realistic, given the combination of socio-cognitive challenges, communication challenges, and narrow interests, to expect fellow autistics to be able to meet one another's social needs—especially as autism severity increases. We therefore shouldn't take double empathy so far that we forget how important it is for non-autistic people to initiate and sustain interactions with autistic people.

Nonetheless, the concept of double empathy does contain several important insights. Part of what makes it hard for autistic individuals to relate to non-autistic individuals is that so many non-autistic interests are social in nature and so much conversation is informal, socially-charged small talk. Non-autistics, for their part, often actively prefer small talk to serious talk. They may have no interest whatsoever in the kinds of subject matter that autistic people find interesting. Indeed, however narrow their interests may be, autistics are often far more likely to share these interests with other autistics than with non-autistics. In addition, the tendency towards more direct, formal language, as we noted earlier, means that there may be fewer communication barriers and breakdowns among fellow autistics—assuming their vocabularies and syntax skills are solid enough that they can generally make themselves understood.

Furthermore, empathy failures at the non-autistic end go even further than Milton has noted. Whether or not non-autistic people actually have disproportionate difficulty predicting or interpreting autistic emotions, it is certainly the case, as we discussed in Chapter 6, that non-autistic people—including under-informed educators and education experts—are prone towards unrealistic expectations and unfair assessments of autistic children, from academic skills to social and behavioral issues. In general, far too few teachers have enough breadth and depth of knowledge about autism not to reflexively fill in the gaps with faulty assumptions or limited stereotypes.

There are a number of stereotypes about autism that are commonly exaggerated into unreasonable assumptions. Some people exaggerate the empathy challenges into a generalized empathy deficit. As we've discussed, however, autism does not entail a lack of basic empathy. Relatedly, some people exaggerate the social difficulties into a generalized lack of interest in people. As we saw Robison and Willey suggest in the last chapter, however, the real problem may be more an issue of not knowing *how* to interact with others or not having the right kinds of opportunities—for example, more structured opportunities—for interaction.

Some people draw on stereotypes that hark back to the movie *Rain Man*. First, they exaggerate the extent to which autistic individuals fear transitions and novelty. Often what's actually at work is not a fear of change, but boredom or a lack of understanding: lack of understanding about what's going on; boredom at how long the transition process is taking. Second, people exaggerate the degree to which the cognitive skills in autism are narrow, rote, "splinter" skills (counting toothpicks instantaneously; memorizing the phone book) as opposed to being part and parcel of a more general intellectual capacity that is limited mainly by language and knowledge deficits.

Finally, some people, harping on those superior rote skills and pitting them against more open-ended, creative processes, make faulty assumptions about creativity. They may cite, for example, the absence of the kinds of creative output that align with non-autistic notions of what's creative—for example, fiction featuring social interactions between human beings. They forget that creativity takes many forms, and can be found, in particular, in Grandin's equipment designs, Robison's acoustic engineering, Jessica Park's paintings, and Stephen Shore's story about pets that "alternated between existing as cats and puppies" and "sold for $47,000 each."

In short, many of us need to inform ourselves better about autism in general and about the particular individuals we're dealing with.

This is also true of society at large: after all, what happens in schools and classrooms is largely a function of broader societal trends, and what happens to autistic individuals after they leave school is largely up to society as a whole.

Who speaks for autism: the challenge of representation

Representing autistic needs to society at large raises the question of who is best poised to speak for autistic people. For some, the answer is obvious. Why not autistic people themselves? It was autism autobiographies, after all, that largely informed our previous chapter. And, indeed, Temple Grandin, John Elder Robison, Liane Holliday Willey, and others are well-positioned and well-equipped to speak on behalf of themselves and other like-minded, high-functioning autistics.

The problem, as we saw with double empathy, boils down to two facts. Autism is a spectrum, and socio-cognitive and communication challenges are central to it. The more severely autistic a person is, the less able he is to communicate for himself, let alone to communicate on behalf of his fellow autistics. And the higher functioning an autistic person is, the more difficult it may be for her to put herself in the shoes of her lower functioning counterparts. Furthermore, in terms of first-hand experience, an autism advocacy group that consists only of high-functioning individuals presents society with an extremely limited representation of autism. To the extent that such a group represents the multiple voices of high-functioning autistics, its members may well be the best spokespeople for their narrow slice of the spectrum. It's far less clear that they are the best spokespeople for the spectrum as a whole.

The question of who should speak for those with moderate-to-severe autism is the subject of fierce debate. This is true whether we're talking about treatments, access to education, needed services, or research priorities. Possible candidates, besides high-functioning autistic advocates, include experts in autism research, people who work directly with autistic individuals, and parents.

First, let's consider the autism research contingent. These people tend to have the most in-depth knowledge of subjects pertaining to the nature of autism—for example, the genetics, the brain differences, or the cognitive, social, linguistic and/or behavioral idiosyncrasies. But as spokespeople for autism, this group has limitations. Academic research is famously "siloed", and however well a researcher knows her specific area, she may be under-informed about others. Researchers, furthermore, tend to focus on deficits. Many do not know autistic individuals as real people. As we've seen, some who've observed autistic individuals in person have leapt to faulty conclusions—for example, that facilitated communication is a valid communication method. In general, researchers may not know enough about the clinical and educational worlds—including issues pertaining to language instruction and academic development—to know what to advocate for there. But autism researchers are at least well-poised to tell society what their respective areas of research show about, say, underlying factors, patterns of symptoms, prognoses, or the efficacy of different treatments and interventions.

What about clinicians and teachers, especially those who work directly with autistic individuals? These people, particularly if they've had broad or longitudinal exposure to many different clients, may be much better positioned to speak on behalf of individuals across the spectrum than anyone else is. But their impressions are susceptible to the distortions of personal experience. There may be a selection bias in who gets referred to and who attends their clinics; or, for teachers, in which students are placed in their classrooms. Over time, some clinicians and teachers may end up specializing in individuals at particular functioning levels, and this may prevent them from developing a deep, generalized expertise in autism as a whole.

In addition, where clinicians are concerned, there's one major caveat. Clinicians operate at many different levels, from direct, hands-on interactions with autistic clients to high-level training, supervising, and directing of therapists. And among the clinical directors and master trainers are the gurus. While relatively small in number, their influence can be substantial, and, in some cases, their public agendas may be compromised by self-promotion and/or the promotion of particular brands of trademarked therapies to which they've attached their names and livelihoods. Those who put personal needs ahead of client needs and personal belief systems ahead of the science, of course, are unreliable as autism advocates.

Then there are parents. When it comes to their own children, parents may well have better insights than anyone else. That, of course, doesn't endow them with generalized wisdom about autism. In addition, some parents, particularly if their children's progress via standard treatments is sufficiently slow, may end up resorting to, and sometimes promoting, quack approaches like FC. That said, most parents are the best advocates for their own children. And a wide enough collection of representative parents can potentially represent the needs of autistic children across the spectrum, as well as the needs of the large number of moderate-to-severe adults who are unable to represent themselves. In particular, parents are reliable advocates for autism-related services. However, they should not be treated as experts on autism treatments or on the general, underlying characteristics of autism.

What do we find among actual parent-run organizations? The earliest one, the Autism Society of America, has professionalized its leadership so that it now includes fundraisers and businesspeople in addition to parents—as well as a president who promotes FC. The leadership of Autism Speaks, also founded by autism family members, has been similarly professionalized. A new group that is run exclusively by autism parents is the National Council on Severe Autism; as its name suggests, this group focuses on severe autism.

So, let's return to the autistic self-advocates: the more verbal, higher-functioning members of the autistic community. Given the various limitations of the other groups, might this contingent be the most qualified to represent certain aspects of autism—particularly the challenges and needs of autistic adults—despite the problems we noted above regarding representation and perspective-taking challenges? Indeed, there is an outspoken group of high-functioning self-advocates who identify as autistic and who answer in a uniform "yes." They argue that they are uniquely positioned to speak, not just on behalf of like-minded, high-functioning autistics, but on behalf of autistic people in general.

Some claim that, despite appearances to the contrary, they have the same core autism traits and autism-related challenges as lower functioning individuals. Some, for example, say they have daily life challenges, difficulties concentrating, and "meltdowns" that are comparable to the daily life, cognitive, and self-regulatory challenges that afflict individuals with severe autism. Some claim to routinely experience being nonspeaking. They explain that, even if they are capable of fluent speech, they sometimes get so tired or overwhelmed that they "run out of words." Or they state that they qualify as nonspeaking inasmuch as they prefer communication modalities other than speech (say, typing). Regarding the other core traits of autism—behavioral and social traits—some have claimed that their true selves would manifest to the world as just as autistic as their so-called lower functioning counterparts. They appear to us as mildly or minimally autistic only because they routinely "mask." That is, they hide their autistic proclivities and attempt to conform to non-autistic standards—perhaps using some of the social mimicry skills we saw Willy describe in the previous chapter.

On the flip side, some of these high-functioning advocates have claimed that lower functioning autistics are actually much higher functioning than they appear: more intellectually and socially intact, and, even if they speak only minimally, more linguistically intact as well. But severe autism, as we noted earlier, severely challenges such views. Those who claim that severely autistic individuals are linguistically intact have had to resort to facilitated communication. That is, they've had to claim that FC is a valid way to communicate and that the articulate and intelligent messages generated by FC are authentically authored by autistic individuals. This, in turn, has allowed them to conclude that even the most severely autistic people with minimal speech are intellectually intact or intellectually superior; already skilled in language and knowledgeable about the world. In terms of autism advocacy, this conclusion, in turn, has allowed the Autism Self Advocacy Network (ASAN) to justify the inclusion of facilitated individuals on its board and to claim that it, ASAN, thus represents individuals across the entire autism spectrum.

But the facts don't support these claims. FC isn't a valid means of communication. Severely autistic people do not generally have normal to above normal IQs, particularly if we include verbal IQ. The socio-cognitive difficulties, by diagnostic definition, increase with autism severity. Successful masking of autistic traits requires a certain threshold of socio-cognitive awareness and social motivation. There is, thus, a world of social, cognitive, and linguistic difference between high functioning autism and severe autism. And the non-speaking episodes and communicative preferences of high-functioning individuals are fundamentally incomparable to the limited linguistic understanding and limited productive language skills of their severely autistic counterparts. In general, then, high-functioning autistic individuals are ill-equipped to represent autism as a whole, particularly if we factor in the perspective-taking skills needed to relate to the very different people that lower functioning autistics, in fact, are.

True neurodiversity: embracing the full breadth of the autism spectrum

So where does that leave us? How do we help society understand what autism is and what autism needs; how do we get society to embrace the full breadth of the autism spectrum?

One approach is through the concept of neurodiversity. In the most general terms, neurodiversity is the notion that there exists a diversity of human cognition—of cognitive styles, of cognitive strengths, weaknesses, and idiosyncrasies—that should be fully appreciated, accepted, and included throughout society. The fundamental goal of the neurodiversity movement, accordingly, is to build awareness of and supports for so-called "neurodivergent" individuals across the gamut of cognitive conditions, autism included. In this generalized, ideal form, neurodiversity is wise and reasonable.

But the reality of the Neurodiversity (ND) Movement as it actually manifests itself in the world today—and which we denote here with capital letters—is different. Where autism is concerned, the membership of the ND Movement, together with its messaging to society, has resulted in a narrow, warped perspective. The underlying problem is that the movement, like any advocacy movement, is naturally dominated by highly articulate, high functioning individuals. True to the spirit of neurodiversity, many of these advocates aren't autistic. They may identify as being neurodivergent in other ways—ADHD, dyslexia, epilepsy, OCD, and Tourette's being some of the more commonly cited conditions. Or they may identify as being "neurotypical" allies of neurodivergent people. But those ND spokespeople who do identify as autistic generally have mild enough symptoms that they often weren't diagnosed until well into adulthood. Some of them are merely self-diagnosed, a phenomenon that the ND Movement fully embraces. Self-diagnosis is accepted as a way around two alleged obstacles: the alleged financial and time costs of getting a medical diagnosis, and the alleged bias by many diagnosticians against diagnosing females as autistic.

Claims about diagnostic bias are prevalent enough that it's worth spending a moment to unpack them. The issue is that boys are four times more likely to be diagnosed with autism. Gender-based prevalence differences, of course, do not by themselves prove gender bias: consider hemophilia, a blood clotting disorder that, as no one disputes, affects far more males than females. And there are other cognitive differences, besides autism, whose rates vary by gender: dyslexia, synesthesia, and colorblindness, for example. Even within the non-autistic population, we find gender differences in traits relevant to autism: male infants and toddlers, on average, are more interested in objects and start talking later, compared to female infants and toddlers who, on average, are more interested in people and start talking earlier. It's true that some of the informal, self-diagnostic, Internet-based autism surveys are skewed by questions that reflect gender-based stereotypes—for example, questions about interests in machines and mechanics. But this is not true of the official diagnostic criteria and screening tools that we reviewed in Chapter 1. These tools focus instead on general behavior patterns that are directly related to autism like how often a child points to things to call attention to them or engages in socially reciprocal exchanges. Thus, the four-to-one ratio of males to females officially diagnosed with autism likely reflects reality rather than bias.

And, yet, the autistic contingent of the ND Movement is far more female-dominated than would be predicted by a four-to-one ratio. This, along with the linguistic fluency and overall functioning level of this contingent, raises concerns about how representative it is of the autism spectrum. On the other hand, there's no reason to expect these people to directly represent autism as a whole. What's important is that they advocate for people across the spectrum and that they don't channel societal supports only towards their own personal needs. The reality, however, is that—in an ironic contradiction of its theoretical ideals—the ND Movement has tended to suppress rather than raise awareness of the diversity of the autistic condition.

This begins with diversity of opinion. At issue, specifically, is the diversity of opinion within the autism world with respect to research priorities, spending priorities, and whether autism is an identity to be honored or a condition to be ameliorated. ND's dominant position is celebratory and anti-treatment. But there are autistic individuals who dissent. They include Jonathan Mitchell, who attests that his autism has prevented him from keeping a job and finding a girlfriend, and Thomas Clements who, while high functioning enough to travel the world, has an older brother who is much more severely affected. Both Clements and Mitchell, in calling for less celebration and more remediation, have become persona non grata in ND circles. So, to some degree, has John Elder Robison. Robison, after spending time with a severely autistic young man, recanted his earlier suggestion that all autistic adults are capable of making major life decisions on their own. (As for Grandin, Willy, and the other autistic memoirists we cited in the previous chapter, their voices are noticeably absent from most of the ND discourse).

A related area in which ND allows little room for dissent concerns cognitive functioning. As we discussed in the previous section, a number of outspoken, high-functioning autistic self-advocates insist that their moderate-to-severely autistic counterparts are much higher functioning than they seem. And it is precisely this view that dominates ND's discourse on autism. Some ND advocates go further, claiming that autism, including non-speaking autism, often involves "superpowers"—or super-human abilities. Buttressing this claim are not just the occasional, often hard-won savant-like skills we discussed in the previous chapter, but also the precocious vocabularies, knowledge, and wisdom extracted from minimally speaking/minimally-verbal individuals through facilitated communication: skills that are purportedly acquired through superhuman listening skills. Furthermore, thanks to the ND-friendly content of some of their facilitated messages (e.g., "People who have intellectual disabilities are assumed to be unintelligent"), some of these facilitated individuals—or, rather, their (unwitting) facilitators—have themselves become respected spokespeople for the ND Movement.

Perhaps nowhere is the gulf between the ideal and reality of neurodiversity greater than in the ND Movement's dismissal of intellectual disability. So vehemently does the dominant ND discourse deny the existence of intellectual disability in autism that it seems at times as if ND advocates consider intellectual disability to be one of the worst of all possible cognitive conditions. A close second, however, are certain debilitating comorbidities that commonly co-occur with autism and that cry out urgently for treatment rather than celebration—for example, epilepsy. Epilepsy is routinely dismissed by ND advocates as unrelated to autism.

Dismissing the more problematic aspects of autism allows ND to embrace autism as an identity. We should add that ND does, additionally, embrace autism as a disability: one that is deserving of accommodations and services. But ND views autism the way that it views all disabilities: as a social construct; a function of societal conditions. Taking this a step further, and tapping into Milton's notion of double empathy, ND also sees autism as a culture, complete with its own special ways of interacting and communicating. As we discussed in the previous section, this conceit works to some extent with small subgroups of high-functioning individuals. But it does not characterize autism as a whole.

Related to its cultural identity conceit are ND's positions on therapeutic interventions and educational placements. Appropriating the discourse of civil rights, ND advocates call for full inclusion of autistic students in general education, as opposed to "segregation" in special ed. classrooms. Relatedly, they tend to reject autism treatments that go beyond low-impact, once-or-twice-a-week speech-language therapy and occupational therapy (OT). Among the more intensive therapies, one is singled out for extreme denunciation: Applied Behavioral Analysis (ABA). Claiming that the ultimate goal of ABA therapy is making autistic children "indistinguishable" from their non-autistic peers, ND advocates have compared ABA to conversion therapy. They've also claimed that ABA is punitive, coercive, and physically abusive, and has led to a legacy of PTSD among ABA "survivors."

As with many of ND's positions, there are some underlying truths. It's true that ABA, as incarnated in the original version of Discrete Trial Training (DTT) (see Chapter 3), has been coercive, punitive, and overly focused on snuffing out harmless autistic perseverations like hand-flapping. But those practices ended long ago. And it is true that abusive ABA sessions conducted by malpracticing therapists have occurred: Similar abuses, sadly, have occurred in many other therapy- and care-providing situations that involve vulnerable populations. But a comparison of ABA vs. FC videos on YouTube shows today's FC to be far more coercive than today's ABA. Furthermore, ABA detractors tend to overlook one of ABA's key roles: namely, as a teaching methodology. Indeed, as we discussed in Chapter 3, ABA is the most evidence-based therapy out there for teaching skills to individuals with autism. Nor is its efficacy limited to autism. The most effective teaching methodologies for students in general—Direct Instruction and Precision Teaching—are based on ABA's behaviorist principles: breaking skills down into subskills and teaching them to mastery.

As for special versus general education, it is true that many special ed. classrooms, autistic support classrooms included, leave much to be desired. Their typically highly dedicated teachers are hamstrung by a combination of understaffing, an extreme range and depth of special needs and behavioral challenges, and (as we discussed in Chapter 7) the one-size-fits-all expectations of Common Core-linked instructional guidelines and accountability tests. But for most of the autistic individuals who have been placed in special ed. settings, full-time general education, which is much more of a one-size-fits-all phenomenon than special ed. is, is not the answer. Most of these individuals lack the linguistic and academic readiness for the reading, writing, and subject-specific demands of general education. If it appears otherwise, it is often only through the illusion of facilitated communication.

Indeed, the illusion of FC is foundational to many ND claims: that there is no such thing as severe autism; that autism is just a different way of being; that no one with autism should be educationally segregated; and that everyone with autism is able to communicate their thoughts, advocate for their needs, and make major life decisions. But beyond helping to fuel this ironically non-neurodiverse view of autism, FC has limited the true neurodiversity of the ND movement in one other way. In combination with the advocacy and awareness statements of ND spokespeople at the mildest end of the autism spectrum, some of whom have never been diagnosed with autism by anyone but themselves, FC has contributed to the growing number of statements that purport to, but do not, represent authentic autistic voices.

One possible reason why this minimally autistic version of autism has prevailed in the ND world is how well it fits in with what society in general would like to believe. As we noted in Chapter 7, the emphasis on mild autism and dismissal of autism severity meshes neatly with broader societal trends. The "social construct" model of disability is popular in academia. The mantra of "presume competence" prevails in disability studies publications and disability rights agendas. An aversion to direct instruction and to placing students according to skill level rather than calendar age dominates the education world. So does the Common Core–inspired notion that all we need to do is provide opportunities for students to "demonstrate understanding."

What this means is that misconceptions about autism are deep-seated within our society, frequently warping the public's perception of autistic challenges and needs, to the great detriment of this vulnerable population. Parents, teachers, and therapists alike have much urgent work to do to raise awareness of the actual therapeutic and educational needs of individuals across the spectrum.

For us, the most important question isn't about who represents autism or about who speaks for whom, but this: How do we ensure that each autistic student has full access to as comprehensive and academically advanced an education as is personally feasible? For that, we must acknowledge the full range of diversity in autism. And we must acknowledge each child where he is and meet him exactly there.

Each child, that is, deserves a careful, in-depth assessment of her strengths and weaknesses in each specific subject and skill area, starting with language. Each child deserves evidence-based therapies and teaching methods that are tailored to those strengths and weaknesses. Each child deserves a calm and cognitively engaging learning environment, with any restless and defiant behaviors recognized as possible signs of anxiety or disengagement; signs that he needs more structure and less auditory and visual clutter, and/or more calming or engaging materials and activities. Each child deserves to have his social challenges acknowledged and addressed. Each child deserves social opportunities that are meaningful to her—however formal or one-sided they may seem to us. Each child deserves recognition for whatever quirky creativity he displays—however much it diverges from neurotypical stereotypes. Each child deserves opportunities to develop his strengths and pursue her interests—however narrow these may appear to the rest of us.

The closer we come to addressing these needs and creating these opportunities for each autistic individual, the closer we will have come to honoring the full breadth of neurodiversity in autism.

References

Crompton, C. J., Ropar, D., Evans-Williams, C. V. M., Flynn, E. G., & Fletcher-Watson, S. (2020, May 20). *Autistic peer-to-peer information transfer is highly effective.* Retrieved from https://journals.sagepub.com/doi/10.1177/1362361320919286

Edey, R., Cook, J., Brewer, R., Johnson, M. H., Bird, G., & Press, C. (2016). Interaction takes two: Typical adults exhibit mind-blindness towards those with autism spectrum disorder. *Journal of abnormal psychology, 125*(7), 879–885. https://doi.org/10.1037/abn0000199

Milton, D. (2018, March 2). The double empathy problem. National Autistic Society. Retrieved from https://www.autism.org.uk/advice-and-guidance/professional-practice/double-empathy

Milton, D. (2021, July 22). Double empathy, explained. *Spectrum.* Retrieved from https://www.spectrumnews.org/news/double-empathy-explained/

Sheppard, E., Pillai, D., Wong, G. T., Ropar, D., & Mitchell, P. (2016). How easy is it to read the minds of people with autism spectrum disorder?. *Journal of autism and developmental disorders, 46*(4), 1247–1254. https://doi.org/10.1007/s10803-015-2662-8